DININ'LEAN®
IN HOUSTON

A Restaurant Guide to Lower Fat/Lower Calorie
Dining in the Houston Area
(Full Service and Fast Foods)

Joanne V. Lichten, PhD, RD/LD

NUTRIFIT Consulting, Inc.
P.O. Box 690452
Houston, TX 77269-0452

Printed in the United States of America

Library of Congress

ISBN: 1-880347-56-3

Copies may be ordered from NUTRIFIT Consulting,
Inc. at the above address or call (713) 955-LEAN.

Cover design and book layout by
Terri Hebert and Marilyn Crawford
Cover illustration by David Roumfort

To Veronica Corona Castillo:
Without your assistance and dedication, this book would not have been written.

To Lorin Lichten:
For your understanding of the long hours needed to write this book and your willingness to eat out often.

HOW TO USE THIS RESTAURANT GUIDE

Many people are under the assumption that it is nearly impossible to "eat right" while "dining out". This book shows that it just isn't so! There are so many restaurants in Houston that offer lower fat and lower calorie choices - and **DININ'LEAN® IN HOUSTON** spells out what those restaurants and menu items are.

The information in this book is as up-to-date as possible. All research was performed between April and July of 1991. Using the restaurant's menu and my questionnaire, I interviewed reliable sources such as chefs, owners, and managers about menu items, portion sizes, methods of preparation, and their restaurant's philosophy about dietary requests.

Before you make a final decision to visit a particular restaurant or to order a particular menu item, consider the following. There is a rapid turnover of restaurants. Restaurants frequently change menus, recipes, and chefs. In addition, there may be errors in the contents of this book due to typographical mistakes or misunderstandings between myself and my sources. So always verify the information in this book before ordering.

DININ'LEAN® IN HOUSTON is a *guide* book that lists some of the lowest fat and lowest calorie menu items available at each restaurant. These are not necessarily exactly what *you* should be eating. As with any book that suggests foods for better health, it is impossible to generalize to the entire population. Always consult with your Registered Dietitian or Medical Doctor regarding how to tailor this restaurant guide to your particular health needs. Bon Appetit!

Dr. Joanne V. Lichten

TABLE OF CONTENTS

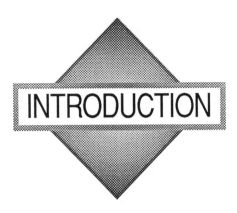

INTRODUCTION

Half of all Americans eat out on a typical day. We eat almost a third of all our calories away from home. Eating out, in the past, used to be a rare social event. Now we "eat out" more frequently because of two career families, luncheon business meetings, lack of time and interest in both shopping and cooking, or other reasons. And...

Statistics show that many Americans want to eat healthier. Americans are constantly trying to lose weight because half of all adults are overweight. The average American gains a pound a year after they reach the age of 25. Because heart disease is the number one killer in the United States, many of us are also concerned with our serum cholesterol.

In fact, about 40% of all restaurant customers are trying to eat healthier food items not only at home but also when eating out. Dining out can no longer be used as an excuse for not complying to the doctor's orders - or keeping the weight down. Because...

Restaurants are responding with healthy foods. A 1988 survey of tableservice restaurants demonstrated that 40% were featuring healthful menu items. Results from another study indicated that nearly half of the restaurants plan to add more nutritious menu items in the future. Even "fast food" restaurants are serving new, good-tasting, healthy foods. And...

DININ'LEAN® IN HOUSTON has made it easier than ever to select the healthiest food on the menu. This book provides you with the background on how many calories and grams of fat you **need** each day, shows you how much fat and calories you actually **eat** each day, and lists the calorie and fat content of many foods.

It furnishes a great deal of information on over 200 individual restaurants: how their foods are prepared, portion sizes served, which menu items are leanest, if smaller portions can be ordered at a discounted price, and whether they would be willing to allow you to special-order.

Why does DININ'LEAN® IN HOUSTON stress low fat menu selections? In the second chapter, you will discover that it is the excess fat in our diet that is killing us with heart disease and keeping us fatter than we want to be. Most people don't realize that:

1. Fats have twice as many calories as carbohydrates and protein.
2. Fats in the foods we eat are very close in composition to the fat on our body. Whenever we eat more fats than we need - they are just "sucked up" by our fat cells.
3. All fats, whether "good" fats (such as margarine or vegetable oil) or "bad" fats (like butter or

lard), have the same number of calories and make us *equally* fat.

4. "Cholesterol Free" *does not* mean the product is calorie-free, lower in calories, fat-free or lower in fat.

5. Simply cutting back on dietary cholesterol is not enough to lower your blood cholesterol - cutting back on fat will.

Therefore, the bottom line is: if you want to lower your serum cholesterol or lose weight, you must decrease your FAT intake!

How this Book is Organized

The second chapter of DININ'LEAN® IN HOUSTON is a discussion of the basics of the science of nutrition. The third chapter contains general guidelines for eating out healthy. Read these sections to learn the basics of how to DINE LEAN.

The remainder of the book is organized into an analysis of over 200 specific Houston area restaurants (which actually represents over 750 restaurants considering multi-locations).

Every restaurant listed in the 1990-1991 Yellow Pages was given an opportunity to respond to the "DININ'LEAN® IN HOUSTON" questionnaire. The owner or manager was telephoned and informed about the book and its purpose. Those that demonstrated an interest were sent a questionnaire.

The restaurant owners and managers were instructed to return the completed questionnaire and a copy of their menu. After analyzing their menu and the responses to their questionnaire, the author interviewed the owner, manager, or chef to discuss their menu items, portions sizes, and methods of food preparation. Finally, using her extensive nutritional knowledge and experience,

each individual restaurant entry was compiled by
the author.

The fourth chapter is on breakfast fare. The next
16 chapters describe those restaurants that serve
lunch (the noonday meal) and dinner (the evening
meal). These are divided into chapters based upon
the type of food served. A chapter is dedicated to
meals that are available for pick-up or delivery. And
the final chapter provides information on Frozen
Yogurt and other frozen desserts.

All of the chapters focus on the Houston
restaurants and provide information of the leanest
(lower in calories and fat) choices at each restaurant. There is no implied comparison of one
restaurant against another.

How to Read a Restaurant Entry

Those participating restaurants that serve a wide
array of leaner breakfast choices are listed under the
chapter **Breakfast**. All restaurants serving lunch and
dinner are further categorized according to the type
of food served (such as Italian, Mexican, or Fast
Food). The restaurants, within each chapter, are
alphabetized for convenience. The following is an
illustrated restaurant entry demonstrating how the
entries have been formatted:

❶ Name of restaurant

❷ Address, in Houston unless otherwise mentioned

❸ Area of town or closest intersection

❹ Phone Number

❺ Dining style is classified as being either Formal,
Informal or Casual. Meals served are noted as B
for Breakfast, L for Lunch, and D for Dinner.

❻ Average Price of a *Dinner* entree

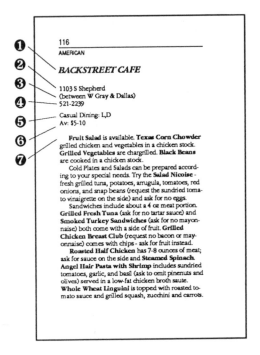

❶ 116

AMERICAN

❷ *BACKSTREET CAFE*

❸ 1103 S Shepherd
(between W Gray & Dallas)

❹ 521-2239

❺ Casual Dining: L,D
Av: $5-10

❻ **Fruit Salad** is available. **Texas Corn Chowder**
grilled chicken and vegetables in a chicken stock.
Grilled Vegetables are chargrilled. **Black Beans**
are cooked in a chicken stock.

❼   Cold Plates and Salads can be prepared according to your special needs. Try the **Salad Nicoise** -
fresh grilled tuna, potatoes, arrugula, tomatoes, red
onions, and snap beans (request the sundried tomato vinaigrette on the side) and ask for no eggs.
    Sandwiches include about a **4 oz** meat portion.
Grilled Fresh Tuna (ask for no tartar sauce) and
Smoked Turkey Sandwiches (ask for no mayonnaise) both come with a side of fruit. **Grilled
Chicken Breast Club** (request no bacon or mayonnaise) comes with chips - ask for fruit instead.
    Roasted Half Chicken has 7-8 ounces of meat;
ask for sauce on the side and **Steamed Spinach**.
Angel Hair Pasta with Shrimp includes sundried
tomatoes, garlic, and basil (ask to omit pinenuts and
olives) served in a low-fat chicken broth saute.
Whole Wheat Linguini is topped with roasted tomato sauce and grilled squash, zucchini and carrots.

❼ Based on the information obtained, those menu
items thought to be the leanest were selected
and **highlighted**. Only the entree was
highlighted - not all the accompaniments. For
example, if the entry reads: **Roast Chicken** with
fresh vegetables, both the roast chicken **and** the
fresh vegetables are considered lean. Be sure to
read on further in the restaurant entry to find out
if other special requests should be made such as:
sauce on the side, without the sauce, without
any oil or fat, steamed rather than sauteed, or no
cheese.

Other menu items that have their first letter capitalized but are not highlighted are *not* recommended items. They are listed to offer more information abut the menu item or it's preparation.

The word "meat", throughout all entries, refers to not just beef but any animal protein source such as pork, chicken, turkey, beef, fish, or shellfish. This term was used to simplify the listing of average portion sizes.

The calories and grams of fat (listed as: # cals/# gms fat) included in a restaurant entry were generally not calculated by the author. These numbers were obtained from the restaurant menu or from the owners, managers, or chefs. Some food companies, most commonly those that serve fast food, provided information on all their products. The calories and grams of fat listed in the introductory sections of the chapters were obtained from USDA food composition tables and scientific literature.

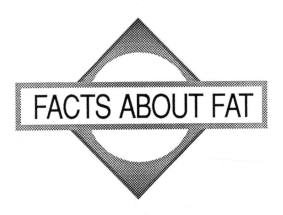

FACTS ABOUT FAT

Did you know that there are 3500 calories in each pound of body fat? Eating just 10 calories extra every day could contribute to one pound gained each year (10 calories X 356 days = 3560 extra calories). That's just 1 hard candy, 1 nibble of a cookie, a sip of soda, or a thin smear of butter. These ten additional calories alone could account for the average one pound many Americans gain each year.

An extra 100 calories each day adds up to nearly a pound each month (100 X 30 days = 3000 extra calories). That is just a third of a doughnut, 8 oz of beer, 8 oz of soda, an extra tablespoon of salad dressing, 2/3 oz of chips, or just 10 french fries.

By the same token, if you eat just 100 calories *less* each day, you can lose a pound a month or 10 pounds a year with very little effort. Throughout this book are additional *minor* changes that can make a *major* impact upon your weight.

A Calorie is a Calorie is a Calorie - Or is it?

Calories come from three basic nutrients: carbohydrates, proteins, and fats.

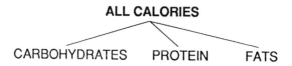

ALL CALORIES

CARBOHYDRATES   PROTEIN   FATS

While carbohydrates and proteins have only 4 calories per gram, fats have 9 calories per gram. Therefore, fats are more than twice as caloric (or fattening) as carbohydrates and proteins.

> 1 gram of carbohydrate = 4 calories
> 1 gram of protein = 4 calories
> **1 gram of fat = 9 calories!**

Because of this caloric difference, you can eat a greater quantity of foods that are low in fat than of high fat foods for the same number of calories. That is why a medium sized apple (high in carbohydrates) has no more calories than a couple of tiny pats of margarine (pure fat).

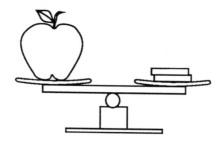

FACTS ABOUT FAT

To further illustrate the point, a cup of white flour has 400 calories and a cup of sugar has 800 calories. But a cup of oil (pure fat) has 2000 calories!

400 Calories   800 Calories   2,000 Calories

Excess fat consumption works against weight control and weight loss efforts in two ways. The first and more obvious is the calories per gram as compared to the other two nutrients. The second and more insidious is the way our bodies process the fats we eat.

All of the three calorie-containing nutrients: carbohydrates, proteins, and fats are changed into calories, the fuel that our body runs on. Whenever we eat more calories (from any source) than we need each day, our body stores the extra calories in our BODY FAT.

But eating an extra 100 calories of carbohydrates or an extra 100 calories of protein does not build as much fat as eating an extra 100 calories of fat. A recent study at the Stanford Center for Research in Disease Prevention demonstrated that dietary fat may be even more caloric than the 4/4/9 ratio indicated.

When we eat more carbohydrates or proteins than we need, twenty three percent (23%) of all the calories are lost in switching the carbohydrates chemically to stored fat. But because the fat that we eat, is very much like the fat that we store on our body, very few calories (3%) are needed to convert it. And basically, extra fat eaten becomes excess fat on our body. So, fats are probably **three** times more fattening than carbohydrates and proteins.

Simple mathematics makes a demonstrable case for controlling fat consumption. By cutting back on the fats we eat, we can enjoy more real food and lose weight painlessly.

Cut Back on Fats to Decrease Your Cholesterol

FACT: HEART DISEASE IS THE #1 KILLER IN THE UNITED STATES.

Half of all Americans die of heart disease. That's why so many people are concerned about their serum cholesterol level. Levels over 200 mg/dl are considered high for most adults. Research demonstrates that lowering your serum cholesterol level can reduce your risk of developing heart disease.

FACT: SIMPLY CUTTING BACK ON YOUR DIETARY CHOLESTEROL INTAKE WILL NOT LOWER YOUR SERUM CHOLESTEROL LEVEL!

Many people think that simply cutting back on the cholesterol content of their food will reduce their serum cholesterol level. While this does have an effect, it is *far more important* to lower your total intake of fat. When you eat *excess fat* your liver simply responds by making *more serum cholesterol.* Cutting back on your cholesterol intake will not necessarily lower your fat intake. But lowering your fat intake usually lowers your cholesterol intake as well.

FACT: THERE ARE TWO TYPES OF FATS.

The fats we eat can be divided into either GOOD fats or BAD fats. Decades ago, we were told to simply replace the BAD fats with the GOOD fats. The

FACTS ABOUT FAT

GOOD fats tend to lower the serum cholesterol while
the BAD fats tend to raise the serum cholesterol.

GOOD FATS	**BAD FATS**
(lower cholesterol)	(raise cholesterol)
Monounsaturated Fats:	Saturated Fats:
Avocado	(Animal)
Cannola Oil	Bacon
Olive Oil	Lard
Peanut Oil	Sausage
Polyunsaturated Fats:	(Vegetable)
Corn Oil	Coconut Oil
Cottonseed Oil	Palm Oil
Soybean Oil	Palm Kernel Oil
Sesame Seed Oil	
Sunflower Oil	Hydrogenated Fats:
Safflower Oil	Hydrog. Vegetable
Shortening	

Unfortunately, so many people believe that
GOOD fats can be eaten in unlimited amounts.
Now we know that it is not that simple. The total fat
content of our diets must be lowered. That's why
the American Heart Association has been saying for
years that we need to reduce our fat intake to less
than 30% of our total calories.

FACT: ALL FATS HAVE THE SAME NUMBER OF
CALORIES.
One level tablespoon of butter and margarine
both have 100 calories. Oil and lard each have 125
calories per level tablespoon. Although the GOOD
fats may be a bit healthier for your heart - they are
both equally fattening!

FACT: ONLY ANIMALS HAVE LIVERS SO ONLY
ANIMALS CAN PRODUCE CHOLESTEROL.

Cholesterol is manufactured in the liver. Since only animals have livers, only animal products can have cholesterol. That is why cholesterol can be found in animal products such as butter, lard, meat, cheese, and eggs.

FACT: *NO* VEGETABLE PRODUCTS HAVE
CHOLESTEROL.

Vegetables do not have livers so vegetables can not produce cholesterol. So vegetable products such as wheat, vegetables, fruits, olive oil, margarine, vegetable oils, and tofu (soy bean curd) do not have any cholesterol. A vegetable oil that claims to have "No Cholesterol" may be misleading if you were to conclude that the product has been modified. Vegetables don't have livers, therefore, vegetables never had cholesterol and never will.

FACT: CHOLESTEROL FREE *DOES NOT MEAN* IT
IS CALORIE-FREE OR FAT-FREE.

"No or low cholesterol" products result from either food that is *naturally* low in cholesterol or from food in which some of the cholesterol has been removed. You can remove the majority of cholesterol from animal products by removing the fat. There is very little cholesterol in skim milk and skim milk cheeses. Egg substitutes are made of just the egg white; the high cholesterol egg yolk has been removed.

But manufacturers of many "no or low cholesterol" foods have just simply changed the type of fat used in a food product. Such as in replacing some or all of the animal fat to a vegetable fat in imitation cheese, crackers, or french fries.

In so many cases, a "cholesterol-free" product has just as much fat as the original - and therefore, just as many calories. Vegetable oil is pure fat. Lard (animal fat) is pure fat. Vegetable oil may be a little healthier for your heart, but it is just as caloric as lard.

FACT: THERE IS NO SUCH THING AS A NO-CHOLESTEROL, NO-FAT OIL.

You can't remove the fat from oil because vegetable oil is 100% fat - removing the oil would leave you with an empty bottle. Diet margarine has less calories only because some of the fat has been replaced with water and then whipped together. You can't cook with diet margarine for that reason; the water simply evaporates. But remember, water has no calories so still 100% of all the calories are coming from fat.

Don't believe it if someone tells you that they are frying with a no-cholesterol, *no-fat* oil, there simply is not such a product. And there is no such thing as a no-cholesterol, *low-fat* oil either.

FACT: FAT-FREE SALAD DRESSINGS ARE REALLY NOT FAT-FREE.

It's true. The Food and Drug Administration allows manufacturers to label foods fat-free if one serving contains less than 1 gram of fat. But one serving is just one level tablespoon. If you eat salads with a large serving of salad dressing, that fat-free dressing could still add up to a significant number of calories and grams of fat.

FACT: THE AMERICAN HEART ASSOCIATION RECOMMENDS THAT AMERICANS EAT NO MORE THAN 30% OF THEIR TOTAL CALORIES FROM FAT.

Simply cutting back on your dietary cholesterol intake *will not* lower your serum cholesterol. That's why the American Heart Association has been recommending for years that we eat less than 30%

of all our calories in the form of fat. Simply replacing butter with margarine and frying with vegetable oil instead of lard, will not lower your cholesterol. You need to cut back on the total amount of fat.

What Foods Are High in Fat?

Most of the fat we eat is not from visible fat such as butter on bread or on a potato. It is hidden from us in the form of egg yolks, whole milk, fried foods, foods prepared with fat, salad dressing, margarine on vegetables, or sauces.

LOW FAT FOODS:

Most Fruits and Fruit Juices (except for Avocados, Coconuts, Olives, Nuts, Seeds, and Peanut Butter)

Vegetables Prepared Without Any Added Fats

Vegetable Juices

Starchy Foods That Are Prepared Without Added Fats such as:

Beans and Peas	Rice
Corn Tortilla	Pasta
Plain Breads	Corn
Most Dry Cereal	Potatoes

Skim or Very Low Fat Milk Products such as:
Skim or Non-Fat Milk
1/2% or 1% Milk
Non-Fat or 1% Milkfat Yogurt
Non-Fat or 1% Milkfat Cottage Cheese
Skim Milk or Very Low Fat Cheese (< 3gms fat/oz)
Non-Fat Frozen Yogurt
Non-Fat Frozen Dairy Products
Egg Whites
Many Egg Substitutes

FACTS ABOUT FAT

Lean Meats such as:
 Fish
 Shellfish
 Chicken, without skin
 Turkey, without skin
 Wild Game, without the skin
 Lean Beef
 Lean Pork

HIGH FAT FOODS:

Cereals with Nuts   Most Granolas
Avocados   Coconuts
Olives   Nuts
Seeds   Peanut Butter

Starchy Foods that are Prepared with Fats such as:
 Fried Rice   Croissants
 Buttered Corn   Danish
 Refried Beans   Doughnuts
 Loaded Baked Potato   Flour Tortillas
 Pasta with a Butter Sauce
 Split Pea Soup with Ham and Cream

Low Fat, Whole Milk, or Cream Products:
 Low Fat (2%) Milk   Whole Milk
 Coffee Creamer   Sour Cream
 Ricotta Cheese   Cream Cheese
 Mozzarella Cheese   Ice Cream
 Yogurt made with Whole Milk
 Cheddar and other Whole Milk Cheeses

Whole Eggs and Eggs Yolks

Fatty Meats such as:
 Prime Rib   Pork Chops
 Hamburger   Sausage
 Poultry with Skin   Hot Dogs

Fried Foods such as:
  Fried Fish   Fried Chicken
  Fried Beef   Fried Cheese
  Fried Okra   French Fries

Non-Dairy Creamers

Salad Dressings

Fats such as:
  Margarine   Butter
  Oil   Lard

How much Fat Could I possibly be Eating?

Picture yourself placing an entire stick of butter on a slice of bread. Roll up that slice of bread and take a bite. Do you think that is disgusting? Well, Americans eat more fat than the equivalent of a stick of butter each day!

Considering that each stick of butter (or margarine) has 88 gms of fat, let's look at a few typical meals eaten out:

Breakfast:

2 Scrambled Eggs	= 14 grams fat
3 Slices Bacon	= 12 grams fat
1 Spoonful Fried Potatoes	= 10 grams fat
1 Small Biscuit, unbuttered	= <u>8</u> grams fat
	44 grams fat

(about 1/2 stick of butter)

An Italian Lunch:

1 Bowl Salad with 3 T Italian Dressing	= 24 grams fat
2 Buttered Breadsticks	= 12 grams fat
Minestrone Soup	= <u>5</u> grams fat
	41 grams fat

(about a 1/2 stick of butter)

FACTS ABOUT FAT

Dinner at a Mexican Restaurant:

1/2 Basket Chips (4 oz)	= 40 grams fat
3 Cheese Enchiladas	= 50 grams fat
Refried Beans	= 10 grams fat
Mexican Rice	= <u>10</u> grams fat
	110 grams fat

(1-1/4 sticks of butter)

These three meals add up to a total of 195 grams of fat or over 2 sticks of butter. How much fat do you eat each day?

Calculating the Percentage of Fats in Foods

The average American eats 35 - 40 percent of all their calories in the form of fat. The American Heart Association recommends that this number be lowered to 30%. How do you know if you are accomplishing that task?

Dietary fats such as margarine, butter, oil, or shortening get nearly 100% of all their calories from fat. On the other hand, most of the fruits, vegetables, and starches in their unadulterated state have less than 10% of all their calories coming from fat.

To calculate the percentage of fat in an individual food, use this simple formula:

GRAMS OF FAT X 9 = CALORIES FROM FAT

$$\frac{\text{CALORIES FROM FAT}}{\text{TOTAL CALORIES}} \text{ X 100 = \% FAT}$$

Fats have more than twice as many calories as the same amount of carbohydrates or proteins. Therefore, the percentage of calories coming from fat will also be disproportionately higher than it would appear from the numbers on a food label. Such as on this label:

1/2% Milk	Whole Milk (3.25%)
Serving Size: 1 c	Serving Size: 1 c
Calories 90	Calories 150
Protein 8	Protein 8
Carbohydrate 11	Carbohydrates .. 11
Fat. 1	Fat 8
$1 \times 9 = 9/90 = .10$	$8 \times 9 = 72/150 = .48$
$.10 \times 100 = 10\%$ FAT	$.48 \times 100 = 48\%$ FAT

Even lean meats can get a large percentage of calories from fat. As you can see, the labeling of a certain percent fat-free (such as 95% fat-free luncheon meats) has *nothing* to do with the American Heart Association's recommendation of 30% fat. The manufacturer is referring to the percentage of the *weight* of the product that is fat-free and not to the percentage of *calories.*

95% Fat Free Meats	Bologna
Serving Size: 1 oz	Serving Size: 1 oz
Calories 35	Calories. 72
Protein 5	Protein 3
Carbohydrates .... <1	Carbohydrates . <1
Fat 2	Fat 7
$2 \times 9 = 18/35 = .51$	$7 \times 9 = 63/72 = .88$
$.51 \times 100 = 51\%$ FAT	$.88 \times 100 = 88\%$ FAT

FACTS ABOUT FAT

Even though vegetables and starches, as they are found in nature, are fairly low fat, adding fats can make a BIG difference.

All you need each day for life is "a dab" of fat, but instead most of us add "just a dab" on everything we eat. And that adds up quickly as you can see in these examples:

Vegetable Salad, Without Dressing	Vegetables Salad With 2 T Dressing
Calories 30	Calories 190
Protein 2	Protein 3
Carbohydrates 4	Carbohydrates 9
Fat 0.2	Fat 16
$0.2 \times 9 = 2/30 = .07$	$16 \times 9 = 144/190 = .76$
$.07 \times 100 = 7\%$ FAT	$.76 \times 100 = 76\%$ FAT

Yeast Roll, No Butter	Yeast Roll With 1 t Margarine
Calories 110	Calories 145
Protein 4	Protein 4
Carbohydrates 22	Carbohydrates .. 22
Fat 1	Fat 5
$1 \times 9 = 9/110 = .08$	$5 \times 9 = 45/145 = .31$
$.08 \times 100 = 8\%$ FAT	$31 \times 100 = 31\%$ FAT

As you can see, many foods are more than 30% fat. This does not mean that you should not be eating them. Instead, try to balance the fat *each day* to no more than 30%. Some foods may be higher than 30% but others will be lower.

An easier way to keep track of the fat in our diet is to know how many grams of fat we should be eating each day.

How much Fat should I be eating?

The average American diet consists of 35 - 40% fat while the American Heart Association recommends that this number be lowered to 30%. Fats contribute to the taste of foods, the texture, and our satiety level (feeling of fullness) but cutting back to 30% is a sensible and achievable level. To calculate 30% of your total calories, use this simple formula:

CALORIES X .30 = CALORIES COMING FROM FAT
CALORIES COMING FROM FAT/9 = GRAMS OF FAT

For example, a person eating 2000 calorie diet each day should try to keep their fat intake to less than 67 grams of fat.

(2000 calories X .30 = 600 calories from fat; 600/9 = 67 grams of fat).
For simplification, use this chart below:

	Calories	30% Fat Level
Women:		
Weight Loss	1000-1200	33-40 gms fat
Maintenance	1500-1800	50-60 gms fat
Men:		
Weight Loss	1800-2000	60-67 gms fat
Maintenance	2500-3000	83-100 gms fat

Now that you understand the basics about watching your fat intake, you will better understand the restaurant entries in this book. But first, read the next chapter on "General Guidelines for Dinin'Lean®" that apply no matter what restaurant you are eating at.

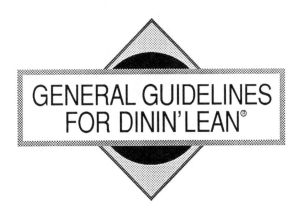

GENERAL GUIDELINES FOR DININ'LEAN®

If you think you are lacking the willpower it takes to dine out low fat, read on. Willpower is not the panacea for weight loss. What you need to prevent overeating is pre-planning skills.

This chapter includes some of the skills that will help you eat healthier when you are dining out. Part of the chapter also focuses on some dietary changes that will save you immensely when it comes to calories and grams of fat. The remainder of the book gives specific guidelines for over 200 restaurants.

Speak to the Manager

It may be difficult to know what to order just by looking at the menu. The staff may also be too busy (or may not know enough about the food) to really help you with your decisions.

So, contact the restaurant ahead of time and ask the manager specific questions about serving sizes and preparation methods. Tell the¡ manager about your nutritional concerns and ask what they can prepare for you. The best time to call the manager is between the hours of 9 and 11 in the morning and between 2 and 5 in the afternoon.

Be Assertive about what Changes You Want

If it seems that the server did not understand your request - repeat it and emphasize your special request such as "without butter" or "sauce on the side".

Send it back if it doesn't come the way you requested it. Remember, **you** are paying for it!

Did Mother say "Never play with your food"?

If the food delivered to your table does not comply to your special request and you do not want to wait for another dish to be prepared, feel free to play with your food. Using your knife, wipe off the extra sauce, trim away the fat, or remove the skin from your chicken. Pour the sauce off your dinner plate and onto an empty bread plate. Use a paper napkin to blot away the extra fat on your slice of pizza.

Get the "Doggie Bag" with Dinner

Since most restaurants serve twice as much food as you really need, ask for a doggie bag as soon as you are served. Put half of the dinner in the doggie bag for tomorrow's lunch. Remember, the starving children in Africa will not benefit from your overeating. If you do not carry out the extra food in a doggie bag, you will carry it out on your "waste" line.

Don't Feel Guilty About Eating

This book was written as a guide to inform you about the food options that are available in restaurants. Use this information to help you decide what you are going to "spend" your calories and grams of fat on.

You don't need to follow each and every suggestion; set your own priorities. One person will order the salad with dressing and the fish fried.

GENERAL GUIDELINES

Another person will eat both the salad and the potato dry and order the fish baked, just so they can "splurge" on a rich, creamy dessert. You decide.

Remember, eating low fat may require some adjustment time - don't just "jump in" or you might find it unpalatable. Make those changes slowly and your taste buds will adapt.

Eat Slowly and Taste Every Bite

Some people eat more than they need simply because they eat at a frantic pace. They don't even taste their food. Do not swallow until you have completely savored the taste of the food. You will enjoy the food so much more and you will end up eating less.

This rule applies especially for desserts. If you have decided to spend the extra calories, take thin slivers of the dessert and savor every bite!

Eat Till You "Feel Fine" - Not Stuffed!

In the past, people went out to eat for special occasions only - that seemed to give them permission to go on an eating binge.

Now that most of us eat at least one meal each day "out" - we need to be more responsible. Start listening to your body. Remember that it takes 20 minutes for the full stomach to tell the brain that it is full. So eat slowly! Allot adequate time for your brain to catch up with your stomach.

Stop when you are comfortable. Don't feel compelled to clean your plate - the restaurant staff will do that for you.

Concentrate on the Atmosphere

Focus on people you are with and the conversation that is going on around you. Then you can concentrate less on the food.

Have a Closing to the Meal

Most of us need a signal that the meal is over. For many of us, it is when the food is gone and the plate is empty. Since restaurants serve more than most of us should be eating, that is a sure way to gain weight.

When you are comfortable (or maybe before) ask for that doggie bag. If you don't plan on taking the extra food home, push your plate aside. Other tactics include salting your food excessively so you will stop nibbling or placing your napkin onto the plate.

Order the "Luncheon" Portion

Some restaurants will allow you to order the "luncheon" portion at dinner for a discounted price. The luncheon portions are generally half the size of the dinner portions.

Some of these restaurants are referenced in this book. Other restaurants stated they would comply if a customer asked, but they preferred not to have it mentioned in the book.

Know the Menu Terminology.

Knowing how to read and interpret the menu can help you to make wiser decisions. If you don't understand a menu item or the description, ask for an explanation. The following definitions will help you make leaner choices.

Leaner ways to cook meats and vegetables:
  Broiling - cooked under an intense heat source
  Roasting - baked in an oven
  Chargrilling - cooking on a rack over charcoal or gas
  Grilling - over charcoal, gas fire, or on a "flat top" grill
  Poaching - simmered in a liquid

Stir-frying - quick cooking method in a small
amount of oil

Boiling - cooked in water

Steaming - cooked in very little water or above the
heated water

NOTE:
- Restaurants may still brush or baste the meats with
fats during or after the cooking process.
- Some meats may be marinated in oil or a high fat
substance which can add a substantial amount
of calories.
- The term Prime refers to meat that is very high in
fat.
- Many restaurants still add margarine, butter, oil, or
other sauces before serving boiled or steamed
vegetables. Request that it be left off.

Higher fat methods to cook meats and vegetables:
Deep fried, or Fried - cooked submerged in oil or
fat

Panfried - shallow-frying in an oil or fat

Sauteing - quickly fried in a little fat

Braising - meat is browned in a fat, then simmered in a covered pan with a little liquid.

Terms that indicate a high fat food:

Crispy	Escalloped
Creamy	Stewed
Buttery	Casserole
In butter sauce	Hash
In a cream sauce	Pot pie
Hollandaise	Au gratin
Creamed	Parmesan
In its own gravy	In a cheese sauce

Don't Drink Your Calories!

Always have a calorie-free beverage such as water, mineral water, club soda, unsweetened iced tea, or a diet soda nearby so you can quench your thirst. These fluids also help satiate your appetite. Nearly all restaurants in this book offered some non-caloric options other than water, coffee, and tea.

Look at the measuring cups in your kitchen to become familiar with fluid ounces. Eight fluid ounces is equivalent to a One Cup measuring cup. This is about the size of a small styrofoam coffee cup. Keep in mind that most of us drink beverages in portions larger than 8 oz.

Most people don't realize how many calories are in the beverages they drink. Look at these comparisons to see how you can save some calories and fat grams:

		CALS	FAT (gms)
Request Skim Milk instead of Whole Milk:			
8 oz Whole Milk		150	8
8 oz Skim Milk		90	0
	SAVINGS:	60	8
Ask for Diet Soda:			
8 oz Soda		100	0
8 oz Diet Soda		1	0
	SAVINGS:	99	0
Lighten your Coffee with Milk:			
1 oz Coffee Cream or		60	6
1 oz Non-dairy Creamer		45	3
1 oz Whole Milk		20	1
	SAVINGS:	25-40	2-5

GENERAL GUIDELINES

	CALS	FAT (gms)
Drink Low Calorie Beverages instead of Mixed Drinks:		
8 oz Screwdriver, Gin & Tonic, Bloody Mary, or Bourbon & Soda	200	0
Diet Soda, Coffee, Tea, Water, Club Soda, Mineral Water	<u>0-1</u>	<u>0</u>
SAVINGS:	**200**	**0**
Order Light Beer:		
12 oz Beer	150	0
12 oz Light Beer	<u>100</u>	<u>0</u>
SAVINGS:	**50**	**0**
Instead of a Wine Cooler, Order Club Soda/Wine:		
8 oz Wine Cooler	160	0
4 oz Wine + 4 oz Club Soda	<u>80</u>	<u>0</u>
SAVINGS:	**80**	**0**
Skip the Liqueurs in Coffee:		
1.5 oz Creme de Menthe + Coffee	180	0
Coffee	<u>0</u>	<u>0</u>
SAVINGS:	**180**	**0**
Order Simple rather than Fancy:		
8 oz Pina Colada, Martini, Manhattan, Daiquiri, or Margarita	500	0
1 oz Rum + 7 oz Coke	<u>190</u>	<u>0</u>
SAVINGS:	**310**	**0**

Make Appetizers the Meal

Many appetizers are fried; you could easily blow your fat allotment before you order the entree! If you are going to eat something fried - order an appetizer portion instead of the entree portion.

If you find some leaner appetizers such as shrimp cocktail or beef strips on a skewer - consider making that your entree. Appetizer meat portions are often only 2 to 4 ounces.

Pasta, in Italian restaurants, is often offered in both the entree and the appetizer portion. Having two or three appetizers for a meal or an appetizer, salad and some bread can be other viable options.

Breads Aren't Fattening

Plain, yeast breads are relatively low in fat and calories. It's the butter and oil that is added that does the damage. Garlic bread can often have twice as many calories as plain Italian bread! Most plain unbuttered breads have only about 75 calories per ounce (an average slice of bread).

Cornbread, croissants, buttered breadsticks, and muffins can add substantially more calories than is in the plain yeast rolls. These are often 100-125 calories per ounce even before you butter them. See the discussion in the chapter on "Salad Bars".

Salads Aren't Always Low Calorie Fare

Raw vegetables are low in fat. But, the dressing and the mayonnaise-ladened salads can really add up the fat and calories.

Salad dressings have about 80 calories per level tablespoon and most restaurants are generous! They frequently put on 3 or 4 tablespoons (that's over 300 calories of pure fat). Oil and vinegar isn't much better - oil has 125 calories per tablespoon. Read the chapter titled "Salad Bars" to discover why selecting a salad can sometimes have more calories and fat than a hamburger and fries.

GENERAL GUIDELINES

Beware of "Low Calorie" Salad Dressings

Don't rely on restaurants to carry very low-calorie dressings. Even if they do have low calorie dressings, they may not be as low as you had hoped.

While regular salad dressings have about 80 cals/9 grams of fat, lower calorie salad dressings may range anywhere from 6 cals/0 gms fat to 50 cals/5 gms fat. Most restaurants select those in the higher range. If a restaurant has a FAT FREE salad dressing, this is listed in the restaurant entry.

Always Ask for Your Dressing on the Side

That way you can control how much is added. A recommended way to get a taste with every bite is to dip your fork into the salad dressing and then into your salad.

There are other Low Calorie Dressings

Vinegar is almost always available although not listed in the restaurant entries. Red Wine Vinegar, Balsamic Vinegar, and Tarragon Vinegar are very flavorful. A squirt of lemon on your salad may satisfy your palate. Picante sauce (at 10 calories per tablespoon) also makes a great low calorie dressing or topping for your baked potato.

Bring Your Own Dressing

Some companies such as Estee, Dieter's Gourmet, Weight Watchers, Skinny Havens, and Pritikin market dressings that are in individual packets. Now you can bring your own dressing!

Stay Away from Fried Foods

Appetizers are notoriously the worst - almost everything is fried. And when you review the examples below, you begin to realize that fried foods just may not be worth it!

		CALS	FAT (gms)
8 oz Fried Fish		550	25
8 oz Baked Fish		240	3
	Savings:	310	22
6 oz Fried Chicken		500	30
6 oz Grilled Chicken Breast		275	7
	Savings:	225	23
10 French Fries		160	8
1/2 c Potato		100	<1
	Savings:	60	8

What "Heart Healthy" really means

Some restaurants use small red hearts or the term "heart healthy" to designate that the menu items are lower in cholesterol and/or fat.

The American Heart Association does not define "heart healthy" for one individual meal. Therefore, these menu items may not always be low enough in fat or calories for your needs. A heart may mean that the dish *can* be prepared lower in cholesterol and fat - but simply ordering the dish without specifying that you want it prepared low fat will give you the higher fat item. Other restaurants used the designation but did not know how many calories or grams of fat were in the food item.

Even if butter is served at the table or used in the cooking, margarine or vegetable oil is almost always available. Request margarine or vegetable oil whenever possible.

GENERAL GUIDELINES

Limit the Meat Portions

Meat is a good source of protein but, unfortunately, it is high in fat - especially saturated fats. The American Heart Association recommends that we only eat 6-8 ounces of animal protein *each day*. That's equivalent to eating a piece of meat the size of a deck of cards for lunch and another piece the same size for dinner. That's plenty of protein for our needs! Unfortunately, meat portions served in restaurants are often 6-8 oz at lunch and 8-10 oz at dinner. Occasionally, you will find luncheon portions closer to 3-4 ounces. Ordering appetizers that have 2 or 3 ounces of meat instead of an entree will help moderate your meat consumption.

Split an Entree and Have an Extra Salad

Again, entrees are much larger than recommended, so consider splitting an entree. Then order an extra salad, a plate of steamed vegetables, or a baked potato.

Simplicity is Best in Entrees

Simply prepared foods are usually the lowest in fats and calories. Butter or oil is often added while cooking the individual servings and can often be omitted if you request. Ask that the vegetables, potatoes, and meats be prepared without added fats.

Broiled foods can be prepared with wine or lemon juice instead of butter. Fish, even with the added fats used when broiling, is usually a better choice than beef. Grilled chicken is almost always offered.

Those Little Extras can Really Add Up

Always ask what is added to the dishes you want to order. Review the chapter on "Salad Bars" to find out how many calories and grams of fat are in salad toppings. The chapter on "Mexican" restaurants discusses the calories in avocados. "Cafes and Delicatessens" addresses the calories and grams of fat in cheese.

Just a few croutons and a sprinkle of cheese can add an extra hundred calories. Is that how you want to spend your calories and fat? Or would you rather have a few bites of dessert?

Order all Sauces on the Side

Most sauces are very high in fat. Unless you know that they are "safe", it is best to order all sauces on the side. That way you can control how much you really want. Dip your fork into the sauce and then into the food for a taste with every bite. This is true for the lemon butter sauce that comes on the fish, the gravy added to the chicken fried steak, the dressing on the salad, and the alfredo sauce on the fettuccine.

Fill up on Fat-Free Fare

Pure unadulterated starches, vegetables, and fruit are very low in fat with a few exceptions.

Plain bread, noodles, potatoes, beans, corn, broccoli, strawberries and melons are all low in fat. It's the toppings that contribute most of the calories and fat grams. A healthy meal includes a small portion of meat and larger amounts of these fat-free fare.

Split Dessert, if You Must

Calories for most desserts range from 500 to 1000 calories per portion. So if you must, split a dessert with another person or several people. Our taste buds are mostly sensitized to those first few bites anyway. So take tiny bites and really enjoy it.

Fruit is a Great Dessert

Fruit makes a low calorie and sweet ending to a meal. Even if fresh fruit is not listed on the menu, it is often available. Make sure it is not covered with cream or liquor or served with cheese. This will foil your good intentions.

Know The Abbreviations and Measurements

Throughout this book, calories and grams of fat are given for specific food items. Measurements such as teaspoon or tablespoon refer to *level* portions not *heaping* spoons!

Take the measuring spoons and cups out of your kitchen cupboard and use them when serving yourself at home so you can become familiar with how much is served in a restaurant. Buy a postage scale to weigh your meat portions at home so you can estimate the portions served at the restaurants.

Common Abbreviations and Measurements:

3 t (teaspoon)	=	1 T (Tablespoon)
4 T	=	1/4 c (cup)
16 T	=	1 c
1 c	=	8 oz (fluid ounces)
3 oz (ounces) meat	=	about the size of a deck of cards
6-8 oz meat	=	size served in most restaurants
lb	=	pound
cals	=	calories
gms	=	grams (measurement of amount of fat)
<1	=	less than 1 gram

BREAKFAST

Most of us are off and running in the morning. Often that means no time for breakfast. No problem, you say, "If I don't eat in the morning, I'll have more calories to "spend" later in the day, right"? WRONG! The research evidence indicates that people who skip breakfast, eat larger meals later in the day when their bodies are the least active. Breakfast skippers appear to be more overweight than those that eat breakfast.

When you skip breakfast, you are telling your body that you are still fasting from the night before. That seems to signal a lowering of your metabolism *all day long*. That's why they call the first meal of the day BREAK FAST - it literally breaks your fast. It really is important to eat something in the morning.

Our weekends are equally disastrous if we sit down to a more leisurely BIG breakfast. Often these meals are loaded in both fat and calories. This might be all right if we were to "Eat breakfast like a king, lunch like a prince, and dinner like a pauper". But how many of us eat dinner like a pauper? Most of us do not!

For the majority of us, the best breakfast is a smaller breakfast than the traditional bacon, eggs, and biscuit meal. What should you eat? A low fat, high fiber, high carbohydrate meal consisting of fresh fruits and juices, low fat cereals and skim milk, low fat breads, and fat toppings within your fat limit. So the next time you think you have no time for breakfast - grab a piece of fruit and a toasted bagel or English muffin. It's not only fast, it's healthy too!

Here are some ideas of the savings you can make in your calorie and fat intake by choosing leaner foods:

	CALS	FAT (gms)
Select Fresh Fruit instead of Fruit Juice:		
Shoney's 1/2 c Orange Juice	54	0
Shoney's 1/2 c diced Cantaloupe	28	0
Savings:	26	0
Order the English Muffin rather than a Biscuit:		
McD's Biscuit w/spread	260	13
McD's English Muffin w/spread	170	4
Savings:	90	9
Select the Egg Platter without Added Meat:		
Arby's Bacon Platter	860	32
Arby's Egg Platter	460	24
Savings:	400	8

	CALS	FAT (gms)
Request Egg Substitutes Instead of Eggs:		
Two eggs scrambled in 1 t margarine	193	15
Egg substitutes scrambled in 1 t margarine	84	4
Savings:	109	11
Have a Bagel rather than a Croissant:		
Burger King's 1.4 oz Croissant	180	10
2 oz Bagel	160	1
Savings:	20	9
Put Jelly on your Toast instead of Margarine:		
Toast with 1 t margarine	109	5
Toast with 1 t jelly	91	1
Savings:	18	4
Enjoy the Fat-Free Muffins:		
WhatABurger's Blueberry Muffin	263	13
McDonald's Fat-Free Blueberry Muffin	170	0
Savings:	93	13
Select Low Fat Milk for Your Cereal:		
3/4 c. Cheerios with 1 c Whole Milk	230	9
3/4 c Cheerios with 1 c 1% Milk	190	3
Savings:	40	6

	CALS	**FAT (gms)**

Compare these Two Pancake Breakfasts:

McDonalds:

Hotcakes w/margarine, syrup	440	12
Hotcakes with syrup only	<u>370</u>	<u>4</u>
Savings:	**70**	**8**

WhatABurger:

Pancakes/Sausage (with syrup, butter)	496	23
Pancakes (without syrup, butter)	<u>288</u>	<u>4</u>
Savings:	**208**	**19**

So for the best low fat breakfasts, choose: fruits and fruit juices, unbuttered low fat breads, egg substitutes, cereal and skim milk, and toppings within your fat limit.

Fresh Fruits, Dried Fruits, and Fruit Juices

Fresh fruits, dried fruits, and fruit juices are great ideas for breakfast; they're high in vitamins and minerals and have virtually no fat. Fresh fruits are high in fiber and fill you up quickly so they are relatively low in calories. Dried fruits are considered high in calories because a raisin has just as many calories as the grape it was made from. But many people have the tendency to eat far more raisins than they would of the fresh fruit.

Fruit juices are also considered to be concentrated in calories. In fact, ounce for ounce fruit juices have the same amount of calories as Coke or Pepsi or any other sugar-sweetened soda. So, if you are watching your weight, you may want to order the small size of juice. Or better yet, enjoy the high fiber benefits of fresh fruit instead. Fresh fruit

also makes an excellent topping for pancakes,
instead of the usual butter and syrup.

Eggs and Egg Substitutes

Eggs are a good source of protein; one egg has
as much protein as one ounce of meat. Unfortunately egg yolks are both high in fat and cholesterol
(egg whites have virtually none). For this reason, the
American Heart Association recommends no more
than 2-3 egg yolks per week.

But, if you like having the protein from eggs
each morning, try the Egg Substitutes. They are
basically colored and flavored egg whites. And
they taste good. Quite a few of the restaurants
listed in this guide offer Egg Whites only or Egg
Substitutes - even if it is not listed on their menu!

Bacon, Sausage, and Hash Browns

Some people add bacon and sausage to their
breakfast because they think that it is high in
protein. But what bacon and sausage mostly
consists of is FAT. Each slice of bacon has 36 cals/
3 gms fat. Each 1 oz sausage patty has 100 cals/8
gms fat. So, bacon and sausage actually get more
than 72% of their calories from fat!

Hash browns or any other fried potato is also
high in fat. Most have more than 40% of their
calories coming from fat.

Milk

Select skim or low fat milk instead of whole
milk at breakfast. This change will substantially
save calories and fat. An 8 oz glass of whole milk
has 8 gms of fat, almost as much fat as 2 t of
margarine or butter, and 150 calories. An 8 oz glass
of low fat milk has 5 gms of fat or the equivalent of
1 t of margarine or butter, and 120 calories. Skim or
nonfat milk has 0-1 gms fat and only 90 calories.

Cereals

Most cold cereals are low in fat provided you select skim or low fat milk. Granola-type cereals or those with added nuts will have substantially more calories and fat. Birchermuesli, a cold cereal, is a blend of oats, fruits, and nuts. Some restaurants use only nonfat plain yogurt in its preparation, therefore, it is fairly healthy (except for the nuts which are high in fat). Most restaurants still prepare it in the traditional Swiss manner using heavy cream or half and half.

Grits and oatmeal, prepared plain, are very low in fat. They have substantially more calories when made with added fats. Always request that it be prepared without butter or margarine. Oatmeal usually is served with milk on the side - always request skim or low fat milk.

Pancakes and Waffles

The batters of both pancakes and waffles have some oil or fat added for tenderness. But they are really not nutritional disasters until the butter and syrup is added. So always ask the server not to add the butter on top when serving pancakes or waffles. And try using a minimal amount of syrup.

Many restaurants are now providing dietetic syrup as an alternative. Applesauce, jelly or jam, sprinkled cinnamon, and fresh fruit also make delicious, lower calorie toppings. A small portion or what some restaurants refer to as a short stack, which may consist of just 3 pancakes instead of 5, is frequently available.

Breads

Breads such as unbuttered sliced toast, English muffins, bagels, and french bread have little or no fat. They each have about 75 cals/0-1 gms fat per ounce. The average slice of bread is 1 oz while the

normal sized (and unbuttered) English muffin or
bagel weighs in at two ounces. There are some
larger bagels (especially at bagel shops) that weigh
3-4 oz (225-300 cals/3-4 gms fat). French rolls,
offered in some bakeries and sandwich shops, can
weigh in at 4-6 oz (300-450 cals/4-6 gms fat).

Croissants, muffins, doughnuts, kolaches, and
turnovers are all high in fat and calories. Each has
about 100-125 cals/4-8 gms fat per *ounce*. Unfortunately, each of these products weigh about 3-5
ounces each!

A baseball-size muffin, weighing in at 3-4 oz,
could add up to at least 300 calories and about 10-15
gms fat. That's even true for most bran muffins. A
medium-sized 3 oz croissant may have 375 cals/15
gms fat - before you add the spread. A large turnover
(5 oz) may have about 625 cals/25 gms fat.

Fats and Other Spreads

Margarine, although just as many calories as
butter, is a healthier fat because it is mostly unsaturated. Each pat (one level teaspoon) has 35 cals/4
gms fat. A small serving of just 2 level tablespoons
of cream cheese has 100 cals/10 gms fat.

Always order your toast dry so you can control
the amount of spread added. Vegetable fats should
be added based on your total fat intake suggested
each day. Putting jelly or jam on your toast will save
you both calories and fat. One teaspoon of sugar-
sweetened or fruit-sweetened jelly or jam has just 16
cals/0 gms fat; 1 t honey has 20 cals/0 gms fat.

The remainder of the chapter focuses on restaurants that provide nutritious and low fat alternatives
for breakfast. For more information on the restaurants (style of dining and average dinner entree
price), please see the respective entry in the other
sections of the book.

ALAIN & MARIE LE NOTRE BAKERY CAFE

1345 S Voss at Woodway &
21 Town and Country Village
975-7633/827-7363

Fresh Fruits (order without cream) and **Juices** are offered. **Cold Cereal** (Cornflakes, Raisin Bran) can be ordered with **Skim Milk**. Homemade **French Rolls**, **Baguettes**, and **Sour Dough Bread** have no fat. **Whole Wheat Bread** has a small amount. Danish, muffins, and tarts are "sinfully rich".

ANCHORAGE

2504 North Loop West
(5 minutes N of Galleria)
688-4411

Request your **Toast**, **English Muffin**, or **Bagel** to be prepared dry without any butter. **Oatmeal** and **Grits** are prepared without added fats. **Dry Cereal** and **Skim Milk** are available.

ARBY'S

	CALS	FAT (gms)
Blueberry Muffin	200	6
Toastix	420	25
Plain Biscuit	280	15
Bacon Biscuit	318	18
Sausage Biscuit	460	32
Bacon/Egg Croissant	389	26
Sausage/Egg Croissant	519	39
Egg Platter	460	24
Bacon Platter	860	32
Sausage Platter	640	41

ARRIVEDERCI ITALIAN CAFE

515 Post Oak Blvd &
1900 W Loop South
622-5775/622-3333

   Fresh Fruit, Fresh Squeezed Juices, and **Fruit Smoothies** are available. The **English Muffins**, **Bagel**, and **Toast** are prepared dry. **Skim Milk** is offered.

BRASSERIE

5150 Westheimer
(Galleria area)
961-1500

A variety of **Fresh Fruits** and **Fruit Juices** are available.

"Good for You" Omelette is a low cholesterol omelette with fresh mushrooms and herbs sauteed in margarine, served with sliced tomato and dry toast. **Cold or Hot Cereal** can be served with **Skim Milk. Grits** are prepared without any fats. Low Fat (2%) Yogurt is offered on Fruit Plate but also comes with large muffin.

BURGER KING

	CALS	FAT (gms)
Croissan'wich w/Egg, Cheese	315	20
Croissan'wich w/Bac, Egg, Ch	361	24
Croissan'wich w/Saus, Egg, Ch	534	40
Croissan'wich w/Ham, Egg, Ch	346	21
Croissant	180	10
Biscuit w/Bacon	378	20
Biscuit w/Sausage	478	29
Biscuit w/Bacon & Egg	467	27
Biscuit w/Sausage & Egg	568	36
Biscuit	332	17
Scrambled Egg Platter	549	34
w/Bacon	610	39
w/Sausage	768	53
French Toast Sticks	538	32
Tater Tenders	213	12
Mini Muffins-Blueberry	292	14

	CALS	FAT (gms)
Lemon Poppyseed	318	18
Raisin Oat Bran	291	12
Danish - Apple Cinnamon	390	13
Cinnamon Raisin	449	18
Cheese	406	16

CAFE VIENNA

5701 Main St
(in Wyndham Warwick Hotel)
639-4552

Fresh Fruits and **Fruit Juices** are offered. **Oatmeal and Grits** are offered without added butter. **Cold Cereals** can be enjoyed with **Skim or Low Fat Milk. Swiss Style Birchermuesli** is a cold cereal that consists of oatmeal, low fat yogurt, raisins, and fresh fruits; the sprinkling of walnuts can be requested to be left off.

Egg Substitutes can be prepared **Scrambled** or as an **Omelet. Yogurt** is low fat - plain or fruited are available. **Toast, Bagels**, and **English Muffin** should be requested dry.

BREAKFAST

CLIFF'S OLD FASHIONED HAMBURGERS

8 restaurants in Houston area
for locations, call:
580-0126

Juices such as pineapple, orange, apple, and tomato are offered. **Egg Substitutes** can be ordered **Scrambled** or as an **Omelet**. **Veggie Omelet** made with **Egg Substitutes** have green peppers, onions, and tomatoes; served with **Grits** (they have no fat).

Oatmeal also has no added fats. **Whole Wheat or Rye Toast** can be prepared dry. Even **French Toast** can be prepared with **Egg Substitutes** and **2% Low Fat Milk.**

DEERFIELD'S

6580 Fannin
(in Marriot/Medical Center)
796-0080

A wide variety of F**resh Fruits** and **Juices** are on the menu. **Cold Cereal** - with fresh fruit and milk (both **Skim and Low Fat** are available) **Oatmeal** or **Grits**. Order dry: **Bagel, English Muffin,** and **Toast.**

Low Cholesterol Omelette (filled with fresh spinach, onions, and green peppers - sauteed in about 1 t margarine and served with sliced tomatoes) served with toast or English Muffin (request dry).

DEVILLE RESTAURANT

1300 Lamar
(Downtown in Four Seasons Hotel)
650-1300

A variety of **Fresh Fruit** and **Juices** are offered.
Bagel or **English Muffin** can be ordered as you
request.

The starred (•) items on the menu are less than
350 calories. They include: **The Alternative**
(choose the leaner menu of fresh fruit plate, shredded wheat with low fat milk, and wheat toast with
margarine); **Oatmeal Brulee**; and **Vegetarian
Omelette** of Cholesterol-free Eggs with Mushrooms, Green Onions, Spinach, and Roasted
Tomato Relish.

EDO'S CAFE ON THE PARK

5 Post Oak Park #120
(Galleria area)
552-0355

Plenty of **Freshly Squeezed Juices** and
Smoothies (made mostly with fresh fruit, juices,
honey, and ice). The **Appetite Quencher** consists
of: fresh strawberries, apples, bananas, Sweet 'n
Low or Nutrasweet, blended with low fat milk but
skim milk can be substituted.

The hot cereals: **Oatmeal, Oatbran,** and **Grits**
are made without fats. Both **Skim and Low fat
Milk** are available with **Dry Cereals. Toast,
English Muffin**, and **Bagels** are prepared as you
request. Margarine is used in this restaurant.

Cholesterol-free Omelet made with 2 egg whites and vegetables are offered. Oatbran muffin, although 90% fat-free, still is high in fat.

FIFTY NINE DINER

3801 Farnham
(Inside loop, off I-59)
523-2333

Fruit Juices and Fresh Fruit are offered. **Egg Substitutes** or "**Egg Whites Only**" can be requested for **Scrambled Eggs** or **Omelets**. **Toast, English Muffins**, and **Bagels** can be ordered dry. **Oatmeal** and **Grits** are offered without added fat.

FOUNTAIN VIEW CAFE

1842 Fountain View
(Galleria area)
785-9060

Plenty of **Fresh Fruit** including **Fruit-A-Lope** which is fresh fruit inside a cantaloupe half. Will prepare "**Egg Whites Only**" upon request - plain or as an omelet with tomatoes, onions, green peppers, mushrooms, and fresh homemade salsa. Ask for **Toast**, **Bagel**, or **English Muffin** to be prepared dry with margarine on the side. **Low Fat Milk** is available for your cereal.

GARDEN COURT/HOUSTON PLAZA HILTON

6633 Travis
(Medical Center)
524-6633

Lots of **Fresh Fruit** and **Fruit Juices**. **Cream of Wheat**, **Oatmeal**, and **Grits** are prepared without any added fats. **Toasted Bagel** and **Toasted English Muffin** come dry with margarine on the side. Both **Skim and Low Fat Milk** are available for your cereal. **EggBeaters** are available upon request.

HEALTH FOUNTAIN RESTAURANT

1331 Augusta Dr.
(in Post Oak YMCA)
266-7600

Fresh Fruit, **Juices**, and **Smoothies** are available for breakfast. Most Smoothies are made with fresh fruit, honey, ice, and juices. Review the components listed on the menu; can be changed if desired. May want to request **Skim Milk** to be used in the **Appetite Quencher** (The Calorie Watcher) instead of low fat milk. The **"Y" Special** is made up of fresh fruit, protein powder, brewer's yeast, honey, ice, juice, and nonfat plain yogurt. Wheat Germ, added to some drinks, is high in fat. Granola is also high in fat.

Homemade Muffins (Blueberry, Apple Oat Bran, Banana Nut) have only about a teaspoon of oil (about 4 grams fat) per muffin and only egg whites are used.

JACK IN THE BOX

	CALS	**FAT (gms)**
Scrambled Egg Pocket	431	21
Supreme Crescent	547	40
Sausage Crescent	584	43
BREAKFAST JACK	307	13
Scrambled Egg Platter	559	32
Hash Browns	156	11
Pancake Platter	612	22
Pancake Syrup	121	0
Grape Jelly	38	0

JOJOS OF TEXAS FAMILY RESTAURANT

6 restaurants in Houston
for locations, call:
440-8831

Fresh Fruits and **Juices** are offered. **Raisin Bran** and **Special K** cereals are available; **Skim and Low Milk** can be ordered. Request **Toast, English Muffin**, and **Bagels** to be prepared dry. **Oatmeal** does not have any added fats (raisins, brown sugar, cinnamon apples, and milk are all on the side). Request **Skim Milk** with the **Oatmeal.**

Egg Substitutes can be ordered scrambled or in an omelette.

Multi-Grain Pancakes are a high fiber alternative but not low in fat; if you order them, request no butter on top. **Low Calorie Syrup** is available upon request.

Low Fat Cottage Cheese is an optional side order.

LA BRASSERIE/DOUBLETREE HOTEL

400 Dallas
(Downtown)
759-0202

A variety of **Fruit Juices** and **Fresh Fruit** (request without cream) are available. **Low Fat Plain and Fruited Yogurt** is offered. **Dry Cereal** can be ordered with **Skim or Low Fat Milk.** **Oatmeal** and **Cream of Wheat.**

Egg Beater Omelette has light cheese and fresh vegetables served open face. It is cooked with a non-stick spray. **Bagel, Toast,** and **English Muffin** can be requested dry.

LA MADELEINE

4002 Westheimer
(Highland Village Center)
623-0645

Sliced Homemade Bread or **Demi-Baguette.** The Baguette has no fat but half of loaf (Demi-baguette) is 6 oz. Order the **Salade de Fruits** or **Berries** without sauce. **Scones** are low fat (4 oz portion has 3 gms fat) and are available in flavors: blueberry, cranberry-orange, and cinnamon.

BREAKFAST

LANCASTER GRILLE

701 Texas Ave
(Downtown)
228-9500

Choose from a wide variety of **Fresh Fruit and Juices**. **The Jogger** includes fresh cantaloupe with cottage cheese, seasonal berries, and six grain toast.

Two **"Cuisine Vitale"** menu choices are available which are low in calories, fat, cholesterol, and sodium: **Cornmeal Pancakes with Raspberry Coulis** or **Fruit Pancakes** served with a warm fruit puree.

LEAF 'N LADLE GARDEN CAFE

14520 L-Memorial Dr
(Dairy Ashford & Memorial)
497-3649

Fruit Salad. Order **Toast, English Muffin,** or **Bagel** to be toasted dry with margarine on the side. **Whole Wheat** (7 grain) **Bread** is available, made without sugar or fat.

Grits have margarine added, request that it be prepared without margarine. **Dry cereal** is available but only with whole milk.

MAMA'S CAFE

6019 Westheimer
(between Fountain View & Green Ridge)
266-8514

Skim Milk with **Assorted Dry Cereal**. **Fresh Fruit** and **Juices** are available. **Grits** and **Oatmeal** prepared without any fats. Order the **Toast** or **English Muffin** with the margarine on the side.

MCDONALD'S

	CALS	FAT (gms)
Hotcakes w/margarine, syrup	440	12
Hotcakes with syrup only	**370**	**4**
Fat-Free Apple Bran Muffin	**190**	**0**
Fat-Free Blueberry Muffin	**170**	**0**
English Muffin w/spread	**170**	**4**
Cherrios	**80**	**1**
Wheaties	**90**	**1**
1% Low Fat Milk	**110**	**2**
Egg McMuffin	280	11
Scrambled Eggs	140	10
Sausage	160	15
Hashbrown Potatoes	130	7
Biscuit w/Biscuit Spread	260	13
Biscuit w/Sausage	420	28
Biscuit w/Sausage, Egg	505	33
Biscuit w/Bacon, Egg, Cheese	440	26
Sausage McMuffin	345	20
Sausage McMuffin w/Egg	430	25
Apple Danish	390	17
Iced Cheese Danish	390	21
Cinnamon Raisin Danish	440	21
Raspberry Danish	410	16

NEW YORK BAGEL COFFEE SHOP

9720 Hillcroft
(at Braeswood)
723-8650

Choose from **Orange, Grapefruit, Tomato, or Apple Juice.** Fifteen varieties of **Bagels** are offered; each is 4 oz. **Cold Cereals** are available with **Skim Milk. Oatmeal** is made without any fat. **Egg Beaters** can be ordered plain or as an omelette.

PROMENADE RESTAURANT/ DOUBLETREE HOTEL

2001 Post Oak
(Galleria area)
961-9300

Fresh Fruit is available ala carte or in a **Tropical Fruit Platter** - fresh fruit with cottage cheese or nonfat plain yogurt (but skip the granola). The **Hot Cereals** are prepared without any fats. **Egg Beaters** are available upon request.

RAZZBERRY'S RESTAURANT

14058 Memorial Drive
(Kirkwood/Memorial Center)
556-9120

Egg Substitutes can be prepared in a variety of ways. Build an Omelette with green peppers, onions, mushrooms, and chives. **Fresh Fruit or Tomatoes** can be chosen to accompany the Egg Substitutes. Request the **English Muffin**, **Bagel**, or **Toast** to be prepared dry so you can add toppings as desired.

SHONEY'S

Fresh Fruit and **Dry Cereal** (except for granola cereal) are low in fat. Nutritional information was provided for some of the other *Breakfast Bar* Items:

	CALS	FAT (gms)
Pancakes (1)	41	0
French Toast	69	3
Syrup, light (ladle)	60	0
Grits (1/4 cup)	57	3
Country Gravy (1/4 cup)	82	7
Cottage Fries (1/4 cup)	62	2
Home Fries, dices (1/4 cup)	53	2
Hashbrowns (1/4 cup)	43	2
Mushroom Topping (1 oz)	25	2
Cheese sauce (ladle)	26	2
Egg scrambled (1/4 cup)	95	7
Biscuit (each)	170	8
Blueberry Muffin (each)	107	3

BREAKFAST

	CALS	FAT (gms)
English Muffin	140	2
with raisin & margarine	158	4
Sausage Patty (each)	136	13
Sausage Link (each)	91	9
Bacon (strip)	36	3
Breakfast Ham	26	1

THE RESTAURANT/THE RITZ CARLTON HILTON

1919 Briar Oaks Lane
(inside 610 on San Felipe)
840-7600

Plenty of **Fresh Fruits. Fitness Cuisine Breakfast** includes: choice of freshly squeezed orange or grapefruit juice OR pineapple, papaya or seasonal fruit; shredded wheat cereal with granola and skim milk; bran muffin; with decaffeinated coffee or tea.

WHATABURGER

	CALS	FAT (gms)
Pancakes/Sausage (with syrup, butter)	496	23
Pancakes (without syrup, butter)	**288**	**4**
Potato & Egg Taquito	311	14
Potato & Egg Taquito w/Ch	358	19
Sausage & Egg Taquito	310	19
Sausage & Egg Taquito w/Ch	357	23
Egg Omelette Sandwich	312	15
Breakfast on a Bun	520	34

	CALS	FAT (gms)
Sausage	208	19
Hash Brown	150	9
Pecan Danish	270	16
Oat Bran Muffin	252	9
Blueberry Muffin	263	13
Biscuit	280	13
Egg (scrambled or folded)	106	8
Biscuit w/Egg & Cheese	458	28

WHISTLER'S WALK

1200 Louisiana
(Downtown)
654-1234

Offers plenty of **Fresh Fruit** in season. **Dry Cereals** are offered with **Skim or Low Fat Milk.** **Hot Oatmeal** or **Grits** have butter on the side (margarine is available on request). **Bagels, English Muffin**, and **Toast** come unbuttered for you to top as desired.

Eggbeaters are available. Two "**Perfect Balance**" breakfasts: **Egg Beater Frittata** - open faced egg beater omelette filled with crisp seasonal vegetables and light cheese (196 cals/3 gms fat) and **Jogger's Breakfast** - 2 large eggs served on a bed of freshly sauteed spinach and accompanied by plain yogurt (323 cals/19 gms fat when eggs are scrambled or 291 cals when poached).

There's no need to "BLOW IT" when eating out at a fast food restaurant. There are plenty of options and most of them take no additional waiting period.

Remember - if you eat just 100 calories a day less than your maintainance calories, you will lose a pound each month. Here are some ideas of how to make leaner choices when eating out in a fast food restaurant:

	<u>CALS</u>	<u>FAT (gms)</u>
Select Small rather than Large:		
Beck's Prime Lg Choc Shake	1048	66
Beck's Prime Sm Choc Shake	<u>655</u>	<u>41</u>
SAVINGS:	**393**	**25**
Jack in the Box Reg Fries	351	17
Jack In the Box Sm Fries	<u>219</u>	<u>11</u>
SAVINGS:	**132**	**6**
Subway's Spicy Italian Sub:		
12" on Italian Roll	1043	63
6" on Italian Roll	<u>522</u>	<u>32</u>
SAVINGS:	**521**	**31**

	CALS	FAT (gms)
Order Diet instead of Regular:		
McDonald's medium Coke	190	0
McDonald's medium Diet Coke	1	0
SAVINGS:	**189**	**0**
Choose the New Lighter Entrees:		
Arby's Regular Roast Beef	353	15
Arby's Light Roast Beef Deluxe	294	10
SAVINGS:	**59**	**5**
McDonald's Quarter Pounder	410	20
McDonald's McLean Deluxe	320	10
SAVINGS:	**90**	**10**
Have it Without Cheese:		
JUMBO JACK with Cheese	677	40
JUMBO JACK	584	34
SAVINGS:	**93**	**6**
Have it Plain:		
Wendy's Hot Stuffed Potato with Sour Cream & Chives	500	23
Wendy's Hot Stuffed Potatoes, plain	270	≤1
Savings	**230**	**23**
Order Grilled Chicken rather than a Hamburger:		
Burger King Whopper without mayonnaise	468	20
Burger King's BK Broiler without honey mustard	230	4
SAVINGS:	**238**	**16**

	CALS	FAT (gms)
Choose Grilled Chicken rather than Chicken Salad:		
Chick-fil-A Chicken Salad Sandwich on wheat bread	379	18
Chick-fil-A Chargrilled Chicken Sandwich	<u>258</u>	<u>5</u>
SAVINGS:	121	13
Select Grilled Chicken rather than Fried Chicken:		
Wendy's Chicken Sandwich	440	19
Wendy's Grilled Chicken Sandwich	<u>340</u>	<u>13</u>
SAVINGS:	100	6
WhatABurger's Whatachick'n Deluxe	671	32
WhatABurger's Grilled Chicken Sandwich	<u>455</u>	<u>16</u>
SAVINGS:	216	16
Order Fish instead of Steak:		
Beck's Prime Steak Sandwich	655	46
Beck's Prime Swordfish Sandwich w/out tartar sauce	<u>364</u>	<u>9</u>
SAVINGS:	291	37
Choose Baked Fish rather than Fried:		
Long John Silvers Fish and Fryes - 3 pc	930	47
Long John Silvers Baked Fish w/paprika - 3 pc	<u>610</u>	<u>12</u>
SAVINGS:	320	35

	CALS	FAT (gms)

Don't Eat the Fried Shell:

	CALS	FAT (gms)
Taco Bell Taco Salad	903	61
Taco Bell Taco Salad without the Shell	484	31
SAVINGS:	419	30

Avoid Double Meat Sandwiches:

Burger King Double Whopper	844	53
Burger King Whopper Sandwich	614	36
SAVINGS:	230	17

Order Sandwiches without Dressing:

Wendy's Grilled Chicken SW	340	13
Above without Honey Mustard	269	7
SAVINGS:	71	6

Choose Frozen Yogurt rather than Soft Serve:

DQ's Reg Vanilla Cone	230	7
DQ's Reg Vanilla Yogurt Cone	180	<1
SAVINGS:	50	7
DQ's Regular Heath Blizzard	820	36
DQ's Regular Heath Breeze	680	21
SAVINGS:	140	15

Choose a Lower Calorie Salad Dressing:

McDonald's Bleu Cheese (pkg)	250	20
McDonald's Lite Vinaigrette (pkg)	48	2
SAVINGS:	202	18

Roast Beef and Turkey are leaner than Cold Cuts:

Schlotzsky's Small Original	578	32
Schlotzsky's Small Roast Beef	394	17
SAVINGS:	184	15

NUTRITION INFORMATION:

All of the nutrition information listed in this chapter was obtained from the respective company's most recent product literature. Numbers have been rounded off to the nearest whole number for simplicity. Review the section on *How Much Fat Should I Be Eating?* in the second chapter to evaluate which fast food menu items fit into *your* nutritional needs.

When no nutritional information is available from the company, a brief summary of the best food choices is listed.

Some food items are not listed if they are adequately covered in other chapters of this book. This is true for soft drinks, fruits, and fruit juices.

ARBY'S

	CALS	FAT (gms)
New Light Sandwiches:		
Light Roast Chicken Deluxe	**263**	**6**
Light Roast Turkey Deluxe	**260**	**5**
Light Roast Beef Deluxe	**294**	**10**
Without mayonnaise	-12	-1
Fresh Express Salads:		
Chef Salad	205	10
Roast Chicken Salad	**180**	**7**
Garden Salad	**109**	**5**
Side Salad	**25**	**<1**
Croutons (1/2 oz pkg)	59	2
Weight Watchers Dressings:		
Creamy Italian (1 oz pkg)	**29**	**3**
Creamy French (1 oz pkg)	**48**	**3**
Regular Roast Beef	353	15

Junior Roast Beef	218	11
Beef 'N Cheddar	451	20
French Dip	345	12
Ham 'N Cheese	330	15
Potato Cakes	204	12
Jamocha Shake	368	11
Curly Fries	337	18
French Fries	246	13

BECKS PRIME

3 locations:
952-BECK

Happy to accommodate dieter's requests.
Grated cheese is on every salad but can be deleted if
requested - this would eliminate most of the fat
grams and many calories. Low fat milk is available.
Average portion of meat is 4 oz.

	CALS	FAT (gms)
Chicken Sandwich	443	18
without mayonnaise	**343**	**7**
with Bacon & Cheese	727	42
Swordfish Sandwich	401	12
without tartar sauce	**364**	**9**
Fresh Garden Salad, lg	**140**	**7**
Fresh Garden Salad, sm	**82**	**5**
Grilled Chicken Salad, lg	**373**	**12**
Grilled Chicken Salad, sm	**315**	**9**
Salad Dressings:		
Lite Italian, 1.5 oz	**24**	**2**
Thousand Island, 1.5 oz	150	15
Blue Cheese, 1.5 oz	270	24
Lite Ranch, 1.5 oz	91	9
Honey Mustard, 1 oz	152	12

FAST FOOD

	CALS	FAT (gms)
Hamburger	517	20
Cheeseburger	729	38
Bacon Cheeseburger	801	44
Beck's Burger	549	22
Hickory Cheeseburger	761	38
Chili-Cheese Burger	786	41
Steak Sandwich	655	46
Bowl of Chili	807	54
Old Fashioned Dog	491	18
Chili-Cheese Dog	786	40
Kraut Dog	518	18
Fries (7 oz)	498	24
Tostados & Picante	516	25
Malts/Shakes		
Vanilla, lg	975	52
Vanilla, sm	574	31
Chocolate, lg	1048	66
Chocolate, sm	655	41
Strawberry, lg	1002	52
Strawberry, sm	626	31

BLIMPIES

All sandwiches and salads are prepared to order. The **Salads** are each under 300 calories (without dressing) and are prepared with same ingredients as the sandwiches except the bread. The salads can be prepared with **Ham** (96% fat-free), **Roast Beef**, or **Turkey** (94% fat-free). Light Sandwich menu is all under 300 calories.

The **Regular Sandwich** is prepared on a 6 inch bun and has 2-1/2 oz of meats *or* 2 oz meat plus 1 oz cheese. The Giant is on a 12 inch bun and has double the meats/cheese as the regular size. **Ham**, **Turkey**, or **Roast Beef** are the leanest sandwiches.

Low fat toppings for the sandwiches are **Lettuce, Tomato, Onions, Oregano, Sweet Peppers, Vinegar, and Pickles**. Oil and mayonnaise can be left off.

BURGER KING

	CALS	FAT (gms)
BK Broiler Sandwich	267	8
BK Broiler w/out sauce	230	4
Side Salad	25	0
Chunky Chicken Salad	142	4
Garden Salad	95	5
Chef Salad	178	9
Salad Dressings:		
Reduced Cal Light Italian	170	18
French Dressing	290	22
Thousand Island	290	26
Bleu Cheese Dressing	300	32
Olive Oil & Vinegar	310	33
Ranch Dressing	350	37
Whopper Sandwich	614	36
Whopper with Cheese	706	44
Double Whopper Sandwich	844	53
Double Whopper with Cheese	935	61
Above 4 ordered without		
mayonnaise	-146	-16
Hamburger	272	11
Cheeseburger	318	15
Bacon Double Cheeseburger	515	31
Above 3 ordered as a Deluxe	+72	+8
BBQ Bacon Double Cheeseburger	536	31
Mushroom Swiss Dble Ch/burger	473	27

FAST FOOD

	CALS	FAT (gms)
Double Cheeseburger	483	27
Burger Buddies	349	17
Chicken Sandwich	685	40
Ocean Catch Fish Filet	495	25
Chicken Tenders	236	13
Dipping Sauces:		
Barbecue	36	0
Sweet & Sour	45	0
BK Am Express Dip	84	0
Honey	91	0
Ranch	171	18
French Fries (med)	372	20
Onion Rings	339	19
Apple Pie	311	14
Vanilla Shake	334	10
Chocolate Shake (syrup added)	409	11

CAFE EXPRESS

3 restaurants at Kirby,
Post Oak Blvd, & W Gray
Call: 963-9222

Self-serve cafe offering a variety of foods. All
sandwiches are served with mayonnaise; request
without mayonnaise. Leanest sandwiches (if
ordered without cheese) are probably: **Roast
Turkey**, **Baked Ham**, **Pastrami**, and **Roast Beef**.
Baked Potatoes. Salads include the **Mixed
Lettuce Salad**, **Shrimp Salad** (tuna and chicken
salads are mixed with mayonnaise, but not the
shrimp), **Pasta Salad with Tomato Vinaigrette**, or
the **Ginger Chicken Salad with Vegetables**

(request Sesame Dressing on the side).

Fettucine with Tomato Sauce can be ordered, although it is not listed on menu; the Tomato Meat Sauce includes Italian Pork Sausage. **Pizzas** can be requested with just onions and half the cheese. Soups are lean: **Chicken with Rice & Vegetables, Black Bean**, and cold **Gazpacho**. The last two have no oil/fats added.

Fresh Fruit is offered. Four flavors of **Frozen Yogurt** are available each day.

CAPTAIN D'S

Nutrition information is not yet available for all products. **Baked Fish Dinner** with rice, green beans, and bread sticks has 622 cals/22 gms fat.

A new program, The Captain's Grille, will be introduced in the fall of 1991 with broiled fish, chicken, and shrimp but no nutritional information is presently available.

CHARLIE'S HAMBURGER JOINT

6 restaurants in Houston area
call for locations:
350-5335

Chicken Sandwich is made with a 4-1/2 oz marinated and grilled chicken breast, and served on a wheat bun with lettuce and tomato. Request to be prepared without mayonnaise; ask that the sandwich buns be grilled without butter.

Chicken Salad is the same grilled chicken served on a bed of lettuce and tomato; request **Light Italian Dressing**.

CHICK-FIL-A

	CALS	FAT (gms)
Chargrilled Chicken(w/bun)	258	5
Chargrilled Chicken Deluxe		
w/lettuce, tomato	266	5
Chick-n-Q Sandwich	206	7
Chick-fil-A Chicken Sandwich	360	9
Chick-fil-A Chicken Deluxe	368	9
Chargrilled Chicken		
Garden Salad	126	2
Tossed Salad	21	<1
with Lite Italian	46	2
with Ranch Dressing	177	16
with Honey French	246	24
with Thousand Island	231	22
Carrot & Raisin Salad-Cup	116	5
Hearty Breast of Chicken		
Soup-Small	152	3
Chick-fil-A Nuggets (8 pack)	287	15
Chick-fil-A Nuggets (12 pack)	430	23
Chicken Salad SW/wheat bread	379	18
Chicken Salad Plate	291	19
Chicken Salad-Cup	192	14
Cole Slaw-Cup	175	14
Potato Salad-Cup	198	15
Waffle Potato Fries (reg)	270	14
Lemon Pie - slice	329	5
Icedream	134	5
Fudge Brownie (w/nuts)	369	19
Cheesecake	299	19
Lemonade - regular	138	<1
Diet Lemonade	32	<1

CLIFF'S OLD FASHIONED HAMBURGERS

8 restaurants in Houston area
for locations, call:
580-0126

Request all sandwich buns to be grilled without margarine. **Grilled Chicken Sandwich** is a 5 oz skinless, boneless chicken breast served on a whole wheat bun with mayonnaise. The chicken breast is dipped in a mixture of lite soy sauce, Worcestershire sauce, and Italian dressing before grilling. Sandwich has about 350 cals/10 gms fat if ordered without mayonnaise or margarine on the bun.

Grilled Chicken Salad has 5 oz of grilled chicken and 2 oz of shredded Monterey Jack cheese on a lettuce bed with vegetables (request without cheese). **Low Calorie Italian Dressing** is available.

Other specials are offered with both chicken and turkey breast such as the 4 oz **Turkey Breast with Swiss Cheese and Hickory Sauce** (request no cheese).

DAIRY QUEEN

	CALS	FAT (gms)
Small Vanilla Cone	140	4
Regular Vanilla Cone	230	7
Large Vanilla Cone	340	10
Regular Chocolate Cone	230	7
Large Chocolate Cone	350	11
Regular Choc Dipped Cone	330	16
Regular Chocolate Sundae	300	7
Regular Vanilla Shake	520	14
Large Vanilla Shake	600	16
Regular Chocolate Shake	540	14
Regular Vanilla Malt	610	14
Banana Split	510	11
Peanut Buster Parfait	710	32
Hot Fudge Brownie Delight	710	29
Nutty Double Fudge	580	22
Small Strawberry Blizzard	500	12
Regular Strawberry Blizzard	740	16
Small Heath Blizzard	560	23
Regular Heath Blizzard	820	36
Straw Waffle Cone Sundae	350	12
Buster Bar	450	29
Dilly Bar	210	13
DQ Sandwich	140	4
DQ Frozen Cake Slice	380	18
Regular Mr Misty	250	0
Regular Yogurt Cone	180	<1
Large Yogurt Cone	260	<1
Regular Cup of Yogurt	170	<1
Large Cup of Yogurt	230	<1
Regular Yogurt Straw Sundae	200	<1
Small Strawberry Breeze	400	<1
Regular Strawberry Breeze	590	1
Small Heath Breeze	450	12
Regular Heath Breeze	680	21
QC Vanilla Big Scoop	300	14
QC Chocolate Big Scoop	310	14

FUDDRUCKERS

9 restaurants in Houston area
for locations, call:
580-0028

Request all sandwich buns to be grilled without
butter. **Grilled Chicken Sandwich** is made with a
5 oz skinless, boneless chicken breast.

New Orleans Fish Sandwich is a 5 oz cut of
North Atlantic Blue Fish and is grilled. Request
remoulade sauce (serving size is 2 T) on the side.
You serve your own toppings, choose: lettuce,
tomatoes, onions, salsa and pickles.

Request **Lite Italian Dressing** or other dressings on the side of the salads. The salads are
prepared within a fried flour tortilla shell - refrain
from eating the shell.

Grilled Country Chicken Salad consists of 5
oz grilled chicken, lettuce, tomato, and green &
red onions (request no eggs, bacon, or cheese).
Chicken Taco Salad - consists of 5 oz grilled
chicken pieces, shredded lettuce, and diced
tomatoes; can request without sour cream (4T),
cheese (1/3 c), and black olives (1-2).

GRANDY'S

Southwestern Grilled Chicken Dinner
consists of 4 oz boneless, skinless, grilled chicken
(130 cals/4 gms fat); rice (90 cals/<1 gm fat), green
beans (35 cals/2 gms fat), and dinner roll (150 cals/4
gms fat). Total is 405 cals/10 gms fat.

Several grilled items will be introduced in the fall
of 1991, possible entrees include Grilled Chicken
Ka-Bob, Grilled Beef Ka-Bob, and Grilled Shrimp.
No nutritional analysis is currently available.

HAMBURGERS BY GOURMET

3802 Yoakum
(Alabama & Montrose area)
524-5721

Chicken Breast Sandwich - 5 oz charbroiled
breast of chicken (request no sauce, remove the
skin, and no butter on the bun). **Chicken Salad** on
Pita bread can be prepared without mayonnaise, if
requested.

Large Baked Potato - ask for just the toppings
you want. **Dinner Salad** has lettuce, cucumbers,
tomato, and carrot (request **Low Calorie Italian
Dressing** on the side).

HARTZ CHICKEN BUFFET

No nutritional information is available. Stores offer **Mesquite Grilled Roasted Chicken** or **Lemon-Pepper Baked Chicken**. The all-you-can-eat buffet includes **Roasted Chicken** (remove skin before eating), **Fresh Steamed Vegetables** (corn, mashed potatoes, and green beans all have added fat), and **Yeast Rolls** (request rolls without oil brushed on top). Some stores have low fat soft serve.

JACK IN THE BOX

	<u>CALS</u>	<u>FATS (gms)</u>
Chicken Fajita Pita		
(w/out guacamole or salsa)	**292**	**8**
Grilled Chicken Fillet	408	17
Ham and Turkey Melt	592	36
Chicken Supreme	641	39
Fish Supreme	510	27
Side Salad	**51**	**3**
Chef Salad	325	18
Taco Salad	503	31
Reduced-Calorie French	**176**	**8**
Buttermilk House Dressing	362	36
Bleu Cheese Dressing	262	22
Thousand Island Dressing	312	30
Hamburger	267	11
Cheeseburger	315	14
Double Cheeseburger	467	27
JUMBO JACK	584	34
JUMBO JACK with Cheese	677	40

FAST FOOD

Bacon Bacon Cheeseburger	705	45
Grilled Sourdough Burger	712	50
Ultimate Cheeseburger	942	69
Sirloin Cheesesteak	621	30
Egg Rolls - 3 piece	437	24
Egg Rolls - 5 piece	753	41
Chicken Strips - 4 piece	285	13
Chicken Strips - 6 piece	451	20
Taquitos - 5 piece	362	15
Taquitos - 7 piece	511	21
Sweet & Sour Sauce	40	<1
BBQ Sauce	44	<1
Guacamole	55	5
Salsa	8	<1
Taco	187	11
Super Taco	281	17
Small French Fries	219	11
Regular French Fries	351	17
Jumbo Fries	396	19
Onion Rings	380	23
Sesame Breadsticks	**70**	**2**
Tortilla Chips	139	6
Hot Apple Turnover	348	19
Cheese Cake	309	18
Double Fudge Cake	288	9
Milk Shakes	320-330	6-7

LONG JOHN SILVER'S

	CALS	**FAT (gms)**
Standard Entrees (baked):		
(w/rice, gr beans, slaw, bread)		
Fish w/paprika - 3 pc	610	12
Fish w/lemon crumb - 3 pc	640	14
Fish w/scampi sauce - 3 pc	660	18
Light Portion Fish		
w/ paprika - 2 pc	300	2
Light Portion Fish		
w/lemon crumb - 2 pc	320	4
Shrimp Scampi	610	18
Chicken	630	17
Entrees:		
Fish and Fryes - 3 pc	930	47
Fish and Fryes - 2 pc	720	35
Fish and More - 2 pc	860	42
Fish and More - 3 pc	1070	53
3 pc Chicken Planks Dinner	860	37
4 pc Chicken Planks Dinner	990	44
Fish and Chicken	930	43
Seafood Platter	860	41
Batter-Dipped Shrimp - 6 pc	800	40
Batter-Dipped Shrimp - 9 pc	970	51
Stuffed Crab - 4 pc	790	34
Homestyle Shrimp - 6 pc	740	33
Homestyle Shrimp - 9 pc	880	41
Ocean Chef Salad	150	5
Seafood Salad	230	5
Side Salad	25	<1
Small Salad	11	0
Lite Italian Dressing	12	<1
Batter Dipped Fish SW, no sauce	380	16
Batter Dipped Chix SW, no sauce	440	17
Baked Chicken SW, no sauce	320	8

FAST FOOD

3 pc Homestyle Fish	830	39
4 pc Homestyle Fish	960	46

A La Carte Items:

Batter Dipped Fish - 1 pc	210	12
Homestyle Fish - 1 pc	125	7
Chicken Plank	130	6
Batter Dipped Shrimp	60	4
Seafood Chowder	140	6
Seafood Gumbo	120	8
Cole Slaw, drained on fork	140	6
Fryes	170	6
Hushpuppies - 1 pc	70	2

LUKE'S HAMBURGER

5 restaurants in Houston area
call for locations:
862-1043

Chicken Sandwich consists of a skinless, marinated chicken breast, grilled and served with lettuce, tomato, onion, and a mustard-mayonnaise sauce served on a whole wheat bun. Can request mustard only. When ordered without mayonnaise, it has 353 cals/9 gms fat.

Chicken Salad has the same grilled chicken served on a tossed green salad. Request without grated cheese or pecans for 200 cals/6 gms fat not including the salad dressing. The **Low Calorie Italian Dressing** has 35 cals/2 gms fat per package.

Side Salad includes greens, tomato wedge, and grated cheese - request it without cheese.

MCDONALD'S

	CALS	FAT (gms)
McLean Deluxe	**320**	**10**
Mclean Deluxe w/cheese	370	14
Hamburger	255	9
Cheeseburger	305	13
Quarter Pounder	410	20
Quarter Pounder w/Cheese	510	28
Big Mac	500	26
Filet-o-Fish	370	18
McChicken	415	19
Chicken McNuggets - 6 pc	270	15
Hot Mustard Sauce	70	4
Barbecue Sauce	50	1
Sweet & Sour Sauce	60	<1
Honey	45	0
Garden Salad	**50**	**2**
Side Salad	**30**	**1**
Chef Salad	170	9
Croutons	50	2
Bacon Bits	15	1
Salad Dressings (pkg):		
Lite Vinaigrette	**48**	**2**
Red French Reduced Calorie	160	8
Bleu Cheese	250	20
Ranch	220	20
1000 Island	390	40
Small French Fries	220	12
Medium French Fries	320	17
Large French Fries	400	22
Vanilla Lowfat Frozen Yogurt Cone	**105**	**1**
Strawberry Lowfat Frozen Sundae	210	1
Hot Fudge Lowfat Frozen Yogurt Sundae	240	3

FAST FOOD

Hot Caramel Lowfat Frozen Yogurt Sundae	270	3
Apple Pie	260	15
Vanilla Lowfat Milk Shake	290	1
Chocolate Lowfat Milk Shake	320	2
Strawberry Lowfat Milk Shake	320	1
McDonaldland Cookies	290	9
Chocolaty Chip Cookies	330	15

PITA EXPRESS

744 Westwood Mall
(Bissonnet and 59)
778-1943

Meat portions are about 4 oz. Mayonnaise and Sesame Seed Sauce (tahini sauce) are often added; both are very high in fat - request dishes without these sauces.

Shish Kabob (beef chunks on skewer) or **Grilled Chicken Breast** are available as a sandwich (on pita bread) or as a plate. The plate comes with french fries and salad - they will give you extra salad *instead of french fries* if requested.

Sandwiches: **Turkey** or **Roast Beef** on **French**, **Pita**, or **White Bread**. **Baked Potatoes** are available; keep toppings to a minimum. **Grilled Chicken Salad** consists of salad and chicken (order dressing on the side).

Tabouli - cracked wheat salad; it does have a small amount of fat added. **Hummus Dip** - mashed garbanzo beans; ask that they not add the oil on top.

Frozen Yogurt is actually **Skinny Dip**.

SBARRO

6602 Fannin
and other locations
790-0709

No nutritional information is available at this time.
Request **Light Ranch Salad Dressing** on the side of
the **Garden Fresh Tossed Salad**. **Fresh Fruit
Salad** is always available.

Lowest fat meal is probably: **Spaghetti &
Tomato Sauce** but includes about 2 cups of spaghetti. All portions are large. This Sbarro features the
Chicken Parmigiana (8 oz breaded and baked
chicken) with tomato sauce and Romano cheese
sprinkled on top instead of mozzarella. In other
products, whole milk mozzarella cheese is used.

Garlic Roll is a little over 3 oz and with added
butter. Pizza slices weigh in at about 7-8 oz. This
location also has **Non-Fat Frozen Yogurt**.

SCHLOTZSKY'S

	CALS	FAT (gms)
Sandwiches		
Small Turkey	**335**	**8**
Small Ham & Cheese	**578**	**13**
Small Original	578	32
Small Roast Beef	394	17
Small Cheese	554	24
Small Philly	462	17
Soups (8 oz)		
Lumberjack Mixed Vegetable	**89**	**3**
Old-Fashioned Chicken Noodle	**98**	**1**
Wisconsin Cheese	286	19

Country Chicken Noodle	124	7
Cream of Broccoli	184	8
Clam Chowder	186	10
Salad dressings (1.5 oz)		
Light Italian	**18**	**1**
1000 Islands	220	21
Creamy Italian	300	20
Buttermilk Ranch	280	31
Honey French	260	17

SUBWAY SANDWICHES & SALADS

Cals/fat are based on a 12" Sub; **figures would be half if you order a 6" roll.** For **Honey Wheat Roll**, add 30 calories and 1 extra gram fat onto the numbers for the sub with **Italian roll.**

	CALS	FAT (gms)
Individual Components:		
Without Cheese	**-84**	**-7**
Without Oil	**-43**	**-5**
Without Mayonnaise	**-102**	**-11**
Turkey Breast:		
Sub-Italian Roll (12")	**645**	**19**
Salad-Small	**201**	**11**
Salad-Regular	**297**	**16**
Roast Beef:		
Sub-Italian Roll (12")	689	23
Salad-Small	222	10
Salad-Regular	340	20
Cold Cut Combo:		
Sub-Italian roll (12")	853	40
Salad-Small	305	25
Salad-Regular	506	37
Spicy Italian:		

	CALS	**FAT (gms)**
Sub-Italian Roll (12")	1043	63
Salad-Small	400	33
Salad-Regular	696	60
BMT:		
Sub-Italian Roll (12")	982	55
Salad-Small	369	29
Salad-Regular	635	52
Subway Club:		
Sub-Italian Roll (12")	693	22
Salad-Small	225	13
Salad-Regular	346	19
Tuna:		
Sub-Italian Roll (12")	1103	72
Salad-Small	430	38
Salad-Regular	755	68
Seafood & Crab:		
Sub-Italian Roll (12")	986	57
Salad-Small	371	30
Salad-Regular	639	53
Seafood & Lobster:		
Sub-Italian Roll (12")	944	53
Salad-Small	351	28
Salad-Regular	597	49
Meatball:		
Sub-Italian Roll (12")	918	44
Steak & Cheese:		
Sub-Italian Roll (12")	765	32
Ham & Cheese:		
Sub-Italian Roll (12")	643	18
Salad-Small	200	12
Salad-Regular	296	18
Veggies & Cheese:		
Sub-Italian Roll (12")	535	17
Salad-Regular	188	14
Salad Dressings (2 oz each):		
Lite-Italian	**23**	**1**

FAST FOOD

	CALS	FAT (gms)
Blue Cheese	322	29
Thousand Island	252	24
French	264	20
Creamy Italian	256	26

TACO BELL

	CALS	FAT (gms)
Bean Burrito w/Red Sauce	**447**	**14**
Beef Burrito	**493**	**21**
Burrito Supreme	**503**	**22**
Combination Burrito	**407**	**16**
Taco	183	11
Taco BellGrande	335	23
Soft Taco	225	12
Soft Taco Supreme	272	16
Tostada with Red Sauce	243	11
Steak Soft Taco	218	11
Chicken Soft Taco	210	10
Taco Supreme	230	15
Nachos BellGrande	649	35
Nachos Supreme	367	27
Nachos	346	18
Enchirito w/Red Sauce	382	20
MexiMelt	266	15
Mexican Pizza	575	37
Pintos N Cheese w/Red Sauce	190	9
Chilito	383	18
Taco Salad	903	61
Taco Salad w/out Shell	484	31
Cinnamon Twist	171	8
Taco Sauce	**2**	**0**
Hot Taco Sauce	**3**	**0**
Salsa	**18**	**0**

	CALS	FAT (gms)
Pico de Gallo	8	0
Jalapeno peppers	20	0
Red Sauce	10	0
Green Sauce	4	0
Sour Cream	46	4
Guacamole	34	2
Ranch Dressing	236	25
Nacho Cheese	103	8

TEPPANYAKI

Willowbrook Mall &
other locations
890-5644

Margarine is used to stir-fry the vegetables and
to brown the meat; sesame seed oil is squirted on
as well. You can request that your food be
prepared without fats - they simply steam in water.
Small and Regular portions are prepared with 2-1/2
oz and 4 ounces meat respectively.

Teppanyaki Chicken, **Teppanyaki Beef**, and
Teppanyaki Seafood (shrimp and crab) is meat
and vegetables over white steamed rice. The
Vegetarian is made with deep-fried tofu - you may
want to request additional steamed vegetables
instead of the tofu.

Beef Noodle, **Chicken Noodle**, and **Seafood
Noodle** is meat and vegetables over steamed
noodles.

TROPIC FROZEN YOGURT

1201 Congress
(Downtown)
228-4100

Window orders only for lunch and dinner.
Order **Lite Italian Salad Dressing** for salads;
dressing is always served on the side. **Side Salad**
and **Chef Salad** both include sprinkled cheese
(probably less than 1/2 oz). **Chef Salad** has 1 oz of
both turkey and ham with 1/2 oz bacon (try to pick
out the bacon and cheese before adding dressing).

Deli Sandwiches include 3-1/2 oz meat. **Turkey**
(94% fat free) and **Ham** (98% fat free) and Swiss are
both prepackaged and made with mayonnaise.
Open the sandwiches, remove the cheese, and wipe
off the mayonnaise.

Baked Potato comes with choice of 3 toppings
- best choices are mushrooms, chives, and sour
cream. **Pickle** and **Bagels** are also available.

Frozen Yogurt comes in 4 flavors; two are
nonfat and two are low fat. Nonfat has 17 cals/fl oz;
low fat has 19 cals/fl oz.

TWO PESOS MEXICAN CAFE

Many items are offered ala carte. **Chicken Fajita**
or **Beef Fajita** is 1-3/4 oz cooked meat in a flour tortilla. Can dress your own with **Tomatoes, Onions,
Jalapenos**, and **Salsa**; **Lettuce** can be requested at
no additional charge. **Chicken Fajita Salad** has
3-1/2 oz of cooked meat and 3/4 oz cheese inside a
fried whole wheat shell - request no guacamole or
sour cream and refrain from eating the shell.

Mexican Rice and **Borracho Beans** have less than 1 gm fat per serving. **Chocolate and Strawberry Frozen Yogurt** are available.

WENDY'S HAMBURGERS

	CALS	FAT (gms)
Grilled Chicken Sandwich	340	13
without Honey Mustard	**269**	**7**
Fish Fillet Sandwich	460	25
without Tarter Sauce	**340**	**11**
Plain Single	340	15
Single With Everything	420	21
Wendy's Big Classic	570	33
Jr Hamburger	260	9
Jr Cheeseburger	310	13
Jr Bacon Cheeseburger	430	25
Jr Swiss Deluxe	360	18
Kids' Meal Hamburger	260	9
Kids' Meal Cheeseburger	300	13
Chicken Sandwich	440	19
Chicken Club Sandwich	506	25
Country Fried Steak Sandwich	440	25
French Fries (small-3.2 oz)	240	12
Chili (regular-9 oz)	220	7
Cheddar Cheese, shredded	110	10
Sour Cream	60	6
Chicken Nuggets (6)	280	20
Nugget Sauces		
Barbecue Sauce	50	<1
Honey Sauce	45	<1
Sweet & Sour Sauce	45	<1
Sweet Mustard	50	1

FAST FOOD

	CALS	FAT (gms)
Hot Stuffed Potatoes		
Plain	**270**	**<1**
Bacon & Cheese	520	18
Broccoli & Cheese	400	16
Cheese	420	15
Chili & Cheese	500	18
Sour Cream & Chives	500	23
Salad Dressings (per 1/2 pkg or 1 ladle):		
Reduced Calorie Italian	**45**	**4**
Blue Cheese	162	18
Celery Seed	126	11
French	108	11
Hidden Valley Ranch	90	11
Thousand Island	126	13
Italian Caesar	144	16
Italian Golden	81	7
Red. Calorie Bacon & Tomato	81	7
Chef Salad	**130**	**5**
Garden Salad	**70**	**2**
Taco Salad	530	23
Frosty Dairy Dessert (sm)	340	10

WHATABURGER

	CALS	FAT (gms)
Grilled Chicken Sandwich	455	16
(without salad dressing)	**385**	**9**
Whataburger Jr	304	14
Justaburger	265	12
Whatacatch	475	27
the above with Cheese	+47	+4
Whataburger	580	24
Whataburger w/Cheese	669	33
Whatachick'n Deluxe	671	32
Whatachick'n Sandwich	575	27
Fajita Taco	301	11
French Fries (small)	221	12
French Fries (regular)	332	18
Onion Rings	226	13
Apple Pie	236	12
Vanilla Shake (small)	322	9

PIZZA

Many people think of pizza as a high fat dish that one should not eat when trying to lose weight or lower their cholesterol. But that simply is not true - if you chose your pizza wisely.

Pizza Crust

The pizza crust is made mostly of flour, yeast, and water so it is very low in fat. But this may change before it is baked. There are two major types of ovens used in cooking pizzas. The old fashioned pizza ovens bake the pizzas without adding any more fat than is already in the pizza crust and its toppings. The pizza is simply placed on the floor of the oven and baked.

The conveyor belt ovens can be a different story. The Thin Crust Pizzas are often placed on a perforated pizza pan without additional fat. In making Pan Pizzas or Thick Crust Pizzas, extra oil is oftentimes added not only *in the pan* to prevent sticking but also *in the dough* to allow quick cooking. So choose either pizzas baked in the traditional old fashioned oven or the Thin Crust Pizza cooked on the conveyor belt oven.

Tomato Sauce

The added tomato sauce is also low in fat. In some of the fancier restaurants, although not commonly seen in pizza parlors, is the brushing of oil onto the crust *before* the sauce is added or *instead of* the sauce. You can request that this oil is simply not added.

Added Cheese

Cheese is added on top of the sauce in amounts of usually slightly less than 1 oz per slice. Mozzarella cheese is the most frequently used cheese, but Provolone and Feta cheese are also used. They range from 5-8 gms of fat per ounce. So, an order of *extra* cheese would not be a healthy request. If you were to eat just 1 or 2 slices of pizza, the 1 or 2 ounces of cheese would not be excessive. The problem is that most people eat 3, 4, or more slices!

You may want to consider requesting that the pizza parlor add only *"half"* of the usual amount of cheese on top or request the pizza to be prepared *"light"* on the cheese. Ask the manager of your favorite pizza restaurant which term is more understandable to their cooking staff. Managers have told me that ordering less cheese is becoming a frequent request from people watching their weight or cholesterol or those with a lactose-intolerance.

Toppings

This is where the calories and fat grams can really add up. Obviously the leanest toppings are the fresh fruits and vegetables such as onions, mushrooms, green and red peppers, broccoli, tomatoes, roasted pepper, spinach, and pineapple. Olives are just about pure fat - so leave them off your Vegetarian Pizza if you really don't care much for them. To give you an idea of how much fat olives have, look at the grams of fat in Domino's Vegetarian Pizza. One slice of the Vegetarian Pizza has just as much fat as their Pepperoni Pizza.

Adding grilled chicken, tuna, crabmeat, or shrimp is a lean protein topping. Hamburger meat or ham would be second best.

The high fat toppings such as pepperoni, bacon, and sausage can more than double the total fat intake.

For the leanest meal, fill yourself up with a salad before eating pizza. Use the lower calorie dressing, if available. Then eat just a couple slices of pizza with plenty of the lower fat fresh fruits and vegetables toppings. If you have a hard time stopping at just 2 or 3 slices, make sure you buy a small enough pizza so there are no extra slices to tempt you.

DOMINO'S PIZZA

	CALS	**FAT (gms)**
(Per Two Slices of a Large 16" Pizza):		
Cheese	376	10
Pepperoni	460	18
Sausage/Mushroom	430	16
Veggie	498	19
Deluxe	498	20
Double Cheese/Pepperoni	545	25
Ham	417	11

GODFATHER'S PIZZA

(Per Slice):	<ins>CALS</ins>	<ins>FAT (gms)</ins>
ORIGINAL CHEESE PIZZA:		
Mini	190	4
Small	240	7
Medium	270	8
Large (hot slice)	370	11
Large	297	9
ORIGINAL COMBO PIZZA:		
Mini	240	7
Small	360	15
Medium	400	17
Large (hot slice)	550	24
Large	437	19
THIN CRUST/CHEESE PIZZA:		
Small	180	6
Medium	210	7
Large	228	7
THIN CRUST/COMBO PIZZA:		
Small	270	13
Medium	310	14
Large	336	16
STUFFED PIE/CHEESE PIZZA:		
Small	310	11
Medium	350	13
Large	381	16
STUFFED PIE/CHEESE PIZZA:		
Small	430	20
Medium	480	23
Large	521	26

IRISH PUB KENNEALLY'S

2111 S Shepherd
(2 blocks N of Westheimer)
630-0486

Sandwiches are made with a minimum of 5 ounces of meat. Ask for the mustard or home-made spicy mustard, instead of mayonnaise.

The leanest meats include: **Roast Beef** (trimmed of all visible fat), **Turkey Breast** (35 cals/1 gm fat per oz), **Corned Beef** (40 cals/2 gms fat per oz), **Pastrami** (40 cals/1 gm fat per oz), and **Baked Ham**. **Wheat Berry**, **Dark Rye**, **Light Rye**, or **French Bread** are available. Sandwiches come with homemade potato chips (can ask to have left off) and pickle slice.

Sauce is added before the toppings on the **Pizza**. Since the pizzas are made to order, specify what you want, such as: mushrooms, bell pepper, and onions and *light* on the cheese.

LITTLE CAESAR'S

	CALS	FAT (gms)
(Per Single Slice of Pizza):		
Cheese Pizza	170	6
With Pepperoni, Green Peppers, Onions, Mushrooms	190	7
Sandwiches:		
Ham and Cheese Sandwich	520	21
Tuna Melt Sandwich	700	37
Italian Sub Sandwich	590	28

Vegetarian Sandwich	620	30
Salads:		
Antipasto Salad	170	9
Greek Salad	140	8
Tossed Salad	80	2

MR GATTI'S

No nutritional information is available at this time. Uses conveyor belt ovens to prepare the pizzas. The **Original, Thin Pizzas** are cooked in an aluminum pan and no oil is added. The Pan Pizzas require extra oil in the dough as well as oil in the pan. So the Pan Pizza ends up having at least 2 T more oil than the thin pizza.

There is about 5 - 5-1/2 oz of provolone cheese on a medium thin crust pizza and 7 oz on a large thin crust. An additional ounce is added to the pan pizzas. Low fat vegetable toppings include: **Green Pepper, Mushroom, Onion, Jalapeno,** and **Diced Tomato**.

PIZZA INN

No nutritional information is available at this time. Most restaurants use the conveyor belt ovens rather than the traditional ovens. To make the **Thin Crust Pizza,** low-lipped pans with perforations are used to force air to penetrate the pizza - so no fats are added. But a considerable amount of oil is added to the pans of the Deep Dish Pizza.

Low Calorie Salad Dressings are available at the **Salad Bar**.

PIZZA HUT

	CALS	**FAT (gms)**
(Per Two Slices of a Medium Pizza):		

PAN PIZZA:

	CALS	FAT
Cheese	492	18
Pepperoni	541	22
Supreme	589	30
Super Supreme	563	26

THIN 'N CRISPY PIZZA:

	CALS	FAT
Cheese	398	17
Pepperoni	413	20
Supreme	459	22
Super Supreme	463	21

HAND-TOSSED PIZZA:

	CALS	FAT
Cheese	518	20
Pepperoni	500	23
Supreme	540	26
Super Supreme	556	25

PERSONAL PAN PIZZA:

	CALS	FAT
Pepperoni (whole pizza)	675	29
Supreme (whole pizza)	647	28

THE POT PIE PIZZERIA

1525 Westheimer
(Montrose area)
528-4350

Request salad dressing on the side for all salads.
Unbuttered Bread can be requested instead of the
usual.

A traditional pizza oven is used for making
their **Pizzas**. Order your pizza *light* on the cheese
and with **Mushrooms, Onions,** and **Bell Peppers**.

Also offered are: **Fettuccine with Red Clam
Sauce** and **Spaghetti Marinara**.

Side orders of: **Sliced Tomatoes, Cottage
Cheese, Homemade Broth-based Soups,** and
Baked Potatoes (with whatever you want to add)
are also available.

CAFETERIAS

Cafeterias are popular places to eat due to their quick service, relatively low cost, and availability of well-balanced, nutritious meals. Since the portion sizes are smaller than most full-service restaurants, you might end up eating less fat. However, unless you are careful, cafeterias can also add quite a bit of fat (and subsequently, more calories) into your daily intake than you think.

First of all, let's discuss what most cafeterias offer on their cafeteria line. Then there's even better news - most cafeterias are willing to help you select lower fat options.

Meats

Cafeterias offer meat portions that are more in line with the American Heart Association's recommended guidelines. Portion sizes are often 4-6 oz. Additionally, most cafeterias offer "half portions". Unfortunately, the meats are often prepared high fat through the process of basting and frying. To prevent the meats from drying out while on display, they are often kept on the service line in a pan with more fats. Still the best choices are usually the baked chicken (remove the skin) and baked fish (remove the toppings). Select those pieces that appear to be sitting in the least amount of oil. Turning down the tartar sauce (1/4 c has 320 cals/36 gms fat) or the gravy will save you considerable calories and fat.

Vegetable and Starches

Just about every vegetable and starch on the serving line has added fats: bacon, oil, margarine, or butter. Other vegetables are covered with cheese or baked in a casserole with additional fats. Some cafeterias are now offering one vegetable prepared plain - without added fats or salt.

Some of the leanest accompaniments are steamed broccoli, plain baked potato, plain rice, corn, green beans, greens, and the like. Ask the server to drain the vegetable well. The higher fat items are the double baked potatoes, stuffing, squash or eggplant casserole, broccoli with a cheese sauce, and fried okra or other fried vegetables.

Breads

Yeast rolls are almost always offered; these breads are lowest in fats. But they are often baked in pans that have fat added and, in addition, they are brushed with fats before being placed on the serving line.

The cornbread, muffins (especially the specialty nut muffins) are considerably higher in fat. Each can add anywhere from 5-10 gms of fat per serving. The pastries are even higher in fat.

For the leanest possible intake, keep to the yeast rolls and do not add any butter or margarine.

Salads

Salads mixed with mayonnaise or other high fat dressings include coleslaw, marinated cucumbers, and spinach salad. Some salads, such as the tossed salad, are displayed plain. When you ask for salad dressing, that's when the fat is added. Keep in mind that each salad dressing ladle is often a 1-2 oz ladle which contains 2-4 T of dressing (150-300 cals/16-32 gms fat). And watch out, some cafeterias add two ladles!

Your best bet is to ask for the dressing on the side. If you want one of the salads already prepared with fat, ask for a portion off the top where the salad is a bit dryer because it has been allowed to drain.

Desserts

Obviously, the fresh fruit that is offered at most cafeterias would be your best choice for a dessert. Beware of "Sugar-Free" Pies, they **may** be appropriate for persons watching their sugar intake. But the *fat content is usually unchanged.* The sugar-free pies end up being just about identical in fat content to the regular pies. You may be saving as little as 50 calories by leaving out the sugar.

The Best News

Fortunately, managers at most of the cafeterias say they are very willing to address the customer's specific nutritional needs. In many cases, you can request foods prepared without fat when you arrive at the cafeteria or call the manager ahead of time. They can steam just about any vegetable and cook the meat portion you need without additional fat.

CLEBURNE CAFETERIA

3606 Bissonnet
(between Buffalo Speedway & Edloe)
667-2386

Casual Dining: L,D
Av: Under $5

Tossed Green Salad with **Diet Italian Dressing**. **Fresh Fruit Salad** is offered everyday.

Offers a wide variety of meats and fishes such as **Half of a Baked Chicken** (remove the skin), **Steamed Catfish** (7-9 oz), Roast Beef (9-10 oz), and **Boneless Breast of Chicken with Rice** (7 oz skinless).

Because of the large meat portions, you may want to split an entree with a friend and have extra vegetables. Vegetables are all prepared with some added fats - select those without sauces or cheese.

Instead of meat, you may opt to order **Cottage Cheese** on a salad. **Rolls**, including **Whole Wheat Rolls**, are large - about 3-4 oz each. **Skim Milk** is available.

FURR'S CAFETERIA

Casual Dining: L,D
Av: Under $5

Willing to prepare special requests. Call the manager of the restaurant to explain your special dietary requests, then they can prepare the food you need when you arrive. Menus and recipes were revised over the past year to decrease the fat.

Kraft Free Dressings are available for your salads. **Fresh Fruits** are always offered.

Meat portions are about 4-6 oz. Chicken is offered in a variety of formats such as **Baked Chicken, Stir-fried Chicken**, or **Spicy Baked Chicken**. **Baked Fish** is offered with a crumb topping or a variety such as **Baked Fish Veracruz** (with a vegetable medley on top).

All **Vegetables** have added fat but some have less than others. Chose from **Yeast Rolls** and **Honey Wheat Rolls**.

Sugar Free Pudding is often available. **Sugar Free Gelatin** is always offered.

LUBY'S CAFETERIA

Casual Dining: L,D
Av: Under $5

Each store prepares food a little differently. If you have a dietary request, they suggest that you talk to the manager at the restaurant. They will usually be able to accommodate your needs.

Some salads such as the **Tossed Salad** are prepared without dressings; others may be available if you ask. **Lower Calorie Dressings** are offered. Each dressing ladle contains 1-1/2 oz (3 T).

Meats are about 4-6 oz. **Baked Chicken** (remove the skin) and **Baked Fish** are often available. **Vegetables** are typically cooked with some fats - select those that have minimal added fats.

LuAnn Platter can be ordered with just about any meat entree - this platter includes a half portion of meat, 2 vegetables, and a roll.

The **Yeast Roll** and **Whole Wheat Roll** are low in fat. The Date Nut Muffin has over 10 gms fat.

Sugar Free Gelatin and **Fresh Fruit** are offered for dessert.

PICCADILLY CAFETERIA

Casual Dining: L,D
Av: Under $5

Willing to accommodate the special dietary requests of their customers. The **Dilly Dish** contains a half portion of meat, 2 vegetables, and a roll. They try to serve at least 1 vegetable each day that is prepared without any added fats or sodium. Meats are generally 5 oz portions.

Best meat selections are the **Baked Chicken** (remove the skin) and the **Baked Fish** (their lemon sauce has no added fats).

No *very* low calorie dressing is available. Each salad dressing ladle is 1 oz (2 T). **Fresh Fruit Salad** is prepared with 5-7 fresh fruits in unsweetened pineapple juice.

Sugar Free Pudding (made with Nutrasweet and nonfat milk) is available in addition to **Sugar Free Gelatin**.

WYATT CAFETERIA

Casual Dining: L,D
Av: Under $5

If you frequent one particular restaurant, Wyatt's encourages you to introduce yourself to the manager. Tell the manager of your special needs and they will be glad to help you select the best choice available - or even prepare it special for you.

Both **Low Calorie Thousand Island and Italian Salad Dressings** are available for the salads. The **Chef Salad** is available in two sizes:

small (3/4 oz of ham and turkey plus 3/4 oz cheese) and large (1-1/2 oz of each meat and cheese).

The average portion of meat is 4-6 ounces cooked. Select from: **Baked Cod** (you may want to scrape off the bread crumb topping), **Baked Chicken** (remove the skin), **Roast Beef** (trim any visible fat), or other leaner daily specials.

All vegetables are typically prepared with some fats. **Diet Jello** is offered everyday, located near the desserts. **Skim Milk** is offered.

The classification of so-called "American" restaurants actually encompasses a broad range of restaurants and menu items. American restaurants offer the more popular menu selections from a wide range of ethnic cuisines. Italian, Mexican, and Chinese along with items normally considered standard American fare such as hamburgers and french fries make for a varied menu.

American restaurants are typically mid-priced restaurants with a casual to informal dress code although many formal service restaurants preferred to be listed in this chapter. When entering an American style restaurant, we expect prompt service in a relaxed environment.

Here are some general guidelines for Dinin'Lean® in American style restaurants:

Soup

Broth-based soups are generally leaner than the creamy variety. Some restaurants are serving "cream" soups made with skim milk and pureed vegetables. These, too, would be a lean selection.

AMERICAN

Appetizers

Most appetizers offered in American style restaurants are fried; these are best avoided. Shrimp cocktail, crabmeat cocktail, or oysters on the half shell are lean; cocktail sauce is also low in fat. These leaner appetizers can be ordered with a salad instead of an entree.

Unbuttered yeast breads are generally low in fat. A standard slice of bread has only 75 calories, but a few slices of bread before dinner can really add up the calories.

Salads

Request salad dressings on the side so that you can control the amount of dressing that is added. Always ask what the salads are comprised of, then request some of the fattier items such as avocado, bacon, egg, cheese, or croutons to be omitted.

Taco salads are frequently served in a fried tortilla shell. A lower calorie/fat alternative would be to request that the salad be served on a plate instead.

Entrees

Most meat entrees are 8-10 oz. You may want to split the entree with another person or request a doggie bag to take half home. The leanest meats are grilled or baked fish, chicken, or turkey.

These items are often brushed with oil so always request little or no oil when preparing these dishes. Sauces are often very high in fat so order the sauces to be served on the side. Leaner sauces include salsas, black bean sauce, and those made from chicken stock and pureed vegetables.

Sandwiches

Sandwiches (with the usual 4 or 5 ounces of meat) frequently offers a smaller serving of meat than an 8-10 oz meat entree. Deli-type sandwiches should be ordered on bread or a roll; croissants are high in fat. Plain sandwiches or dressed with mustard are recommended choices. If other dressings are desired, request the spread on the side.

Hamburgers and grilled chicken sandwiches are often served with buttered and grilled buns. Ask that the buns be grilled dry. If the price of a sandwich includes chips or fries, request a substitute such as a small salad, steamed vegetables, or fresh fruit. Some restaurants even offer a discount for ordering the sandwich without the chips or fries.

Pastas

Pasta noodles are low in fat but the sauces and other toppings can really add on the calories. Red tomato sauces are generally the best choices for a topping. When topped with meat, ask how it will be prepared. Often the meat can be steamed instead of sauteed.

Accompaniments

Ask for steamed vegetables and request no butter to be added. Baked potatoes can be prepared dry. Mashed potatoes can be ordered without gravy or with gravy on the side.

Dessert

Fresh fruit may be available for dessert even if it is not listed on the menu.

AMERICAN

ANTHONY'S RESTAURANT

4611 Montrose
(between Bissonnet & Richmond)
622-6778

Formal Dining: L,D
Av: $15

Caters to a clientele with special food preparation requests. Willing to weigh and measure as needed. Start with **Clams and Mussels fra Diavolo** - steamed with tomatoes, garlic, and herbs.

Lunch menu rotates but always offers 3-4 **"Spa"** menu items (prepared with little or no fat) with 250-300 calories for pasta and 400-500 for entrees (3-4 ounces meat).

Pasta "Red Duke" - tomatoes, basil, garlic, and sundried tomatoes (omit pinenuts). **Penne Rustica** - pasta with roasted vegetables and spring hen (2-3 oz).

Whole Red Snapper - ask for sauce on the side. **Hearth Roasted Spring Hen** - ask that skin be removed and sauce on the side. **Grilled Salmon Ponzu** - has sauce with no fat (low sodium soy sauce, balsamic vinegar, herbs). **Open Fire Roasted Veal Loin** - sauce has olive oil and cheese, ask for it on the side. **Grilled Red Snapper** - ask for sauce on the side. **Salmon Carpaccio** - olive oil is not added to this dish; it is added at the table if desired.

BACKSTREET CAFE

1103 S Shepherd
(between W Gray & Dallas)
521-2239

Casual Dining: L,D
Av: $5-10

Fruit Salad is available. **Texas Corn Chowder**
grilled chicken and vegetables in a chicken stock.
Grilled Vegetables are chargrilled. **Black Beans**
are cooked in a chicken stock.

Cold Plates and Salads can be prepared according to your special needs. Try the **Salad Nicoise** -
fresh grilled tuna, potatoes, arrugula, tomatoes, red
onions, and snap beans (request the sundried tomato vinaigrette on the side) and ask for no eggs.

Sandwiches include about a 4 oz meat portion.
Grilled Fresh Tuna (ask for no tartar sauce) and
Smoked Turkey Sandwiches (ask for no mayon-
naise) both come with a side of fruit. **Grilled
Chicken Breast Club** (request no bacon or may-
onnaise) comes with chips - ask for fruit instead.

Roasted Half Chicken has 7-8 ounces of meat;
ask for sauce on the side and **Steamed Spinach**.
Angel Hair Pasta with Shrimp includes sundried
tomatoes, garlic, and basil (ask to omit pinenuts and
olives) served in a low-fat chicken broth saute.
Whole Wheat Linguini is topped with roasted tomato sauce and grilled squash, zucchini and carrots.

AMERICAN

BLACK EYED PEA RESTAURANT

17 in Houston area
for locations, call:
784-8674

Casual Dining: L,D
Av: $5-10

Yeast Rolls (2 oz each) and/or Cornbread are
served to the table. **Dinner Salad** and **Charbroiled Chicken Salad** should be requested
without cheese or croutons. **Charbroiled Chicken
Salad** is prepared with 5 oz of skinless chicken.
Charbroiled Chicken Breast Sandwich is 7 oz;
dressings are brought to the table.

Leanest entrees (each at 6-7 oz) are three. **Charbroiled Chicken Breast** is pre-marinated. **Baked
Whitefish** - either remove the mayonnaise-type
sauce or order without sauce but expect a 10
minute wait. **Charbroiled Halibut Steak** - request
without butter baste.

All vegetables and side dishes are prepared with
some fats or oil. Those lowest in fat (less than a teaspoon of fat) are: **Green Beans**, **Kernel Corn**, and
Glazed Carrots. **Fresh Green Beans**, **Boiled Cabbage**, and **Green Peas** can be prepared without
any fats if requested but will take an additional 15
minutes.

CAFE ANNIE

1728 Post Oak Blvd
(Galleria area)
840-1111

Formal Dining: L,D
Av: $20 & over

Request salad dressings on the side. Unbuttered bread is served with meals.

Low fat menu items are prepared upon request. Chefs are experienced in cooking flavorful low fat meals including special seasoning and sauces. They ask that you inform the server *exactly* what your special needs are and they will guide you in your selections. Typical meat portions are: 7 oz at lunch and 8 oz at dinner. Sometimes, smaller portions can be served.

The menu changes daily but you can chose from a variety of elaborate, flavorful dishes prepared to your specific needs. Perhaps an appetizer of **Pasta with Fresh Chopped Tomatoes and Seasoning**. Frequently, soups are prepared low in fat; the cream is added just before serving and can be left off. Salads include about 2-3 oz of meat in addition to vegetables. Request salad dressing on the side.

Entrees include a wide variety of fish, chicken, and wild game. **Beef Filets** can be cut to any size such as a 3-4 oz cut, perhaps with a low fat **Roast Tomato Sauce**. **Grilled Quail** may be offered with a low fat **Smoked Chile Sauce**. **Roasted Rabbit** can be prepared with a lean **Tomatillo Sauce**. **Fresh Fruit** for dessert.

CAFE VIENNA

5701 Main St
(in Wyndham Warwick Hotel)
639-4552

Informal Dining: B,L,D
Av: $10-20

Request salad dressings on the side for the **Cafe Salad** and other entree salads. **Diet Vinaigrette** is available. **Pico De Gallo Salad** contains 2 or 2-1/2 oz of grilled chicken, mixed greens, jicama, and oranges (request without cheese). **Fresh Fruit Plate** is served with **Low Fat Yogurt** or **Cottage Cheese. Shrimp Cocktail** with Spicy Salsa (request no avocado).

Grilled Chicken Croissant (about 4 oz chicken) should be requested on **French Roll** instead. Can be requested without pesto & cheese. Lunch also offers a **Pasta Bar** where you can ask the chef to concoct just about any dish. Select from a variety of **Pasta Noodles**, **Vegetables**, meats such as **Grilled Shrimp** or **Grilled Chicken**, and sauces such as **Marinara Sauce**.

Average portion of meat is 6 oz. **Blackened Snapper** with pico de gallo has about 1 t oil. **Fresh Grilled Gulf Shrimp** with basil & garlic. A 7 oz **Filet Mignon** can be ordered at lunch. **Spinach Fettucine with Grilled Chicken** can be requested without any oil. **Grilled Breast of Chicken** can be ordered with **Rice** or **Vegetables** instead of potato salad.

All entrees are served with **Rice** or **Baked Potato** (evenings only). **Steamed Vegetables** are available without added fats. Both **Skim and Low Fat Milk** are available. **Fresh Fruit**.

CLEMENTINE'S EATING PARLOR

6448 W FM 1960
(near Willowbrook Mall)
440-5310

Casual Dining: L,D
Av: $5-10

    Tossed Green Salad - order **Low Calorie Italian or Ranch Dressing** on the side. They serve only **Low Fat Sour Cream** with their **Baked Potato**. Meat portions are about 8 oz.

    Breast of Chicken Sandwich - request no mayonnaise, or light mayo on the side. **Fajita Salad** can be served on a plate instead of the fried flour shell; (omit the cheese and avocado).

    Other lower fat choices include: **Clementine's Fruit Surprise** -fresh fruit platter served on a bed of lettuce with creamy cottage cheese and 4-5 oz of grilled turkey breast and **Summer Teriyaki** - marinated chicken breast served with rice (ask that mushrooms be sauteed in water only). Other chicken dishes include fried foods or very large portions of meat and other protein.

    Daily specials can often be prepared low in fat, if requested.

AMERICAN

DOVERS/DOUBLETREE HOTEL

400 Dallas
(Downtown)
759-0202

Informal Dining: L,D
Av: $10-20

Mixed Field Greens with vegetables (request dressing on the side). Offers a variety of **"Naturals"** (meals restricted in cholesterol, fats, and sodium) for both lunch and dinner.

At lunch: **Chicken Brochette** - strips of chicken woven on skewer with vegetables, and pineapple; charbroiled and served on a bed of rice (no fats are added).

At dinner: **Chicken Tomatillo** - charbroiled chicken breast, and tomatillo salsa (green tomatoes pureed with a touch of jalapeno); **Poached Salmon** - prepared with wine and herbs; or **Tuna Steak** - charbroiled and dressed with raspberry vinegar.

For accompaniments request **Plain White Rice** or **Plain Baked Potato**, and **Fresh Vegetables** (request that it be prepared without any butter or oil).

Fresh Fruit Plate or **Sorbet** (made with fruit) is available for dessert.

DUCKS & COMPANY

1200 Louisiana
(Downtown in Hyatt Regency)
654-1234

Formal Dining: L,D
Av: $16-22

For lunch, meat portions are about 6 oz. **Salad Bar** includes fresh fruits and vegetables; **Lite Italian Salad Dressing** is available. Two **"Perfect Balance Meals"** are offered: **Asparagus Chicken** - poached skinless breast of chicken stuffed with asparagus and served with cous cous and fresh seasonal vegetables on an asparagus coulis (511 cals/16 gms fat) and **Broiled Fresh Seasonal Fish** - quickly broiled fish with poached seasonal vegetables (328 cals/2 gms fat).

For dinner: **Garden Salad** - ask for the dressing on the side.

Alaskan Claw Cocktail - five jumbo snow crab claws served with cocktail sauce. Dinner meat portions are about 8-10 oz.

Grilled Seafood (Swordfish, Tuna, or Salmon) ask for sauces on the side. **Red Pepper Coulis** is pureed red peppers, spices, and no fats. **Grilled Chicken Breast** - order sauces on the side (made with liquors, it is high in sugar but has no fats).

The **"Perfect Balance Meals"** are also available at dinner. Dinners are served with **Baked Potato** (request what you want on it), or **Steamed Long Grain and Wild Rice** and **Fresh Seasonal Vegetables** (request to have it steamed without margarine). For Dessert: **Fresh Fruit**.

AMERICAN

FIFTY NINE DINER

3801 Farnham
(Inside loop, off I-59)
523-2333

Casual Dining: B,L,D
Av: $5-10

Salad dressings are served on the side for **Dinner Salad** and **Grilled Chicken Salad** (request no bacon bits, eggs, cheddar cheese, or croutons). **Unbuttered Bread** and margarine are served with meals.

Average portion of meat is about 6 oz. Leanest menu items are: **Turkey Sandwich** (request no mayo and substitute **Vegetable of the Day** instead of stuffing & gravy). **Chicken Sandwich** (grilled with honey mustard on the side. **Hawaiian Chicken Plate** - grilled, marinated boneless breast of chicken served on a bed of **Rice**, with vegetable, and dinner salad. If you order mashed potatoes, request without gravy.

Low Fat Milk is available. **Fresh Fruit** is offered for dessert.

FOUNTAIN VIEW CAFE

1842 Fountain View
(Galleria area)
785-9060

Casual Dining: B,L
Av: $5-10

For starters or for a light meal there is a variety of fruit. **Fruit-A-Lope** - a half cantaloupe filled with fruit. **Fresh Fruit Salad** - ask for poppy seed dressing on the side. **Fruit & Yogurt** with low fat vanilla yogurt. **Fruit & Cottage Cheese**.

There are several leaner sandwiches. **Grilled Chicken Sandwich** - skinless breast, hold the mayo. **Ham, Roast Beef, or Turkey Breast Sandwiches** (request without mayonnaise or cheese) - skip the basket of high fat additions.

Grilled Chicken Salad is available but ask for without avocado and the dressing on the side. Or have the **Pasta & Chicken Salad** - dressing comes on the side.

AMERICAN

GREAT CHARCOAL CHICKEN COMPANY

1000 Campbell Rd
(at I-10)
468-1212

Casual Dining: L,D
Av: $5-10

Offers **Crystal Lite Lemonade** in addition to **Diet Coke**. **Smoked Chicken Plates** are brushed with cottonseed oil and smoked with skin on - 1/4 chicken is about 3-4 ounces, remove skin before eating. May request white meat only.

Side orders lowest in fat: **Steamed Peas and Carrots** (currently not shown on menu) and **New Potatoes** - request both without butter. **Hot bread** is available without butter - just ask.

Charcoal Grilled Chicken Diet Plates (best choice is the **Original and Lemon-Peppered**) are about 5 ounces cooked. Request the chicken breasts not be brushed with oil prior to grilling. Plates include **Tomatoes** and small **Green Salad** (request without croutons and **Diet Ranch Dressing** on the side). No bread is brought to the table, when you order the diet plates, to tempt you.

JAGS

5120 Woodway at Sage
(Galleria area)
621-4765

Informal Dining: L
Av: $10-20

Ask for **Light Vinaigrette Dressing** on the side of your salad. **JAGS Salad** is a green salad. **Caesar Salad JAGS** includes 5 oz grilled chicken breast; request no croutons or cheese (less than 1 oz). **East/West Salad** (wholesome grains and corn).

Beginnings: **Lentil Soup** and **Spring Vegetable Soup** have little or no fat. **Pasta Romano** - linguini with tomatoes, basil, and romano cheese (cheese can be left off). **Ravioli Rienzi** - vegetable filled pasta, spicy fresh tomato sauce, vegetable confetti. Both **Skim and Low Fat Milk** are available. Average portion of meat is 6-7 oz; smaller portions can be ordered for a discount.

Seared Salmon with a non-fat cucumber salsa. **Steamed Vegetables** served with brown rice and ginger sauce. **Roasted Gobbler Sandwich** - turkey sandwich (request without avocado, dressing, or bacon). **Fresh Fruit** is available for dessert.

AMERICAN

JOJOS OF TEXAS FAMILY RESTAURANT

6 restaurants in Houston area
for locations, call:
440-8831

Casual Dining: B,L,D
Av: $7-12

Buttered bread is usually served, ask for **Unbuttered Bread** instead. **Lower Calorie French and Italian Dressings** are available. Request the salad dressing to be served on the side for all salads such as the **Green Garden Salad**. **Chicken Fajita Salad** - 6 oz chicken meat atop greens with other vegetables (request no cheese, guacamole, sour cream, and olives). Or order these on the side so you can control the amounts.

Order the **Tortilla Soup** without cheese or tortilla strips, it still has chicken and vegetables in it. **Skim and Low Fat Milk** is also offered.

Steamed Vegetable Plate comes with a **Teriyaki Sauce** and garlic cheese bread. Request no butter on buns when ordering the **Chicken Sandwich**. This is a 6 oz broiled chicken breast with either barbecue or teriyaki sauce. Ask for the **Vegetable Du Jour** instead of usual high fat accompaniments.

Very little oil is added to the **Stir Fry Chicken**, just a light brushing on the pan. **Rainbow Trout** - 7 oz grilled (request broiled without butter). **Alaska Crab Legs** - 8 oz (request no drawn butter). **Ocean Cod** - 6 oz filet, lightly breaded and grilled. A 6 oz **Top Sirloin** is also available.

Fresh Fruit can be ordered for dessert.

KAPHAN'S

7900 S Main
(at Kirby)
668-0491

Formal Dining: L,D
Av: $10-20

Texas Gulf Shrimp Cocktail, Texas Crabmeat Cocktail, Cold Boiled Shrimp, and **Oysters on the Half Shell** come with cocktail sauce.

Order **Light Ranch Dressing** for your salad, on the side. Meat portions at lunch are 6 oz and 8-10 oz at dinner. **Luncheon Portions** are available at dinner time for a discounted price.

For lunch: **Grilled Chicken Breast served with a tangy Marinara Sauce over Capellini** (thin pasta) or have the **Shrimp over Capellini** with the same red sauce. If you want **Broiled Breast of Chicken *or* Broiled Gulf Shrimp Kaphan's Mushrooms over Rice**, ask them to "saute the mushrooms without any oil". **Broiled Filet of Catfish or any other fish** - ask for preparation without oil or butter and substitute **Plain Rice** instead of Augratin potatoes.

For dinner: broiled dishes such as **Chicken, Whole Flounder, Deep Sea Scallops**, and **Catfish** can be prepared without any oil, if requested. The **Grilled Fish** needs a little oil for preparation. **Lobster Tails** - request no drawn butter. **Fresh Fruit** is available for dessert.

KING RESTAURANT & DELI

17637 El Camino Real
(Clear Lake area)
488-1802

Casual Dining: B,L,D
Av: $5-10

You put on your own salad dressings at the
Soup/Salad/Spud Bar. **No Fat Italian Dressing** is
available.

Average meat portion is 6 oz at both lunch and
dinner.

None of the sandwiches are "dressed" - you put
on the dressings that you want. Deli Sandwiches:
Roast Beef (request without cheese), **Ham** (order
without cheese), or **Turkey**.

Graceland's Grilled Chicken - chicken breast
with lettuce, tomato, onion on a roll or bread. **Rock-
ahula Sandwich** - pineapple-marinated chicken
breast with grilled pineapple slice, sprouts, tomato,
lettuce, and onion. **Graceland's Vegetable Garden
Sandwich** - lettuce, tomato, onion, cucumber, and
sprouts on whole wheat bread.

These dishes are lean: **Fun in Aculpulco** - lime-
marinated chicken and **The Mansion's Mandarin
Chicken** - with orange marinade. Both are served on
a bed of herb rice with vegetable of the day. **Vegetable of the Day** is steamed, request no butter.

Platters include **Soup/Salad/Spud Bar**, **Dinner
Roll**, and **Veggie of the Day**: **Grilled Catfish**,
Blackened Catfish (with no oil), **Blackened Chick-
en**, **King Creole** (grilled catfish with creole rice), or
Grilled Chicken Platters. **Fresh Fruit** is available
on the salad bar.

LA BRASSERIE/ DOUBLETREE HOTEL

400 Dallas
(Downtown)
759-0202

Casual Dining: B,L,D
Av: $5-10

The Brasserie Salad consists of vegetables (request dressing on the side). Offers a variety of **"Naturals"** (food choices that are lower in fats, cholesterol, and sodium) for both lunch and dinner.

Choices include: **Stir Fry Chicken/Beef/or Shrimp** - strips of chicken served over steamed rice; **Charbroiled Mahi Mahi** - served with fresh vegetables and steamed rice; or **California Fruit Plate** - fruits with sorbet or cottage cheese.

For accompaniments request **Plain White Rice** or **Plain Baked Potato**, and **Fresh Vegetables** prepared without any butter or oil. **Fresh Fruit Plate** or **Sorbet** is available for dessert.

AMERICAN

LANCASTER GRILLE

701 Texas
(Downtown)
228-9500

Formal Dining: B,L,D
Av: $20 and over

For lunch chose from several **"Cuisine Vitale"** entrees which are said to be low in calories, fat, cholesterol, and sodium. Cuisine Vitale entrees change seasonally to ensure the freshness of their foods.

They include: **Fresh Gulf Crabmeat with Celery Root Salad in a Mustard and Lemon Dressing** (312 calories), **Grilled London Broil Salad with Mixed Beans and Haricots Verts** (477 calories), **Breast of Capon with Scallions and Wild Mushrooms** (422 calories), and **Fresh Tuna with Tomato Mint Salsa** (281 calories).

The new dinner menu includes other selections from **"Cuisine Vitale"**. **Fresh Fruit** is available for dessert.

MAGNOLIA BAR & GRILL

6000 Richmond
(Galleria area)
781-6207

Informal Dining: L,D
Av: $8-15

    Request **Unbuttered Bread** instead of usual buttered bread. **Boiled Shrimp** appetizer is 4 oz. **American Field Salad** consists of greens and raw vegetables - order salad dressing on the side.

    Three menu items are identified, with a small heart symbol, as being Heart Healthy . **Cold Crab Pasta Salad** has no dressing. **Baked Chicken** is half a chicken (request skin to be removed) and comes with strawberries and steamed vegetables. **Steamed Vegetables** have no added fat. **Poached Gulf Red Snapper** is 5 oz and is served with strawberries and steamed vegetables. Other entrees are served with **Yam Slice** (grilled), Corn Masque (high in fat), and **Steamed Vegetables**.

    There are other lean choices. All pasta can be ordered without sauce, sauce on the side, or with tomato sauce. **Pasta Diablo** can come with or without the shrimp. Fish can be prepared **Poached, Mesquite,** or **Grilled** such as: **Catfish, Snapper, Salmon, Trout, Shrimp,** or other specials of the day. Meat portions are about 8 oz. Can request **Fresh Fruit** for dessert.

AMERICAN

MAMA'S CAFE

6019 Westheimer
(between Fountain View & Green Ridge)
266-8514

Casual Dining: B,L,D
Av: $5-10

Corn Muffins are served with meals. Since just about all entrees are cooked to order, most items can be deleted or added at the request of the guest. **Fresh Vegetables** are steamed in batches and margarine or bacon is added - to get "fat-free" will require a wait. **Baked Potato** comes with margarine, sour cream, and chives - ask to have what you want left off.

Sandwiches are dressed with mayonnaise - be sure to request without mayonnaise. **Grilled Chicken Sandwich** or **Turkey Sandwich** - thin sliced breast of turkey served on a fresh hoagie bun (leave off the cheese).

House Salad (ask for dressing on the side). **Vegetable Platter** - plate of any three vegetables (all are prepared with fat). **Homemade Vegetable Soup** (vegetables are sauteed before adding to beef stock) or **Soup & House Salad**. **Boneless Chicken Breast** - marinated and seasoned in our special sauce, comes with two fresh vegetables. **Grilled Catfish** - floured and sauteed in a little fat.

POST OAK GRILL

1415 S Post Oak Ln
(Galleria area)
993-9966

Casual Dining: L,D
Av: $8-15

The appetizer: **Spicy Shrimp Brochette**
comes with a fairly low fat sauce of tomatillo salsa
made with blanched tomatillos and chicken stock.

Request salad dressings on the side for the
Fresh Mixed Greens and other salads. **Warm
Grilled Chicken Salad** - mixed greens, grilled
chicken (4-5 oz), apples, grapes (request without
pecans or roquefort chunk). **Ethel's Warm Grilled
Salmon** - mixed greens, grilled salmon (4-5 oz),
orzo pasta, and sweet red onions.

Angel Hair with fresh Roma tomatoes and garlic can be prepared without any oil. **Angel Hair**
with seared scallops in a spicy tomatillo sauce is low
in fat.

Fish is sprayed with a non-stick spray prior to
grilling; chicken breasts are dipped in oil. Entrees
include about 7 oz of meat. **Grilled Salmon** with
cilantro tomato salsa. **Lemon Pepper Chicken**
comes with fresh spinach (request plain rather than
sauteed) and fettuccine (order it plain rather than in
garlic butter). **Grilled Rosemary Chicken** with
roasted garlic comes with rice or rice pilaf. **Steamed
Vegetables** can be requested to be prepared without fat. **Fresh Fruit** is available for dessert.

POTATOE PATCH

2504 FM 1960 E
(1/2 mi E of Hardy Toll Rd)
443-3530

Casual Dining: L,D
Av: $5-10

Salad dressings are served on the side for all salads. **Lower Calorie Dressings** are available. **House Salad** can be ordered without cheese, egg, bacon, or croutons. **Club Salad** consists of strips of broiled chicken; request no chicken tenders or bacon.

Average portion of meat is 8 oz but smaller portions can be ordered for a discount. **Hawaiian Chicken** is marinated in herbs and spice, topped with teriyaki sauce, and served over a bed of rice and vegetables (request no cheese). **Shrimp & Snow Crab Legs** - 1/2 snow crab legs & 8 gulf shrimp (no drawn butter). **Broiled, Baked,** or **Blackened Fish** is often on the daily specials. For beef, a 6 oz **Filet Mignon** is offered.

Vegetables are steamed, seasonings are added, but no added fats are used. **Baked Potatoes** can be served dry or as you request. **Low Fat Milk** is available.

PROMENADE RESTAURANT

2001 Post Oak Blvd
(in the Doubletree Post Oak Hotel)
961-9300

Informal Dining: B,L,D
Av: $5-15

Boiled Gulf Shrimp is available - choose to have the **Cocktail Sauce** instead of the Creole Remoulade Sauce.

They have a homemade **Fat-Free, Low Calorie Vinaigrette** - be sure to ask for it with your **Post Oak Tossed Green Salad** or the **New England Style Grilled Chicken Salad**. **California Fresh Fruit Salad** consists of fresh fruit with either yogurt (nonfat available) or cottage cheese.

Build your own **Deli Sandwich** - request **Roast Beef, Smoked Ham, or Turkey Breast** on white, wheat, rye, or french bread - they serve the condiments on the side. Instead of french fries, ask for **Steamed Vegetables** with no butter.

Four **Naturals** are available for entrees. Each are said to be lower in fat and calories. Meat portions are 6-7 ounces and come with two **Fresh Steamed Vegetables** (request no butter). Choose from: **Vegetarian Stir fry with Steamed Angel Hair Pasta, Steamed Breast of Chicken with Fresh Salsa, Grilled or Poached Filet of Salmon,** and **Steamed Seafood Marinara**. Request **Fresh Fruit** for dessert.

RITA'S TEXAS CAFE

1045 N Gessner &
7927 FM 1960
464-3666/890-6800

Casual Dining: L,D
Av: $5-10

Willing to provide special orders but has some specific heart-healthy items specified on menu. **Dinner Salad**, request **Lite Italian Salad Dressing** (dressing comes on side for all salads).

Chicken entrees include: **Charbroiled Chicken Salad** -charbroiled, boneless, strips of skinless chicken breast on top of fresh salad vegetables; **Charbroiled Chicken**-comes with charro beans, Texas toast, and dinner salad; and **Chicken Sandwich** (request no cheese and honey-mustard dressing on the side).

Other lower fat choices include: **Turkey Sandwich** (request honey mustard dressing on the side), **Straight Chili** (with meat) or **Chili and Beans**.

THE RIVER OAKS GRILL

2630 Westheimer
(at Kirby)
520-1738

Formal Dining: D
Av: $10-20

Unbuttered Bread is brought to the table - margarine can be requested instead of butter.

Meat portions are 6-8 oz. Vegetables come with the entrees - can request **"Steamed Vegetables"**.

The following entrees can be grilled without any fat, if requested: **Grilled Salmon**, **Grilled Swordfish** with sauce on the side, **Pork Tenderloin** with black bean sauce, and **Grilled Chicken**. **Red Snapper**, because of its delicate nature, tends to fall apart if grilled - it may still be requested grilled, or lightly sauteed in oil - but skip the butter/wine sauce.

Veal Piccata can be prepared with lemon and sherry wine (but request no butter). **Grilled Quail** is marinated and then grilled.

Baked Potatoes are available; they will ask you what you want on it. **Pico de Gallo** is a low fat topping for the potato or on your entree.

AMERICAN

ROTISSERIE FOR BEEF & BIRD

2200 Wilcrest
(1 block N of Westheimer)
977-9524

Formal Dining: L,D
Av: $10-25

Appetizers include: **Oysters on the Half Shell**, **Jumbo Gulf Shrimp Cocktail**, and **Fresh Native Lump Crabmeat** - ask for cocktail sauce.

Potato chips are served along with other breads during lunch; salmon pate comes with dinner.

For lunch: **Mesquite Grilled Red Snapper** or **Breast of Chicken** have no added fat. **Fettucine with a Spicy Seafood Sauce** has very little oil. Vegetables are stir-fried; request **Steamed Vegetables** instead, request that no fat be added. **Rice** is available without added fats. Luncheon portions for meat are about 8 ounces; 16 ounces at dinner (delicacies are smaller). Half portions are available for some items at a discount.

For Dinner: **Grilled Pheasant**, **Cackle Bird**, **Wild Boar** (plum sauce has no oils), **Venison**, **Roast Duckling** (remove skin and visible fat), and **Spring Lamb**. **Fresh Fish of the Day** and **Fresh Shellfish** can be broiled or grilled without any added fats.

Entrees come with a **Salad**, **Garden Fresh Vegetable** (request steamed), and rolls. Half order of **Tournedos of Beef Armagnac** is available if you want beef; this cut is from the tenderloin. **Fresh Fruit** is available for dessert.

RUBY TUESDAY

7925 FM 1960
(in Willowbrook Mall)
955-1772

Casual Dining: L,D
Av: $5-10

Salad Bar offers **Raw Vegetables**, **Pickles**, **Turkey Ham**, and **Fruits**; other items may be requested. **Baked Potato** is about 11-12 oz and can be prepared as you like. Request sandwiches without mayonnaise. Ask them to remove the skin off the **Chicken Teriyaki Sandwich.**

Ruby's Grilled or Blackened Fish, Cajun Chicken, and **Chicken Teriyaki** come with french fries. Substitute **Steamed Broccoli** or a **Sprout Salad** with Vinaigrette on the side instead of the fries.

Three nutritionally balanced "PhD" dishes are offered. **PhD Open Faced Chicken Breast Sandwich** - grilled chicken breast served on warm Italian bread with melted mozzarella cheese and a side of yogurt dressing (made with nonfat yogurt) has 458 cals/16 gms fat. Can be requested without cheese for an additional savings in cals/fat.

PhD Steamed Vegetable Plate consists of steamed broccoli, cauliflower, carrots, yellow squash, and a baked potato served with a side of yogurt dressing for 404 cals/2 gms fat. **Tuna Stuffed Tomato** includes a tomato stuffed with tuna salad served with wheat crackers, broccoli, cauliflower, carrot sticks, and fresh fruit for 383 cals/ 15 gms fat. Can request the tuna to be prepared with half the mayonnaise or none at all.

AMERICAN

SHONEY'S RESTAURANT

3 restaurants in Houston area
for locations, call:
890-2485

Informal Dining: B,L,D
Av: $5-10

Offers a large **Salad Bar** with a variety of raw
vegetables, protein sources (cottage cheese, ham),
and fresh fruit that could make a complete meal.
Low Calorie Salad Dressings are available.

Soups that are low in calories and fat (less than
85 cals/3 gms fat per 6 oz) include: **Tomato Vegetable**, **Chicken Rice**, **Tomato Florentine**, **Bean**,
Cream of Chicken Vegetable, **Chicken Noodle**,
Vegetable Beef, **Chicken Gumbo**, and **Onion**.

The leanest dinner *entrees* are: **Charbroiled
Chicken** (239 cals/7 gms fat), **Hawaiian Chicken**
(262 cals/7 gms fat), **Baked Fish** (170 cals/1.4 gm
fat), **Light Baked Fish** (170 cals/1.4 gms fat), **Charbroiled Shrimp** (138 cals/3 gms fat), and **Boiled
Shrimp** (138 cals/3 gms fat).

The above numbers do not include accompaniments. A **Baked Potato**, plain, has 264 cals/<1 gm
fat. **Rice** (137 cals/4 gms fat).

For sandwiches: **Fish Sandwich** (323 cals/13
gms fat), **Baked Ham Sandwich** (290 cals/10 gms
fat), and **Charbroiled Chicken Sandwich** (451
cals/17 gms fat) are lowest in calories and fat.
Choose **Fresh Fruit** from the salad bar for dessert.
Or the **Chocolate Pudding** (162 cals/4 gms fat) for
1/2 c serving.

SPINDLETOP

1200 Louisiana
(Downtown in Hyatt Regency)
654-1234

Formal Dining: L,D
Av: Over $20

For lunch: **Spindletop Salad** has a variety of vegetables - ask for **Lite Italian** or **Raspberry Lite Vinaigrette** on the side. **Fresh Fruit Plate** - a seasonal selection of fresh fruits and berries served with plain yogurt (skip the banana nut bread to save much fat).

Chicken Breast Burger - mayo comes on the side. **Grilled Pacific Swordfish** and **Grilled Breast of Chicken** should both be ordered with sauce on the side.

For dinner, appetizers include: **Shrimp Cocktail** and **Grilled Sea Scallops** (order sauce on the side).

Entrees include: **Live Main Lobster** - request no drawn butter, and **Grilled Swordfish**. The **Seafood Sampler** consists of 4 oz grilled swordfish, 2 scallops, 2 shrimp, and 2 oysters rockerfeller (the oysters are much higher in fat than the others) - sauce is on the side. **Scallopini of Veal** - ask for it to be sauteed in very little oil with marsala wine and mushrooms on the side.

Entrees (for both lunch and dinner) are served with Rainbow Fettucini (tossed with about a half teaspoon of butter) or **Steamed Long Grain and Wild Rice** *and* **Fresh Vegetables** (request to be steamed, with no butter added). **Fresh Fruit** is available for Dessert.

STABLES RESTAURANT

7325 S Main at Greenbriar &
3734 Westheimer
795-5900/621-0833

Informal Dining: L,D
Av: $10-20

For salads, request their **Fat-Free Dressing**.
The **Dinner Salad** is a variety of vegetables. Re-
quest no eggs or cheese on their **Grilled Italian
Chicken Salad** or **Grilled Lemon Peppered
Chicken Salad**. Ask about the soup - sometimes
the creamy ones may be prepared with skim milk.

The Chargrilled Chicken Sandwich can be a
lean choice if you ask that the skin be removed,
leave off the cheese, *and* substitute (instead of
french fries and onion rings) **Baked Potato** or
Steamed Vegetables (request no fats added).

Request that the skin be removed from chargrilled chicken items. Chicken choices (about 6
ounces cooked) include: **Chargrilled Breast of
Chicken**, **Chicken Kabobs**, and **Chargrilled
Lemon Peppered Chicken**.

You may request fish to be broiled with white
wine, lemon juice and herbs, but no oil. Seafood
choices include: **Chargrilled Gulf Shrimp**, **Cana-
dian Scallops** (request sauce on the side), and
Broiled Seafarer's Platter.

STRAWBERRY PATCH

5839 Westheimer
(Galleria area)
780-7352

Casual Dining: L,D
Av: $10-20

There are three leaner Chicken Breast (but still 10 oz each) dishes; request that the skin be removed. **Chicken Teriyaki** - marinated in pineapple soy sauce & mesquite-grilled; served with wild rice pilaf. **Chicken Dijon** - mesquite-grilled chicken; topped with mushrooms and red peppers (ask for without avocado or cheese). **Blackened Chicken Orleans** - chicken breast blackened with Cajun spices, request without oil; top with plain seafood instead of the sauteed seafood. Request all chicken dishes to be served with the sauce on the side. All are served with fresh vegetables that are prepared with butter; you may request **Steamed Broccoli** instead.

Request salad dressing on the side for **Patch Salads** or **Grilled Chicken Breast Salad** (10 oz chicken on a bed of lettuce; request no tortilla strips and dressing on the side).

Filet Mignon - 6 oz cut is offered. **Shrimp or Crab Salad** - boiled shrimp or crabmeat (each are about 4 oz meat) on a bed of crisp romaine lettuce; topped with pineapple, red pepper; request cocktail sauce for a topping.

Fish servings are about 8-10 oz each. Popular **Catch of the Day** items: **Salmon** (can be requested without breading and mesquite grilled) and a **Blackened Fresh Fish** - ask for fresh crawfish as topping (instead of etouffee). **Fresh Strawberries**.

AMERICAN

VARGO'S

2401 Fondren
(1 block N of Westheimer)
782-3888

Formal Dining: L,D
Av: $19 - $25

Lunch: **Grilled Chicken Breast** with pineapple and other fresh fruits; **Chicken Salad** with fresh vegetables; **Crab Salad** (ask for oil and vinegar dressing on the side); or **Grilled Rainbow Trout** (request without butter). Both the **Vegetable of the Day** and the **Potato of the Day** (or **Pasta** or **Rice**) can be prepared without any fats.

Dinner begins with a **Complimentary Relish Tray** (consists of pickled vegetables and cheese - you may want to stay away from cheese) *and* either a **Fresh Fruit Cup** or a **Mixed Green Salad** (order **Low Calorie Ranch Dressing** on the side). **Jumbo Gulf Shrimp Cocktail** is available for an appetizer.

The grilled menu items can be prepared without any butter if requested: **Fresh Red Snapper, Gulf Shrimp Kabob, Rainbow Trout** (ask for Meuniere sauce on the side), and **Grilled Chicken Breast** on a bed of rice pilaf. **Salmon Filet** - poached (ask for sauce on the side) and **Fresh Red Snapper Albert** (baked with vegetables on top but no fat is added) are also available. Fish portions are about 8 ounces; Filet Mignon is also 8 ounces.

Fresh Green Beans, Louisiana Dirty Rice (**Plain Rice** can be substituted), Whipped Potatoes, Spiced Apples, and **Hot French Bread** accompany all entrees. **Fresh Strawberries** are available in season.

WHISTLERS WALK

1200 Louisiana
(Downtown in Hyatt Regency)
654-1234

Casual Dining: B,L,D
Av: $7-20

Garden Salad - greens, carrots, zucchini, cucumbers, and red cabbage (ask for **Light Italian** or **Vinegar** on the side). **Shrimp Cocktail** - five shrimp comes with cocktail sauce (available for dinner only).

Lunch and Dinner both offer two **"Perfect Balance Meals"** (low in calories): **Broiled Fresh Seasonal Fish** - with crushed herbs and spices, garnished with bouquet of seasonal vegetables (328 cals/2 gms fat) or **Asparagus Stuffed Chicken** - poached skinless breast of chicken stuffed with asparagus and served with cous cous and fresh steamed vegetables on an asparagus coulis; sauce is a vegetable puree and has no added fats (511 cals/ 16 grams fat).

Another option at dinner: **Charbroiled Fresh Swordfish** - ask for butter sauce on the side. Request to be served with **Plain Baked Potato**, **Plain Rice or Wild Rice** and **Steamed Vegetables** (no butter is added to these dishes).

FRENCH & CONTINENTAL

Continental and French style restaurants typically offer fancier dining than American style restaurants. The tables are often set with cloth napkins.

This is where you really get waited on but the pace is a lot slower. You can expect to spend two or three hours dining in some of the Continental/ French restaurants. Many special occasions are celebrated in Continental restaurants because of this distinctive ambience and extraordinary service. Predictably, the price tag is often higher.

French cuisine once considered haute cuisine, was noted for rich sauces such as Bearnaise, Mornay, and Bechamel. These sauces are high in butter, eggs, and cream.

The newer cuisine, nouvelle cuisine, is lighter and healthier. You are much more likely to find grilled, blackened, poached, and stir-fried foods. Due to customer demand, vegetable sauces are also more common now.

Continental restaurants are more likely to offer specific lower fat dinners as noted on their menu. Special requests are also more accepted because food is prepared just for you, not in advance as is often the case in the less expensive restaurants.

Here are some general guidelines for Dinin'Lean® in French and Continental restaurants:

Appetizer

If you want a fried appetizer, split the order with a friend. A broth-based soup such as clear consomme or vegetable soup would be a good, filling starter.

Breads

Specialty breads are often served at the table such as garlic rolls, croissants, cheese toast, cinnamon rolls, or herb bread. All are high in fat even before the butter is added. Unless the rest of the meal will be low in fat, there items are best avoided. Plain breads are often available if requested. Some restaurants even offer the newer no-fat, no-cholesterol muffins as an option.

Sandwiches

Chose those sandwiches made with pita bread, sliced bread, or on a yeast roll instead of a croissant. Order the sandwiches to be prepared dry or with mustard. Ask for the dressings (such as mayonnaise, honey mustard, or ranch dressing) to be served on the side so you can control how much dressing gets added.

Salads

Continental restaurants frequently serve a salad with a variety of greens and other vegetables. Ask what additional components are added. You may want to omit the added nuts, avocado, cheese, olives, or croutons because of their high fat content.

Quite a few of these restaurants make their own non-fat vinaigrette. Or ask for the many flavorful varieties of vinegars (such as red wine or tarragon vinegar) that are frequently available. If these are not available, order the salad dressing on the side.

Crab or Shrimp Louis is often simply a salad with the seafood on the top. This would be a recommended low fat choice. Ask for the cocktail sauce for a dressing.

Entrees

Fish and seafood are very lean choices. Watch out for the drawn butter with the seafood or the butter than may have been brushed on the fish. Upon request, these can both be omitted. Fish may also have toppings of sauces or sauteed seafood such as crab. Ask for your fish to be prepared without this or order the topping on the side.

Chicken and other poultry can be lean choices if the skin and visible fat is removed. White meat is leaner than the dark meat. Wild game is very lean. Again, order all sauces on the side.

If you want beef, order the smallest filet. Often this is available in a 4 or 6 oz cut even if it is not specified on the menu.

Accompaniments

Steamed or grilled vegetables are leaner choices than sauteed or fried vegetables. Even steamed vegetables are often covered with butter or a sauce; request these to be prepared without added fats or sauces.

Order baked potatoes without the toppings or on the side. Rice pilaf has some added fat but plain rice is often available.

Pastas are best ordered with a red sauce or requested to be prepared with very little oil.

Dessert

Fresh fruit is usually available even if it is not listed on the menu. Sorbet and frozen yogurt are not calorie free but they are usually low in fat.

Most other desserts are often very rich. It is best to share these fattening desserts with a few of your friends because one serving is often 500 calories to over 1000 calories per portion. Spicing your coffee with liquor might offer the sweet touch you need with far less calories.

CONTINENTAL

THE BROWNSTONE

2736 Virginia
(at Westheimer)
520-5666

Formal Dining: L,D
Av: $20 and over

They are willing to honor any guest's requests. **Cholesterol/Fat-Free Muffins** come to the table along with other high fat items. **Seasonal Fruit Plate** - dressing is served on the side. **House Gourmet Green Salad** ask for dressing on the side or request their fat-free **Tarragon Dressing** which is made with honey, tarragon, and lemon juice - no oil. Other salads include: **Grilled Herbed Breast of Chicken** on gourmet greens and **Pecan Smoked Chicken** over spinach and gourmet greens (chicken portions for these salads are about 5 oz cooked).

Entrees include: **Mahi-Mahi, Swordfish,** other **Fresh Fish of the Day** (fish can be grilled - request sauce on the side) and **Grilled Herbed Breast of Chicken**. Meat portions are about 6 oz. at lunch; 10 oz at dinner. **Petite Filet** is 6 oz at lunch or dinner.

Bow Tie Pasta with Marinara Sauce is available as either an appetizer or an entree. **Steamed Vegetables** - request no added fats. Entrees are accompanied by **Potato of the Day** (can be prepared as desired) or **Basmati Rice** (no fats are added). **Fresh Kiwi and Strawberries** are available for dessert (request without the Midori).

CALYPSO

5555 Morningside Dr
(Rice Village)
524-8571

Casual Dining: L,D
Av: $8-12

Serves Carribean cuisine. Honey Muffins that come to the table are made with brown sugar, honey, eggs, and whole milk - not low calorie! But there is so much else that is low fat and healthy.

More than not, the fish and poultry is grilled with no oil. To saute, very little oil is used along with some chicken stock - but you can always request only chicken stock or wine.

Court Bullion de Martinique - braised fish, crab, and shrimp in a sauce of tomato, garlic, shallot, and lime. **Fish Dominica** - sauteed fillet topped with onion, tomato, cilantro, lemon, and sour cream (just a dollop). **Boston Beach Shrimp** - large skewered shrimp marinated with traditional Caribbean spices, then grilled.

Raspberry-Tamarind Chicken - sauteed chicken breast with raspberry-tamarind sauce. **Jerk Chicken** - grilled chicken with blend of fiery peppers and exotic Caribbean spices.

Entrees come with **Vegetables** and **Rice** of the day. Rice has no added fat. Black beans have some fat - can substitute **Vegetables Sauteed in Water/Chicken Stock.**

Fresh Fruits are available for dessert.

CHEZ EDDY

6560 Fannin
(4th Floor in Scurlock Tower)
790-6474

Formal Dining: L,D
Av: $10-20

Chez Eddy's food is all heart healthy cuisine.
The restaurant, owned by the Methodist Hospital
System, offers meals with fewer calories because
they follow the American Heart Association's
guidelines for fat, cholesterol, and sodium. They
add no extra fat or sodium in their cooking. Each
entree has less than 12 grams of fat.

It is possible to select meals under 500 cals or
even under 300 cals that include salad with salad
dressing, an entree, vegetable, and dessert. One
choice at 540 cals: **Grilled Salmon Antonio** (with
a green peppercorn sauce), **Vegetable of the Day**,
Chez Eddy House Salad (served with almond herb
dressing), and **Coupe Chez Eddy** (vanilla frozen
yogurt with fresh strawberry sauce, fresh strawberries and fresh kiwi). **Bread** and margarine are also
brought to the table but not calculated in the
example.

Other entrees include: **Grilled Thai Chicken
Salad** (served with spicy Thai vinaigrette), **Tenderloin of Beef Marchand de Vin** (4-5 oz cut),
Salmon and Crab Cakes (served with fresh dill
sauce), and **Grilled Wild Boar with Plum Sauce**.

Other lower calorie/fat desserts include: **Choco-
late Brownie with Frozen Vanilla Yogurt**, **Fresh
Seasonal Fruit with Sorbet**, and **Chez Eddy
Cheesecake**.

CHEZ GEORGES RESTAURANT

11920 Westheimer
(at Kirkwood)
497-1122

Formal Dining: L,D
Av: $10-20

Hors D'Oeuvres: **La Terrine de Legumes "Pierre et Jean"** - vegetable terrine with fresh tomato pulp has no added fat. **Effeuille de Saumon Marine aux Herbes que J'Aime** - 3-4 oz salmon marinated with herbs (specify to be prepared without oil).

Entrees are served with potatoes (which are prepared with cream) and **Steamed Vegetables** (request no butter). Can order extra vegetables *instead of* potatoes.

La Fricassee de Grenouilles et d'Ecrevisses sur un Nid d'Aubergine - deboned frog legs and sauteed crawfish on a top of eggplant, with mixed fresh herb sauce (request for without butter sauce). **Le Red Snapper Grille au Fenouil** - 8-10 oz grilled red snapper (ask for no butter sauce). **Grilled Salmon** and **Grilled Sole** are also available.

Le Filet Mignon de Veau a la Tomate, Citron Vert et Basilic is specified on the menu as "low calorie" but it is still a 10 oz filet prepared with 1 t olive oil.

Fresh Fruit is available when in season.

CONTINENTAL

CHEZ NOUS

217 Ave G, Humble
(next to NE Medical Center)
446-6717

Formal Dining: D
Av: $10-20

Salade Maison (Seasonal Greens) is tossed with
French dressing in kitchen (chef estimates about 1
T) or **Sliced Tomato & Scallions**. Each day's
Specials includes at least one lean appetizer (such
as **Navasota Melon Soup**, **Andalousean
Gazpacho**, or **Hot Summer Squash Soup**) and
two lean entrees (such as **Grilled Blue Marlin
Steak** with pinto, kidney, and black bean salad;
Yellowfin Tuna Steak with corn and cilantro salsa,
or **Breast of Chicken** stuffed with cilantro).

Grilled Vegetable Plate - mesquite grilled
vegetables with angel hair pasta can be individual-
ized to those customers desiring not to eat meat.

Smallest beef dish is the **Tournedos Bordelaise**
(7-8 oz beef tenderloin flambe - request Bordeause
Mushroom Sauce on the side). The entrees are all
accompanied by 2 **Vegetables** (sauteed in chicken
stock or steamed) <u>and</u> Risotto (rice dish) or **Potatoes** (request to be prepared plain).

Low fat milk is available. **Fresh Fruit** is
available for dessert.

DELMONICO'S/WESTIN GALLERIA

5650 W Alabama
(Galleria area)
960-6558

Casual Dining: L,D
Av: $17-24

Average portion of meat is 8 oz for lunch & 10 oz for dinner (even in salads). Smaller portions can be ordered for a discount. Order **Low Calorie Vinaigrette** or other dressings on the side of your salad. For lunch: **Texas Cobb Salad** - grilled skirt steak, blackeyed peas, corn kernels (request without cheese) or **Herbed Chicken Breast Salad** (order without avocado or pecans).

Instead of fried potatoes - request **Steamed Vegetables**; no butter is added. **Chargrilled Chicken Sandwich** with steamed Tri-color peppers (request no mayo). **Pan Seared Corn-meal Coho Salmon** - request not to be breaded and prepared with very little oil; **Chili Verde Sauce** has no oil. Other **Grilled Fish** may be available. **Petit Filet** is 6 oz at lunch (request without cream sauce). **Grilled Maple Marinated Chicken Breast** with wild rice cakes and sauce on the side.

Dinner always includes a **Light-n-Lively Entree** of the Week which is calculated by the chef to be under 300 calories. Other selections at dinner: **Pan Seared Norwegian Salmon** (request without butter sauce); **Swordfish Steak with Chili Verde Sauce**; or **Lobster Tails** (request without drawn butter). **Grilled Chicken Breast** has Steamed Tri-color peppers with Tuscan beans (request no oil). Both **Skim and Low Fat Milk** are available. **Fresh Fruit** or **Sorbet** available for dessert.

GARDEN COURT/HOUSTON PLAZA HILTON

6633 Travis
(Medical Center area)
524-6633

Formal Dining: B,L,D
Av: $10-20

French Rolls are served with butter on the side. Offers a lean **Chicken Vegetable Soup** or **Clear Consomme**. For salads: **Garden Court Salad** - request no olives or **Spinach Salad** - has only fresh spinach and mushrooms (ask for dressing on the side).

Order the **Grilled Chicken Sandwich** without avocado or cheese. **Fresh Fruit Salad Platter** is served with cottage cheese. **Grilled Breast of Chicken** with rice and steamed vegetables. Request **Steamed Vegetables** to be prepared without fats.

Other luncheon items include a 6 oz meat portion including a 6 oz **Filet Mignon**. Eight oz meat portions are served at dinner.

Several low fat dinner choices are available. **Stuffed Baked Shrimp** - 5 jumbo shrimp stuffed with just crabmeat, ask for sherry sauce on the side. **Norwegian Salmon Steak** - an 8 ounce grilled salmon steak served with rice and vegetables. **Red Snapper** - ask for without sauteed crawfish, served with rice and vegetables.

Low Fat Frozen Yogurt or **Fresh Fruit** is available for dessert.

LANTERN INN

12448 Memorial Dr
(between Gessner & Beltway 8)
465-5684

Formal Dining: L,D
Av: $10-20

Lunch: Order dressing on the side for the salads.
Chef Salad has 2 oz turkey or chicken breast and 1/
2 - 1 oz cheese; request no cheese, but add more
meat (if desired). **Lantern Salad** has 3 oz crabmeat.
Spinach Salad includes 2 oz smoked shrimp or 1 -
1/2 oz salmon.

Chicken Sandwich is made with 3 oz chicken,
lettuce, and tomato in a pita - no dressing has been
added. **Grilled Salmon** is a 4 oz serving and is
served with sauteed spinach (request boiled
instead) and rice with sauteed vegetables. **Chicken
Sausage** is made from only 2 oz chicken breasts
and seasonings. It is served over pasta with a onion,
bellpepper, and tomato sauce.

Dinner: **Shrimp Cocktail** (3 oz), **Smoked
Salmon** (2 oz), **Lump Gulf Crabmeat Cocktail** (2
oz), or **Beef Steak Tomato** (ask for dressing on the
side). Fish portions are 6-8 oz; 5-6 oz for chicken or
veal. A **4 oz Tenderloin Steak** can be requested.

Lobster Tail is poached with white wine/water,
then baked in the oven. **Red Snapper** can be
prepared the same way. **Broiled Fillet of Gulf Red
Snapper** can be ordered without sauce. **Fresh
Salmon** - request grilled with lemon juice. **Blackened Catfish** can be prepared without any oil.
Grilled Chicken or Veal. Fresh Fruit is available.

CONTINENTAL

LE CAFE ROYAL

425 N Beltway 8
(in Hotel Sofitel)
445-9000

Formal Dining: L,D
Av: $20 and over

Plain Bread is served with butter. Entrees come with **Mixed Green Salad** (request salad dressing on the side), **Vegetable of the Day** (request steamed without oil), and **Rice or Potato of the Day** (both can be prepared plain, if requested). Meat portions are 5-6 oz at lunch; 8 oz at dinner. Reduced portions are available for a discount including a *four* oz **Filet Mignon**.

Lunch: **Salade Monte-Cristo** - with 4 oz lobster and **Salade Neptune** -1-1/2 oz crabmeat, fish, shrimp and scallops should be ordered without egg and with salad dressing on the side. **Salade de Fruits Frais** includes fruit with plain low fat yogurt (to save calories, order without honey).

All fish can be grilled. Ask for **Grilled Scallops and Shrimp** in reduced grapefruit juice but no butter. **Grilled Red Snapper or Swordfish** without butter or oil. **Grilled Salmon** without the sauce. **Grilled Chicken** is available without sauce and skin.

Dinner: **Arlequin de Saumon et de Sole en Habit Vert** is steamed fish and vegetables "rolled-up" (request butter sauce on the side). **Grilled Swordfish**, **Shrimp**, **Red Snapper**, or **Mixed Grill de Poisson** (assortment of grilled seafood) should be requested without sauce. **Fresh Fruit** for dessert.

MEDITERRANEAN RESTAURANT & BAR

2425 W Holcolmbe Blvd
(Medical Center area)
662-8302

Casual Dining: L,D
Av: $10-20

Boiled Shrimp Cocktail with cocktail sauce for an appetizer. **Dinner Salad** consists of greens, cucumber, and tomato; request **Light Dressing** on the side.

Sopa de Ajo - garlic soup does have some egg but no added oil. **Crema de Mariscos** - is not a cream soup, but rather seafood and vegetables. **Sopa de Pescado y Mariscos con Arroz** - seafood and rice soup.

Espinacas Salteadas Con Pinones y Pasas - spinach with raisin and pinenuts has no added fat, but pinenuts are still high in fat. **Grilled Fish** can be prepared without any oil, only lemon and salt such as grouper, red snapper, and any special fish from Spain. **Medio Pollo Parrilla Al Limon** - half grilled chicken with lemon. An 8 oz cut of **Grilled Veal** is also available.

Fresh Fruit is available for dessert.

CONTINENTAL

QUAIL HOLLOW INN

214 Morton, Richmond
(30 minutes SW of Houston)
341-6733

Formal Dining: L,D
Av: $10-20

At lunch, cheese toast is brought to the table, but **Unbuttered Bread** is served with dinner. **Shrimp Cocktail** is available. Lowest fat sandwiches are: **Ham, Turkey, and Roast Beef Sandwiches** - ask for no cheese and no mayo.

Ask for dressing on the side for all the salads. **Chinese Chicken Salad** (ask for chicken to be broiled and ask to omit cashews and crunchy chinese noodles). **Crab or Shrimp Louis** (ask for no eggs). **Fruit Plate** comes with cottage cheese or sherbet.

A couple items are available at both lunch and dinner. **Grilled Chicken Breast** (ask to have skin removed). **Pacific Snapper Filet** (ask to have prepared low fat using cajun style spices and non-stick spray). The average portion of meat is 6-8 oz.

Dinner: request **Broccoli** without Hollandaise sauce. **Duckling** - remove skin and ask for the sauce on the side. Lean game meats (request sauce on the side) include: **Venison Pepper Steak**, **Scallops of Wild Boar**, and **Broiled Quail with Filet of Rabbit** . Dinners are served with soup (not always lean), **Salad** (request dressing on the side), **Baked Potato**, and Vegetable du Jour (*always* has butter/oil added).

Fresh Fruit is offered for dessert.

RAINBOW LODGE

#1 Birdsall
(between Memorial Park & Downtown)
861-8666

Formal Dining: L,D
Av: $10-20

Always willing to prepare according to the customer's request. Request the salad dressing on the side for all the salads.

Valley Salad (jicama, carrots, and red onion) is low in fat if you ask to omit the avocado and ask for the cilantro lime vinaigrette to be served on the side. **Tossed Salad** should be requested without tortilla strips. **Grilled Chicken with Arugula** is grilled chicken tossed with mixed greens, arugula, and jicama. **Low Fat Milk** is available.

For lunch, there's a **Grilled Chicken Sandwich** - ask for no spread and no cheese or a **Steamed Vegetable Platter** - ask for no butter to be added. A **Light Luncheon Special** is grilled chicken, house salad, potatoes, and steamed vegetables.

Other choices include **Orvis Salmon** - request the crabmeat be sauteed in white wine instead of butter or the **Weezie Chicken** - request the chicken and vegetables be sauteed in white wine or chicken stock and that lime butter not be ladled on top.

Fresh Fruit is available for dessert.

CONTINENTAL

RAZZBERRY'S FOOD AND SPIRITS

14058 Memorial Drive
(Kirkwood/Memorial Center)
556-9120

Casual Dining: B,L,D
Av: $5-10

Soups are homemade; many are broth-based. **Chicken Noodle Soup** is made with lean chicken breast. Ask for the **No-Fat Vinaigrette** to be served with the **House Salad** or the **Marinated Breast of Chicken Salad**.

Fresh Fruit Salad is served with cottage cheese. **Skim Milk** is available.

Breast of Turkey Sandwich or **Club Sandwich** (ham and turkey) are made to order - tell them what you want on it. **Marinated Breast of Chicken Sandwich** is served on a bun.

For dinner: **Grilled Breast of Chicken** (4-5 oz), **Baked Catfish Fillet**, or **Catch of the Day** is served with **Baked Potato** (ask for margarine or other toppings on the side) and **Vegetables** (can be ordered without butter if you call ahead).

Luncheon portions can be ordered at dinner for a discount.

RED LION

7315 Main
(at Greenbriar)
795-5000

Informal Dining: L,D
Av: $10-20

 With your salad, request the **Yogurt Ranch Dressing**, it has no fat. **Low Fat Milk** is available. **Yeast Rolls** are served with margarine on the side, try to ignore those cinnamon rolls.

 Many menu items can be prepared low in fat and calories according to **The Living Heart Diet** by Dr. DeBakey. Make the request that they be prepared this way.

 Lunch offers the: **Crabmeat & Vegetable Platter**. For dinner: **Hearts of Palm** and **Hearts of Artichoke** - request vinaigrette dressing on the side.

 Heart-healthy entrees for dinner include: **Grilled Breast of Chicken** served with seasonal fresh fruit or vegetables; **Churchill's Peppered Chicken** marinated in lemon juice and black pepper then char-grilled, served with rice; **Snapper Ponchartrain** broiled and topped with Creole Sauce; **Orange Roughy Almondine**; **Broiled Orange Roughy**; and **Filet Mignon Petite Cut** - a heart healthy 4 ounce cut. **Fresh Fruit** for dessert can be arranged.

THE RESTAURANT/THE RITZ CARLTON HILTON

1919 Briar Oaks Lane
(inside 610 off San Felipe)
840-7600

Formal Dining: B,L,D
Av: $20 and over

"**Fitness Cuisine**" (meals that are lower in fat, cholesterol, and sodium) is offered at lunch and dinner.

The **Fitness Cuisine** appetizers are: **Chilled White Gazpacho** or **Heart of Bibb Lettuce** with **Vegetable Vinaigrette**.

There are three **Fitness Cuisine** entrees: **Grilled Chicken Breast with Papaya Al Pesto**; **Veal Piccata with Ratatouille**; or **Poached Norwegian Salmon and Warm Vegetable Salad with Cardamon Vinaigrette**.

The **Fitness Cuisine** desserts are **Passion Fruit Sorbet with a Minted Raspberry Coulis** or **Seasonal Fruit with a Poppy Seed Yogurt**.

For dinner, **Fitness Cuisine** is not listed on the menu but is available upon request. Or simply ask for any dinner entree to be prepared in a low fat manner.

RIVOLI RESTAURANT

5636 Richmond
(Galleria area)
789-1900

Formal Dining: L,D
Av: $20 and over

Request **6 Grains Bread**. **Green Garden Salad**: request salad dressing on the side. **Gulf Shrimp Cocktail** with **Red Sauce**. **Chilled Andolusian Gazpacho**. **Sliced Tomato with Lump Crabmeat and Asparagus Tips** - request vinaigrette on the side. A dinner hor d'oeuvres is **Blackened Gulf Shrimp** - ask for no sauce. **Fruit Plate** is served with cottage cheese or sherbet and honey dressing.

Average meat portion is 6-8 oz; smaller portions are available. **Grilled Norwegian Salmon, Broiled Gulf Red Snapper**, and **Grilled Dover Sole** - request these without sauce. **Grilled Peppered Chicken Breast with Rosemary. Steamed or Grilled Vegetable Plate**-request without sauce. Entrees are served with 3 vegetables (request steamed or grilled) and a potato-request steamed or grilled.

At dinner, many of the above dishes are available. In addition: **Grilled Tournedos** (without sauce) can be requested in a smaller portion. **Grilled Tuna with Tomatillo Salsa, Grilled Swordfish Steak** - ask for without lemon butter. **Broiled Sea Scallops** - request dry. **Blackened Redfish** does require about 1/2 T of oil.

Fresh Fruit or **Sherbet** is available for dessert. **Raspberry Souffle** - skip the sauce. Both **Skim Milk** and **Low Fat Milk** are available.

CONTINENTAL

RUDI LECHNER'S RESTAURANT

2503 S Gessner
(1 block N of Westheimer)
782-1180

Informal Dining: L,D
Av: $5-10

For the traditional German foods, they are willing to cook **Steamed Vegetables** without any fats, broil or bake foods instead of frying, remove poultry skin and trim visible fat, and to serve the sauces on the side. Inquire about their leaner menu suggestions.

But for much lower fat food (but not necessarily the traditional German taste), try the items below listed on their "**Light & Right Cuisine**" menu. Meat portions are about 6 oz but little or no fats have been added; chicken stock and herb seasoning are used for flavor instead.

Chicken Breast and Fettuccine tossed with Vegetables or **Fettuccine tossed with Vegetables** in chicken stock are both lean. **Vegetable Plate** is served with boiled potatoes and pasta.

The following "**Light & Right Cuisine**" dishes are served with **Steamed Vegetables** and **Boiled Potatoes** (or **Rice**): Skinless, Boneless, Grilled Chicken Breast; Fresh Fish of the Day; or **Lean Flank Steak** grilled with peppers, onions, and tomatoes.

All "**Light & Right Cuisine**" menu items include **Fresh Fruit** available from the **Salad Buffet** or **Frozen Yogurt of the Day** (about 4 oz). **Skim Milk** is available.

THE TEXAS CLUB

601 Travis
(Downtown)
227-7000

Formal Dining: L
Av: $10-20

This private athletic and dining club caters to members who are concerned about what they eat. They pride themselves on honoring every customer request. **Whole Wheat French Bread** is served with butter or margarine on the side.

The Club recommends four leaner choices: **Chicken San Antonio** - a marinated boneless skinless chicken breast (6-7 oz.) served with a puree of black beans (beans have no added fat). **Red Snapper Caudabec** - fillet of fresh fish (6-7 oz.) broiled with seasonings and a touch of margarine, served with fruit cocktail and steamed vegetables. **Pasta Primavera with Grilled Chicken** (fresh pasta and vegetables topped with grilled chicken and **"Red Sauce"**. **Filet Mignon** - grilled filet mignon (6 oz.) served with a natural brown sauce with fresh mushrooms.

Steamed Vegetables, **Steamed Rice**, and **Boiled Potatoes** can be requested without any added fats.

Fresh Fruits and **Nonfat Frozen Yogurt** are available for dessert.

CONTINENTAL

TONY'S RESTAURANT

1801 Post Oak Blvd
(Galleria area)
622-6778

Formal Dining: L,D
Av: $25+

Willing to do any special ordering for customers.
Salad Maison - argula, radicchio and endive in
tomato basil vinaigrette (request that **vinaigrette be
prepared without oil**). **Pasta Leggera** - sundried
tomatoes, broccoli, mushrooms, olive oil, and garlic
(256 calories) for an appetizer.

Menu changes monthly but always has fresh fish
such as snapper, shrimp, salmon, and lobster.
Poultry such as duckling, and chicken breast are
also available. Veal can be prepared lower in fat as
can the lean wild game birds such as pheasant and
quail. Be sure to ask lots of questions so you can
allow them to adapt the menu item to your nutritional needs.

Meat portions are 6-10 oz but smaller portions
are available at a discounted price. **Fresh Steamed
Vegetables** upon request. **Fresh Fruit** is available
for dessert.

THE VICKER'S INN RESTAURANT

122 S 1st Street
(in La Porte)
471-6505

Informal Dining: L,D
Av: $10-20

Request salad dressing to be served on the side.
Unbuttered Honey Wheat Rolls are served in
addition to bread rounds (buttered slices) and pate.
Meat portions are 6-8 oz at lunch and 6-10 oz at
dinner. **Steamed Vegetables** (without any butter)
can be requested. Dutchess Potatoes are creamed
and then piped onto a cookie sheet and baked
(each has about 1/2 T margarine and a small
amount of egg). Rice pilaf has added fat. Willing to
prepare special requests for their customers.
Lunch: **Baked Chicken Breast on a Lemon
Sauce** has 1/2 T margarine. **Baked Chicken Breast**
has no added fat (request no sauce). **Charcoal
Grilled Fish** requires a little margarine to prevent
sticking. A combination **Plate** is available: **Fish,
Steamed Vegetables, and Fresh Fruit** (request
poppyseed dressing on the side).
Dinner: **Grilled Shrimp Brochette, Grilled
Angus** (6 oz filet), **Grilled Fish**, and **Grilled
Chicken Breast**-request with sauce on the side.
Fresh Fruit for dessert.

CAJUN/CREOLE

Cajun foods are those originating from the Acadian French immigrants living in southern Louisiana. Creole foods can be broadened to those foods prepared by a person of European parentage born in the West Indies, Central America, or Gulf States.

Most of us think of Cajun and Creole foods as being spicy and flavorful. Fish is the most common "meat" seen on Cajun and Creole restaurant menus and is added to salads, soups, and sauces. Roux, a mixture of melted fat and flour, is frequently used for thickening sauces for meats, gravies or etoufees, and soups such as gumbo.

Fish can be fried, stuffed, blackened, or pan broiled with possibly a sauce on top. Blackened fish can be relatively low in fat although some restaurants add a great deal of oil.

Fried fish has about twice as many calories as grilled or broiled fish. This calorie difference makes a major impact because fish portions are generally about 8-12 oz portions. Stuffed fish are often prepared with additional fat and are best avoided.

To blacken meats, the meat is dipped in oil and then in a spice mixture containing the hotter spices such as garlic, cayenne, and white pepper. Some restaurants put oil in the pan or brush on oil and then sprinkle the meat with the spices. Then the meat is cooked in a very hot skillet or on the grill that the outer portion gets crusty and blackened; the inside stays moist and juicy. The meatier fish such as salmon and swordfish hold up best. Blackened chicken would be fairly lean while blackened beef would be much higher in fat.

Pan broiled fish is prepared with more fat than

when charbroiled. The butter and cream sauces atop seafood is very high in fats and calories. If you want the taste of the sauce, order it on the side and dip your fork into the sauce and then into a piece of fish. Etoufees are made from roux-based gravies and are very high in fat.

Here are some general guidelines for Dinin'Lean® at Cajun/Creole restaurants:

Appetizers

Boiled shrimp, boiled crawfish, and oysters on the half shell are low fat choices. Choose the red sauce for dipping. It is best to avoid the many fried appetizers that are offered, share them with a friend, or have them instead of an entree.

Salads

Vegetable salads should be ordered with the dressing on the side. You may want to omit the other high fat components such as cheese, olives, and croutons. Seafood salads prepared with mayonnaise or other salad dressings should be ordered dry.

Entree

The meat that is lowest in fat is the mesquite-grilled, charbroiled, or broiled. Blackened fish is low in fat if your ask that the meat be blackened in very little or no oil. Skip the butter or cream toppings or ask for them on the side.

Sandwiches

Po Boys (or Peaux Boys) are typically fried, or possibly sauteed, meat sandwiches served on french bread or a hoagie bun. The dressing is usually a cocktail sauce and tartar sauce mixture; lettuce, tomato, and pickles are often added. You may be able to request a Po Boy sandwich prepared with broiled fish and dressing on the side.

Accompaniments

Usually one vegetable is prepared steamed; ask for it without sauce or butter. Red beans and rice are common and may be a low fat choice depending on the individual recipe used. Dirty rice is prepared with a variety of meats including chicken liver, gizzards, sausage, and pork. This selection is not low fat nor low cholesterol; plain rice is a recommended alternative. Baked potatoes are often very large but can be prepared dry.

Dessert

Fresh fruit may be offered and would definitely be the best choice for dessert. Bread pudding, pecan pie, pralines, and other rice desserts are best shared with may friends.

ATCHAFALAYA RIVER CAFE

8816 Westheimer
Call for other locations
975-7873

Informal Dining: L,D
Av: $5-10

Menu items termed "Lite Cajun Fare" are offered for lunch, but they are *not all light in fat and calories*. **Vegetable Saute** uses 3 oz olive oil (request *steamed* vegetables instead) served over steamed rice. **Stuffed Tomato Trio** - includes three tomato halves stuffed with shrimp, crabmeat, and chicken mixed with a **Cajun Lite Dressing** made of lowfat yogurt and cocktail sauce.

Chicken Feaux Deaux Deaux - 6 oz grilled chicken breast with fettuccine, white wine, garlic, onion, and mushrooms. **Grilled Scallops Fettucine Murot** is prepared the same way except with 12 oz of scallops. **Lemon Peppered Catfish** - 8 oz filets dipped in buttermilk and grilled. These three dishes are served with the **Vegetable Du Jour** (request steamed vegetables instead).

Lower fat appetizers include: **Oysters on the Half Shell, Boiled Shrimp, and Shrimp Cocktail**. Salads include: **Dinner Salad, Blackened Chicken Salad, Shrimp Salad**, and **Crabmeat Salad** (order the salad dressing on the side).

Request the following fish to be prepared *without* any fats: **Grilled Shrimp Thibodeaux, Grilled Seafood en Brochette, Blackened Redfish, Blackened Soft Shell Crab, Atchafalaya Redfish, Redfish Pontchartrain, Redfish Confetti**, and **Grilled Chicken Au Vin. Fresh Fruit** is available for dessert.

BRENNAN'S RESTAURANT

3300 Smith Street
(Downtown)
522-9711

Formal Dining: L,D
Av: $10-20

This is a Creole Restaurant. Request salad
dressing on the side for all salads. Fish portions
range from 4-7 oz while chicken portions are almost
10 oz.

Special requests will be honored but some menu
items are prefixed with a heart to signify that they
are lower in fat. **Gulf Coast Seafood Gumbo** is
prepared without the usual roux. **Marinated
Lentils and Corn with Roma Tomatoes over
Roasted Eggplant** is in a vinaigrette that is lower in
oil. Eggplant has been sprayed with a non-stick
spray and grilled.

Grilled Gulf of Mexico Mahi Mahi is served
over sauteed vegetables (request *steamed* vegetables instead). **Grilled Norwegian Salmon** is
served on a roasted tomatillo salsa. **Grilled Swordfish with a Provencale Vinaigrette** is topped
with a light sauce of oven dried tomatoes, greek
olives, basil, and rice vinegar. **Roasted Pheasant &
Sea Scallops Soubise** is served with a onion leek
sauce, wilted watercress, and sea scallops.

Specialties of the day can often be prepared light
such as **Fish en Papillote** - baked with vegetables
in parchment without oil.

Fresh Fruit is offered for dessert.

FLOYD'S LOUISIANA SEAFOOD KITCHEN

4730 Richmond
(Galleria area)
621-6602

Casual Dining: L,D
Av: $10-12

Appetizers: **Shrimp Cocktail, Lump Crabmeat Cocktail, Boiled Shrimp, Oysters on the Half Shell,** and **Boiled Crawfish.**

Shrimp (6) or **Lump Crab Salad** (4 oz) is typically prepared with Thousand Island Dressing; order it dry with dressing on the side instead.

Order the **Lettuce & Tomato Salad** without olives and the **Dinner Salad** with dressing on the side. **Baked Potatoes** are served dry. **Vegetables** are usually sauteed (request *steamed* instead).

Broiled Fish is an 8 oz portion cooked on the grill (request that it be grilled with very little margarine, dry, or poached). Choose from: **Catfish Filet, Fresh Gulf Shrimp, Broiled Trout,** and **Whole Gulf Flounder**. Each comes with a **Baked Potato.**

Pasta with Vegetables are also offered - request vegetables to be steamed.

CONTINENTAL

PAPPADEAUX SEAFOOD KITCHEN

5 restaurants in Houston area
Call for locations:
782-6310

Informal Dining: L,D
Av: $10-20

Honoring special requests are very normal for
this restaurant. Salad dressings are served on the
side for *most* salads.

The Greek Salad is prepared at your table so
you can request no olives and ask for the dressing
on the side. The **Louisiana Shrimp, Crabmeat, or
Combination Salads** are simply fresh boiled
seafood on lettuce mix. **Dinner Salad** is tossed
greens (request no croutons).

Hot appetizer: **Whole Boiled Crawfish**
(available seasonally). Cold appetizers: **Cold Boiled
Shrimp, Fresh Gulf Oysters, Mixed Oysters &
Shrimp, Shrimp Cocktail**, and **Crabmeat
Cocktail**. The cocktails or the orders of 6 shrimp or
oysters includes about 2-1/2 - 3 oz of meat. Red
sauce comes with these orders.

Baked Potato is a huge 16-22 oz but can be
served dry. **Steamed Rice** or **Steamed Broccoli**
(for an additional charge) can be substituted for the
dirty rice that comes with many dishes.

Fish and chicken are served blackened or
charbroiled (mesquite grilled). About 1 T of butter
(can request olive oil or margarine instead) is
needed to blacken the meats.

Many fish have toppings of etouffee; blackened
oysters; shrimp & crabmeat; or other high fat
toppings. You can request plain boiled shrimp or
crabmeat or a similar topping instead.

CAFES & DELICATESSENS

Cafes and delicatessens are generally smaller restaurants serving a variety of foods including sandwiches, salads, and soups. Other entrees are also offered.

To eat lean, you may want to split a sandwich and have an extra salad, cup of broth-based soup, or some fruit. Another idea would be to order just a half of a sandwich along with an extra slice of bread. Then you can divide the meat to make a whole sandwich with only half the meat.

Here are some other general guidelines for Dinin'Lean® at Cafes and Delicatessens:

Soups

Broth-based soups are much lower in fat than the cream soups. Choose the broth soups including vegetable soup, chicken noodle soup, and vegetable beef soup. Creamy soups such as cream of broccoli or potato soup would be far more caloric. Homemade cream soups can have as much as 500 calories per one cup portion.

Salads

Vegetable salads are low in fat; request the

dressing on the side. Caesar salads are prepared with a high fat creamy cheese dressing, but this too can be served on the side.

Chicken, tuna, and shrimp are low in fat by themselves. But when you add mayonnaise at 100 calorie per level tablespoon - such as in chicken, tuna, or shrimp salad - the calories are so much higher. For example, tuna salad will have about 400 cals/19 gms fat per 1/2 c depending on how much mayonnaise is used. Eggs already have a great deal of fat so egg salad would be higher in fat than is recommended.

Sandwiches

There are many people that, when dieting, take off the bread and eat just the meat. If anything, they should be doing the opposite. Breads such as sliced breads, baguettes, bagels, rolls, and pita bread are low in fat (150 cals/1-2 gms fat per 2 oz portion). On the other hand, a small 3 oz croissant has about 350 cals/18 gms fat - even before you add the meat and toppings.

Deli meats range from 40-100 calories per ounce and most sandwiches are made of 4-6 oz of meat. The leanest cuts are turkey, chicken, ham, and roast beef. Cheese, bologna, chopped liver, salami, and similar meats are on the upper level of 100 cals/9 gms fat per ounce. Corned beef and pastrami may be lean or very fatty depending on the extent of the marbling of fat.

The lowest fat dressings are mustard, ketchup, and horseradish. Ask for your sandwich without the other dressings or order them on the side.

Accompaniments

Potatoes, cabbage, and macaroni are low in fat but when mayonnaise is added, both the calories and grams of fat are much higher. One half cup of potato salad will have about 200 cals/12 gms fat, coleslaw has about 160 cals/10 gms fat, and macaroni salad is about 220/15 gms fat. But these numbers will vary greatly depending upon how much mayonnaise or salad dressing is added. For an indication, ask the server if their salads are moist.

If the meal is normally served with potato salad, cole slaw, chips or other high fat accompaniments, ask for a substitute such as a tossed salad, sliced tomatoes, fresh fruit, or a big pickle. Lower fat pretzels or popcorn may also be available.

Other foods

Quiches are egg pies. The pie shell, the eggs, cream, and cheese added are all high in fat. Therefore, quiches are best avoided. Grilled or baked fish or chicken would be healthier alternatives. Blackened chicken and fish may also be offered in some cafes; often they are fairly low in fat.

Desserts

Fruit plates are often offered; skip the cheese if it is on the plate. Custards are made with milk and egg and have about 200 cals/5 gms fat per half cup portion. This would be a better choice than most other desserts such as the pastries, tarts, cookies, and eclairs.

CAFES AND DELICATESSENS

ALAIN & MARIE LE NOTRE BAKERY CAFE

21 Town and Country Village
(on Memorial at West Belt)
827-7363

Casual Dining: B,L,D
Av: $4-6

Homemade **French Rolls**, **Baguettes**, and **Sour Dough Bread** have no added fat. **Whole Wheat Bread** has a very small amount of fat. Danish, muffins, and tarts are "sinfully rich".

Garden Salad consists of romaine lettuce, cucumber, and radish (request salad dressing on the side). Order sandwiches without mayonnaise: **Roast Beef**, **Turkey**, and **Smoked Ham** (request no cheese). Ask them to be served on the low fat breads listed above rather than the croissants. **Sorbets** are available for dessert.

Diet Mousse Cakes can be ordered in advance. Each 1/8 slice of a 6" cake has 104 cals/1 gm fat and 108 cals/6 gms fat for the **Strawberry** or **Chocolate Mousse Cake** respectively. The mousse cakes use fructose for sweetening; the chocolate cake also has Equal Brand Sweetner.

BUTERA'S

3 restaurants in Houston
for locations, call:
790-0637

Casual Dining: L,D
Av: $5-10

Two locations offer a **Salad Bar** with plenty of **Raw Vegetables**. **Diet Creamy Tarragon** and **Diet Blue Cheese** are homemade with low fat yogurt and lowfat imitation sour cream. **Lite Vinaigrette** is also offered.

At least one **Broth-Based Soup** is offered each day; **Vegetarian Vegetable Soup** is always available. Soup cup size is 8 oz.

Deli sandwiches are available on **Kaiser Roll, Pumpernickel, 7 Grain Bread**, and **French Bread**. **Turkey** and **Ham** are the leanest meats; portion size is 3.5 oz. They will ask you what dressing you want.

Fresh Fruit is always offered. **Lowfat and Nonfat Frozen Yogurt** (Columbo brand) is available at the Medical Center restaurant only.

CAFES AND DELICATESSENS

EDO'S CAFE ON THE PARK

Five Post Oak Park #120
(Galleria area)
552-0355

Casual Dining: B,L
Av: $5-10

This is an Italian cafe. Sandwiches are served dry (server will ask what you want on it). **Light Mayonnaise** is used on all sandwiches instead of the regular. **Tuna Salad** or **Chicken Salad** are mixed with the light mayonnaise. But a lower fat **Turkey Sandwich** is also available.

Homemade Salads and **Diet Dressing**. The Ranch Dressing is made with buttermilk and low fat yogurt. **Fresh Fruit Salad** is available plain or with **Lite Frozen Yogurt**.

Lower fat soups: **Vegetable** and **Minestrone**. Homemade broth is refrigerated the day before and the fat is skimmed off. This de-fatted broth is then used for sauteing vegetables and in the soups. No animal fat is used in this restaurant.

Baked Potato - available with usual toppings or with steamed vegetables. **Organic Rice** and **Steamed Vegetables** each has just about 1 t of oil for the *whole batch*.

Freshly squeezed Juices and many **Smoothies** are made with fresh fruit, juices, honey and ice - see menu for all the ingredients. You may want to substitute skim milk for those using low fat milk.

Cookies are large, about 4 oz, and although organic, still are high in calories. **Frozen Yogurt** or **Fresh Fruit** is available for dessert.

GOURMET HOUSTON

809 Studemont
(at Washington)
862-8678

Casual Dining: L
Av: $5-10

Fresh Seasonal Fruits are offered. **Soups** are homemade; two are available each day. Most soups are chicken broth-based (with fat skimmed); puree soups do have cream and would be high in fat.

Roast Beef, Breast of Turkey, and Smoked Country Ham Sandwiches are made to order on **Honey Wheat, Herb,** or **Marble Rye Bread**. Meat portion is 3 - 3-1/2 oz; cheese (if added) is a 1 oz portion. Request these sandwiches to be made without mayonnaise.

Other salads and sandwiches on the menu are mayonnaise or oil-based.

JASON'S DELI

2611 S Shepherd
(at Westheimer)
520-6728

Casual Dining: L,D
Av: $5-10

Sandwiches are available with a variety of meats, vegetables, and breads. Special requests will be honored - "If we have it, we will make it". Average portion of meat is 5-1/2 ounces but you can request *half the meat* at a reduced price. Mustard is usually standard on the sandwiches; other dressings are on request.

Traditional sandwiches include: **Breast of Turkey** and **Smoked Turkey. Chick on Bun** can be prepared using unmarinated chicken, if requested. **Shrimp Ahoy** - shrimp salad in a pita (307 cals/11 gms fat) comes with fresh fruit. **Pita Plus** - turkey, alfalfa, tomatoes, and avocado has 364 cals/18 gms fat when ordered without the ranch dressing (if requested without avocado there is another 153 cals/15 gms fat less).

Slender Jane - a stuffed baked potato with sour cream, topped with garden fresh chopped vegetables, and alfalfa sprouts (364 cals/8 gms fat). **Steamed Vegetables** are available. Salad dressing is served on the side of the **Small Dinner Salad** or self-serve for the **Salad Bar. Low calorie Ranch Dressing** is available.

Shrimp Salad has 283 cals/17 gms fat. **Marinated Chicken Breast Salad** (request no cheese, avocado, or black olives). **Bagels** (163 cals/1 gm fat) can be purchased without cream cheese (cream cheese would add another 148 cals/13 gms fat). **Fresh Fruit Plate** had 412 cals/0 gms fat including the dressing (which accounts for 42 of the calories).

LA MADELEINE

4002 Westheimer
(Highland Village Center)
623-0645

Casual Dining: B,L,D
Av: Under $5

Request salad dressings on the side for all salads. Ask what the components are in the **Salade Du Jour** before selecting. Usually at least one **Soupe De Jour** is broth-based such as: **Chicken Gumbo** (not made with roux), **French Onion Soup** (request no bread and cheese), **Gazpacho**, **Vegetable**, or **Boullabaise** (request without garlic aioli).

Sandwiches should be requested with **Sliced Homemade Bread** or **Demi-Baguette**. The Baguette has no fat but half of loaf (portion size for the sandwiches) is 6 oz. Request sandwich to be prepared with **Turkey**, **Roast Beef**, or **Ham** (order without cheese and dressings on the side).

Salade de Fruits or **Berries** without sauce. **Scones** are low fat (4 oz portion has 3 gms fat) and are available in flavors: blueberry, cranberry-orange, and cinnamon.

LEAF 'N LADLE GARDEN CAFE

14520L Memorial Drive
(at Ashford)
497-3649

Informal Dining: B,L,D
Av: $5-10

Lowest fat entree salads: **Grilled Chicken Salad** (5 oz chicken) or the **Garden Vegetable Salad**. Order the **Low Calorie Italian Dressing** or **Salsa**. A heart healthy **Soup of the Day** is available - even the "cream" soups are made with non-fat milk.

All sandwiches are on **Whole Wheat** (7 grain) bread with lettuce, tomato, and about 1 T mayonnaise (request no mayonnaise). Heart healthy sandwiches are: **Breast of Turkey**; **Garden Vegetable** (tomato, cucumbers, mushrooms, and 2 oz cheddar cheese with lettuce, spinach, and alfalfa sprouts); and **Breast of Chicken**. Side dish options are probably best kept to the **Fruit Salad** or **Green Salad** (ask for dressing on the side). Meat portions for entree salads and sandwiches are all about 4 ounces.

Pasta dishes include: **Pasta Primavera** in a tomato sauce, **Chicken Breast Marinara**, and **Spaghetti Marinara**.

NEW YORK BAGEL COFFEE SHOP

9720 Hillcroft
(at Braeswood)
723-8650

Informal Dining: B,L
Av: Under $5

Tossed Salad or **Sliced Tomato**: order **Low Calorie Italian Dressing** on the side. **Unbuttered Bread** and butter are brought to the table; margarine is available upon request. **Skim Milk** is available. Fifteen varieties of **Bagels** are offered, each bagel weighs 4 oz. Your choice of bagel: **Plain, Poppy, Sesame, Onion, Garlic, Pumpernickel, Rye, Bialy, Salt, Cinnamon Raisin, Wholewheat, Blueberry, Black & White, E.T., & Oat Bran**.

Sandwiches are served with condiments on the side; cole slaw and pickle comes with all sandwiches. **Light Bread** is available upon request. Lowest fat sandwiches are: **Cold Roast Beef, Turkey Breast** (97% fat-free), **Imported Ham**, or **Charbroiled Chicken Breast** (it is *not* marinated. The **Hot Kosher Style Corned Beef** and **Hot Kosher Style Pastrami** have both been trimmed. Average portion of meat is 4 oz.

An **Individual Can of White Tuna** can be purchased for a very low fat alternative. Other low fat extras include: **Cottage Cheese and Peaches, Applesauce**, and **Fresh Fruit**.

SUNSET TEA ROOM CAFE

2606 Sunset
(at Kirby)
666-9032

Informal Dining: L,D
Av: $5-10

Whole Wheat Mini Loaves are brought to the table. Butter is served but margarine is available upon request. **Guiltless Gourmet's No Oil Baked Chips** can be ordered with the **Guiltless Gourmet's No-Oil Salsa, No-Oil Black Bean Dip,** or **No-Oil Pinto Bean Dip**. Lowfat milk is available.

For lunch: **The Earl** - 6 oz boneless, skinless, grilled chicken breast filet served with fresh vegetables and crisp green salad; **The Windsor** - grilled chicken breast sandwich (ask for no cheese) and a cup of fresh fruit; **The Duchess** - grilled chicken salad, made with chicken breast and a large garden salad (order without cheese); and **The Duke** - broiled or grilled fresh fish. Request salad dressing on the side for each of these menu items.

The Char-Grilled items available for dinner include: **Grilled Fish, Chicken, Shrimp, Scallops, and a Grilled Combo**. These dishes come with **Rice Pilaf** and **Steamed Vegetables** (request them to be served plain, without margarine). **Grilled Chicken Breast Sandwich** (request without cheese or mayonnaise) is also available with a cup of fresh fruit.

Fresh Fruit is offered for dessert.

TERRACE CAFE

1300 Lamar
(Downtown in Four Seasons Hotel)
650-1300

Informal Dining: L,D
Av: $5-10

The starred (*) menu items are lower in calories. Appetizer and entree are less than 555 calories:

Appetizer: **Assorted Garden Greens** with choice of dressings (request salad dressing on the side).

Entrees: **Vegetable Club** with radish sprouts, peppers, tomato, onion, lettuce, avocado, and cholesterol-free tarragon mayonnaise (because of high fat content, may want to omit avocado and the mayonnaise). **Smoked Chicken Salad** with leaf lettuce greens, radicchio, and brioche.

Fresh Seasonal Fruits can be ordered without the marscarpone cream (soft, unripened cheese) and strawberry glaze.

WALL STREET DELI

6 restaurants in Houston area:
for locations, call:
649-8310

Casual Dining: B,L
Av: Under $5

Selections may differ depending on store size.
Offers **Crystal Light** in addition to diet soda. Both
Skim Milk and **Low Fat Milk** are available.
Bagels are offered (3 oz each).

Deli sandwiches are made of 3 oz meat on either
a 4 oz roll (**Wheat Nut Roll**, **French Bread**,
Wheat Hoagie, **Rye Hoagie**) or on **Wheat Berry
Bread**. **Turkey** is 97% fat-free; ham is 89% fat-free.
Request lettuce, tomato, pickles, mustard, and
onions - no mayo or other dressings.

Grilled Chicken Breast is 5 oz when raw
(boneless and skinless) served on french roll - you
select your own toppings.

Some stores have a 70 item salad bar including
Tossed Salad with **Fat-Free Ranch Dressing**,
Spinach Salad with Light Italian Dressing, an
array of fresh cut **Raw Vegetables**, and cold/hot
Pasta (some without any oil at all such as the
Meatless Tomato Sauce). At least 2 **Broth-Based
Soups** are offered each day. **Fruit Salad** is avail-
able. **Frozen Yogurt** (2 fat-free and 2 low fat) is
the Columbo brand.

ZINNANTE'S DELICATESSEN

9806 Hillcroft
(between Braeswood & Willowbend)
723-7001

Casual Dining: L,D
Av: $5-10

Sandwiches are made to order; can be ordered
with mustard or vinegar only. **Turkey**, **Ham**, and
Roast Beef are available. **Tossed Salad** has
dressing on the side.

Pasta & Chicken - marinated chicken blackened (request to be prepared without oil) in skillet
with vegetables, marinara sauce, and linguine
added, topped with sprinkling of Romano cheese.
Blackened Catfish - seared in black skillet (request
to use as little oil as necessary) with okra, marinara
sauce, and linguine.

CHINESE

Chinese cooking combines many of the American foods that we are familiar with such as mushrooms, broccoli, chicken, and shrimp with some not so common Oriental foods such as water chestnuts, bamboo shoots, and soy sauce.

Stir-frying with fat or oil is the cooking method most commonly used. Individual components (meats and vegetables) are cut up, occasionally precooked, and then combined for specific dishes. Most Chinese restaurants are able and willing to prepare food to your dietary specifications.

There are four main regions of China; each region has its own unique cuisine. Cantonese style comes to us from southern China. The flavors are mild and subtle.

Bejing/Peking in northern China is noted for the sweet and sour sauces, plum, or hoisin sauces.

Szechuan and Hunan cooking is from western China. This area is noted for the hot and spicy foods flavored with chilies, garlic, and hot red peppers.

Shanghai, in Eastern China, uses a combination of soy sauces, wine, and sugar. Braising of foods, in

Shanghai cooking, is often referred to as red cooking.

Dishes are typically served with rice as is common in southern China. Northern China is better known for their wheat products such as noodles.

Here are some general guidelines for Dinin'Lean® in Chinese restaurants:

Appetizers/Soups

Hot and sour, won ton, and chicken and rice soups are all lean choices. Egg drop soup includes eggs; this makes for a high cholesterol, high fat soup.

Entrees

Usually 1-2 tablespoon of oil (and sometimes lard) is used to stirfry the food. Some restaurants use as much as 4 T. All of the restaurants in this book use vegetable oil in their cooking. Foods are cut up ahead of time and/or semi-cooked in the fryer. Individual orders are stir-fried in the wok when ordered. Be sure to ask what their preparation techniques are for your favorite dish.

Most restaurants will steam your dish by cooking it in water or chicken broth, if requested, but the food will not taste exactly the same. Usually steamed dishes are served without a sauce, but you can request a sauce to be made of only thickened broth - and no oil. Or request a specified amount of oil, and then ask them to use chicken broth if more liquid is needed.

Meats are higher in fat and calories than vegetables. So it makes sense to order dishes that have more vegetables than meat. If a dish you want is made up of mostly meat, ask the restaurant to replace some of the meat with vegetables. Most restaurants will be happy to oblige.

Most restaurants do not measure the nuts that are added to some dishes, but rather described it as being a handful. This amount will vary but is generally about 1/4 c. Peanuts, almonds and cashews are all high in calories and fat (250 cals/20 gms fat per 1/4 c serving).

As a rule, House Specialties should be avoided. These higher priced items are usually dishes consisting of large portions of meat and little or no vegetables. These selections are usually high in both fat and calories.

Accompaniments

Noodles and rice, steamed or boiled, are very low in fat. Fried rice and lo mein (fried noodles) have added fat. The amounts will vary depending on the restaurant. When fried rice is offered with the dish you order, request steamed rice instead. Lo Mein is lowest when ordered with just vegetables or chicken instead of beef or pork.

Buffets

It is probably best to stay away from eating at the buffet. Most foods are either fried or prepared with a large amount of fat. Offering these foods make it is more economical for the restaurants to fill you up fast for the "all you can eat for one price offer".

Definitions:

Black Bean Sauce - a thick, brown sauce commonly used in Cantonese cooking. It is made of fermented soy beans, wheat flour, and salt.

Chop Suey - Chow Mein without the fried noodle topping.

Hoisin - a thick sauce that is both sweet and spicy. It is made from soybeans, sugar, garlic, chili, and vinegar.

Tofu - a soft cheese made from soy beans. Although it has little flavor by itself, it soaks up the flavor of the foods in the dish. It is a high protein source and moderate in fat content.

MSG - Monosodium Glutamate is a flavor enhancer. Some people are sensitive to the agent and report hot flashes, sweating, and headaches shortly after eating foods prepared with MSG. To reduce the symptoms, simply request that no MSG be added to your dish. Other components within the dish may still contain MSG, such as if they add chicken broth for making a sauce.

Oyster sauce - thick sauce made of oysters and soy sauce frequently used in Cantonese cooking.

Plum sauce - thick sauce that is both spicy and sweet-and-sour. It is made from plums, apricots, hot peppers, vinegar, and sugar.

Sweet and Sour Sauce - thick sauce made from sugar, vinegar, and soy sauce.

CHEF CHAN'S HUNAN CHINESE

17833 Kuykendahl
(near Cypresswood)
370-3884

Informal Dining: L,D
Av: $10-20

About 2-3 t of oil are used for each dish. All dishes can be cooked with no oil or very little - just ask. For appetizers: **Steamed Dumplings** - order of six; filling is made with 50% vegetables and 25% each of shrimp and beef. **Chicken Soong** is chicken and vegetables rolled in lettuce. Sauces come on the side.

Some meat portions are 8-12 oz. Listed below are those with only 5-6 oz meat and *more* vegetables (40% meat/60% vegetables). You can request even less meat and more vegetables.

Seafood: **Lake Tung Ting Shrimp** - mushrooms, water chestnuts, and broccoli; **Shrimp and Snow Pea Pods**; and **Baby Shrimp and Chicken with Brown Sauce** - water chestnuts and snow pea pods.

Beef & Lamb: **Beef with Broccoli**; **Beef with Bamboo Shoots & Chinese Mushrooms**; and **Sliced Lamb with Scallions**.

Poultry: **Chicken Sticks with Lemon Flavored Sauce** (with celery and bell pepper); **Chicken with Pineapple** (and snow pea pods); **Shredded Chicken with Snow Pea Pods**; and **Sliced Boneless Duckling with Broccoli**.

Cantonese meals: **Moo Goo Gai Pan**; **Chicken with Mixed Vegetables**; and **Beef with Mixed Vegetables**. **Vegetables dishes** (except for Eggplant Family Style) are low in fat. For dessert: **Lychees** are chinese fruit packed in sugar syrup, but low in fat.

CHINA KITCHEN

18525 Kuykendahl Rd, Spring
(at Louetta)
376-4167

Informal Dining: L,D
Av: $5 - 10

Prior to final preparation, vegetables are steamed. Meat is cooked with about 2 T oil - request meat cooked without any oil. Luncheon portions are about 4 oz meat, as much as 8 oz at dinner. Lunch Specials include eggroll (request more vegetables instead) and fried rice (request steamed rice instead). The Lite Lunch is egg roll and fried rice only. Entrees with the least amount of meat include: **Chicken Chow Mein** (request no crispy noodles), **Moo Goo Gai Pan**, and **Beef with Broccoli**.

Dinner: Steamed Dumplings are available for appetizers but oil is added along with mostly pork and beef (some vegetables) before it is steamed. Perhaps enjoy these as an entree instead.

Vegetable dishes include: **Budda's Delight** - 10 kinds of vegetables including napa cabbage, snow peas, and bamboo shoots; **Snow Peas with Water Chestnuts**; **Broccoli with Oyster Sauce**; and **Bean Curd Szechuan Style**. Other vegetable dishes have deep fried tofu.

Other dishes that have more vegetables than meat include: **Shrimp with Broccoli**, **Shrimp with Snow Peas**, **Kung Pao Beef** (request no peanuts), **Beef with Broccoli**, **Szechuan Beef**, **Moo Goo Gai Pan** - chicken with mushrooms, **Chicken with Broccoli**, and **Chicken with Cashew Nuts** (request no cashews).

CHOPSTICKS D'LITE

1040 Uvalde &
3304 Center, Deer Park
455-6688/479-0066

Casual Dining: L,D
Av: Under $5

Chicken and beef are trimmed of all visible fat and skin. Components (meat & vegetables) are cooked in hot water prior to being mixed for individual orders. Some oil is added to stirfry individual orders. Most dishes can be prepared without oil if the customer requests.

Request Chopstick's Platters with **Steamed Rice** instead of fried rice. Leanest are: **Chicken Chow Mein** (request no fried noodles), **Moo Goo Gai Pan** - Mushroom Chicken, **Kung Bao Chicken** - marinated chicken with Chinese vegetables stir-fried with dry red pepper in an Kung Bao sauce, **Pepper Steak**, **Broccoli Beef**, **Hunan Beef**, **Shrimp Vegetable** - Chinese mixed vegetables stir-fried with shrimp in clear wine sauce, **Hunan Shrimp**, **Kung Bao Shrimp**, **Triple Deluxe** - beef, chicken, and fresh shrimp stir-fried with vegetables, and **Vegetable D'Lite**.

Frozen Yogurt is Columbo brand (both low fat and Lite yogurt are used).

DANIEL WONG RESTAURANT

3130 Richmond
(Buffalo Speedway & Kirby)
523-4111

Casual Dining: L,D
Av: $5-10

Offers a **"Special Menu for Low Calorie Dishes"**. No MSG or sugar is used in any of these dishes. If you have a special dietary request, they ask that you tell the waiter so preparation of your meal can be exactly to your liking.

The calories in the **"Low Calorie Dishes"** do not include the rice - only the dish specified. About 1/2 c. rice is served with these dishes. Approximately 1 T oil is added to these dishes but you can request them to be steamed without any oil, if desired.

Sliced Beef with Broccoli - in a rich seasoning sauce (528 cals). **Mushroom Chicken** - pieces of chicken, fresh mushrooms, Chinese dried mushrooms, snow peas, and carrots melded with a sauce (338 cals). **Fresh Asparagus Chicken** (282 cals). **Lamb with Green Onion** (203 cals). **Monk's Delight** - six different Chinese vegetables with fried cubes of fresh bean cake and a special sauce (311 cals). **Mushroom with Heart of Tender Green** - prepared Chinese black mushrooms combined with white and straw mushrooms and "heart of tender green" (238 cals).

Other dishes included in the Low Calorie section, (no calories listed): **Spicy Dry Tofu with Crisp Vegetables**, **Fresh Tofu with Vegetables**, and **Stir Cooked Mixed Fresh Vegetables**.

EGG ROLL'S

21181 Tomball Parkway
(NW Houston)
370-1088

Casual Dining: L,D
Av: Under $5

This Cantonese-style restaurant offers many entrees which are mostly vegetables and very little meat. They say this is closer to how the Chinese from Canton really eat - and this combination also makes meals that are lower in fat.

About 1 T of oil is used in the menu items listed below, less can be requested, or they can be steamed without any oil.

These menu items that follow are more than 70% vegetables. **Moo Koo Gai Pan** - with mushrooms, bamboo shoots, and broccoli; **Steak Kew** - same except with Beef; and **Chow Hai Kew** - same except with shrimp.

Hot & Spicy Chicken, Hot and Spicy Beef, and **Hot and Spicy Shrimp**.

Tomato Chicken Cantonese - with tomatoes, bell peppers, onions, and garlic and **Pepper Beef** - like the previous except with beef. **Chicken with Broccoli** and **Beef with Broccoli. Snow Pea and Beef. Subgum Mixed Vegetables** - vegetables only.

Roast Pork with Cabbage has very little pork (5-10%) but about 2 T oil is needed for preparation.

EMPRESS OF CHINA

5419-A FM 1960 W
(Champions area)
583-8021

Formal Dining: L,D
Av: $10-20

Uses Nouvelle Chinese Cuisine methods
featuring menu items that are lower in calories.
Willing to prepare special requests; you can even
specify your calorie and fat limits for the chef.

There is a variety of vegetable dishes: **Seasonal
Fresh Vegetables**, **Sauteed Mushrooms and
Snowpeas**, **Shi Lin Delight**, **Snowpeas with
Water Chestnuts**, and **Tofu with Assorted
Vegetables**. Meat entrees are still about 6 oz at
lunch and 12 oz at dinner so you may want to
request less meat & extra vegetables. Dishes that
consist of about half vegetables include: **The Clash
of the Titans** - sliced prawns, breast of chicken and
beef sauteed with crispy vegetables in special
brown sauce and **Chicken Sauteed with Mushrooms** - chicken slices stir-fried with mushrooms,
snowpeas, and other vegetables in a white sauce.

**Steamed Salmon with Fresh Ginger &
Scallions** has 8 oz of meat and no vegetables. **Sand
on the Snow** - white chicken meat, flambed with
black pepper, garlic, and sherry includes 8 oz of
meat and a garnish of broccoli. These dishes can be
requested to be made with more vegetables.

Most traditional dishes have been adapted to
contain less fat such as: **Crabmeat Fettucini with
Caviar** (the light white sauce is made with 1/3 third
half & half - the other 2/3 is chicken stock).

HAPPY ALL CHINESE VIETNAMESE RESTAURANT

2502 W Holcolmbe
(Medical Center area)
660-0020

Casual Dining: L,D
Av: $5-10

Willing to cook the way the customer requests to meet their dietary needs. *Fried* noodles are served at all tables!

Food is generally cooked ahead of time (vegetables are steamed and meat is boiled). Then about 2t of oil is added in the stirfrying process and sesame oil is sprinkled on top. Ask that they leave off the sesame oil. Meals are served with **Steamed Rice**.

Steamed dumplings are available; the **Vegetable Steamed Dumplings** would be the leanest. **Szechuan Pickled Chicken Salad** has no oil, but a spoonful of peanuts are sprinkled on top (can request no peanuts).

Cold Spring Rolls - (peanut sauce is very high in fat). **Steamed Whole Fish** is probably the leanest House Specialty, but still has about 8-10 oz meat. **Eggplant with Spicy Garlic Sauce** - eggplant is stirfried; sauce has no fat.

Nine **"Weight Watcher's Choice"** menu items are cooked in a steamer and served with special sauces on the side: **Broccoli and Snow Peas, Mixed Fresh Chinese Vegetables, Chicken with Snow Peas and Vegetables, Chicken with Broccoli and Snow Peas, Shrimp with Snow Peas and Vegetables, Shrimp and Scallop with Mixed Vegetables, Fish Fillet with Broccoli and Snow Peas, Fish Fillet with Fresh Vegetables**, and **Weight Watchers Special** - shrimp, scallop, chicken, and mixed vegetables. You may create your own dish as well.

HUNAN CAFE

14520 Memorial Dr
(SW Houston)
558-5616

Formal Dining: L,D
Av: $5-10

Their philosophy is that "caring makes the difference". Willing to make special dietary orders. MSG is not used in any of the food items with the exception of the soups. Can request that MSG be left out of soups as well. Meat portions are 8 oz but can be reduced (with more vegetables added) upon request.

Vegetables are boiled in chicken stock; meat is cooked in oil, then strained and rinsed. Individual orders are then stir-fried in the sauce (consisting of mostly soy sauce and cornstarch). All items can be steamed with the sauce on the side if requested.

Chicken: **Sand on the Snow** - chicken slices with black pepper, **General Tso's Chicken** - chicken chunks with hot sauce, **Yu-Hsiang Chicken**, **Chicken with Snow Peas**, and **Moo Goo Gai Pan**.

Shrimp: **Kan-Shao Shrimp** - sauteed in fresh ginger, garlic, wine, and spicy tomato sauce, **Yu-Hsiang Shrimp**, **Shrimp with Snow Peas**, and **Shrimp with Vegetables**.

Vegetables: **Broccoli in Garlic Sauce**, **Snow Peas & Waterchestnuts**, **Mixed Vegetables**, and **Chinese Mushrooms & Bamboo Shoots**.

HUNAN DYNASTY CHINESE RESTAURANT

8330 S Main
(Medical Center)
669-1168

Casual Dining: L,D
Av: $5-10

Upon request, they will omit the fat, MSG, sugar, or salt.

Low Fat Milk is available. Average meat portion at lunch is 3 - 3-1/2 oz; 6-7 oz at dinner.

Five **Diet Dinners** are offered; each is prepared in a steamer and served with Kung Bao, Garlic, Brown or Light sauce. They are: **Hunan Mixed Vegetables**, **Broccoli Chicken**, **Moo Goo Gai Pan** - chicken breast with Chinese vegetables, **Shrimp with Chinese Vegetables**, or **Scallops with Chinese Vegetables**. You can request other dishes to be prepared the same way.

Typically, about 1-2 T oil is used to stir-fry dishes. The dishes consisting of more vegetables than meat are listed below. **Scallops in Garlic Sauce**, **Scallops in Velvet Sauce**, **Shrimp with Garlic Sauce**, **Shrimp Chow Mein** (request no fried noodles), **Shrimp Chop Suey**, or **Chicken with Garlic Sauce**. Vegetable dishes include: **String Bean Szechuan Style**, **Szechuan Broccoli**, and **Vegetable Chow Mein** (request no fried noodles) and **Vegetable Chop Suey**.

Low Fat Frozen Yogurt is offered for dessert.

NORTH CHINA RESTAURANT

879 Frostwood
(near Memorial City)
464-6774

Formal Dining: L,D
Av: $5-10

Foods are prepared Mandarin-style (northern China). Meats are first precooked without oil. Then oil (about 1 T) is used to stir-fry all the ingredients together. All dishes are prepared individually so customer's requests can be accommodated - orders can be steamed. Nutrasweet and potassium salt are available as substitutes, if requested. Liquids are thickened with cornstarch unless requested.

The owner suggested the dishes that are mostly vegetables and only 2-4 oz of meat. These include all the vegetable dishes such as: **Black Mushrooms with Chinese Cabbage, Snow Peas with (Water) Chestnuts**, and **Bamboo Shoots with Black Mushrooms**.

The lowest fat tofu dishes are: **Mushroom with Bean Curd, Family Bean Curd**, and **Stewed Bean Curd**. All of the noodle dishes are 90-95% vegetables such as: **Noodles with Chop Suey & Soup** and **Chicken Chu Mein**.

Other lower fat dishes are: **Kung Pao Shrimp or Chicken** (request no peanuts), **Curry Shrimp, Moo Shu Shrimps, Garlic Chicken, Chicken with Mushrooms, Fried Pork Shreds** (isn't fried - this was a mistake in translation) and **Snow Peas with Beef**.

Fresh Fruit is available for dessert.

RESTAURANT 801

801 Congress
(Downtown)
222-1688

Informal: L,D
Av: $5-10

Luncheon specials are served with **Hot and
Sour Soup** or **Wonton Soup**, Fried Rice (request
Steamed Rice instead), and Fried Spring Roll. The
leanest luncheon specials may be **Assorted
Vegetables, Sauteed Chicken with Vegetables**,
and **Sauteed Shrimp with Vegetables**.

Serves Hunan-style food so meat portions are
large (about 10 oz). Can request to be served with
less meat and more vegetables.

Dishes are stir-fried with 1-2 oz (2-4 T) vegetable oil. Request to be prepared with less oil or to
be steamed. Four entrees are listed on the menu as
Diet Favors. Request these dishes **Steamed** with
**Light Sauce: Garden Vegetables, Chicken with
Vegetables, Shrimp with Fresh Mushroom**,
and **Beef with Snow Peas**.

Vegetable dishes include: **Fresh and Dry
Mushrooms, Buddha's Delight, Snow Peas and
Water Chestnuts, Sauteed Green Beans,
Sauteed Garden Spinach**, and **Sauteed Aspara-
gus. Home Style Bean Curd** should be requested
with plain, not fried tofu. Eggplant with Garlic
Sauce is prepared with fried eggplant which is later
soaked in water.

Fresh Fruit is available for dessert.

ROYAL PALACE

14535 Memorial Dr
(SW Houston)
493-3030

Formal Dining: L,D
Av: $7-19

Serves Cantonese Cuisine. Willing to serve the customer's special requests. Start with: **Wonton Soup, Wor Wonton Soup** - with shrimp, chicken, and vegetables, or **Chicken Corn Soup. Vegetable Dumplings** are made with a small amount of egg, but no oil.

Steamed Rice is served with entrees. **Steamed Whole Fish** and **Grilled Fish** are available.

Dishes include about 5-6 oz meat with a large amount of vegetables. About 1 T is used in the stir-frying of most entrees. If it is requested to be "prepared without oil" the wok will be *brushed* with oil instead.

Those entrees with the largest percentage of vegetables are: **Pineapple Chicken, Chicken with Broccoli, Chicken with Snow Peas**, and **Moo Goo Gai Pan. Beef with Broccoli** and **Pepper Steak. Shrimp with Vegetables,** and **Shrimp with Broccoli.**

Vegetable dishes are: **Mix Vegetables,** Snow **Peas with Water Chestnuts, Chinese Mushrooms and Bamboo Shoots, Chinese Kal-Lan in Light Sauce**, and **Sauteed String Beans**.

Walnut Chicken and Almond Chicken both have a fistful of nuts that contribute a large amount of fat - but this amount can be reduced or eliminated upon request.

SHANGHAI RESTAURANT

9116 Bellaire Blvd
(SW Houston)
771-8082

Formal Dining: L,D
Av: $5-10

Meats are fried briefly in corn oil and then drained; vegetables are boiled in chicken stock. The dish is then cooked to order in a sauce. To avoid excess fats, order the vegetable dishes or the menu items with less meat and more vegetables.

Luncheon Specials are served with **Hot & Sour Soup** and **Steamed Rice** - request no egg roll. **Vegetable Delight** is all vegetables. **Moo Goo Gai Pan, Shrimp with Snow Peas, Fresh Shrimp with Mixed Vegetables** and **Chicken with Garlic Sauce** are each about half vegetables and half meat. You can request even less meat and more vegetables.

Other entrees which can be requested with extra vegetables include: **Beef with Snow Peas, Chicken with Snow Peas, Scallops with Garlic Sauce**. The Kung Pau dishes have no vegetables and a sprinkling of peanuts; this dish can be ordered with more vegetables but no peanuts.

Vegetable dishes include: **Buddha's Delight, Bamboo Shoots with Black Mushroom,** and **Three Delicacies Mushroom. Bean Curd in Black Bean Sauce** includes tofu which has not been fried. The Bean Curd with Hot Spicy Sauce has pork; the Bean Curd with Vegetables has fried tofu.

SHANGHAI RIVER RESTAURANT

2407 Westheimer
(at Kirby)
528-5528

Formal Dining: L,D
Av: $10-20

Wonton and **Vegetable Soup** are lowest in fat.
Vegetable Dumplings are steamed vegetables
wrapped in an egg roll wrapper and steamed -
sauce is on the side.

Six **"Diet Favors"** are listed on the menu. They
are prepared in the steamer and served with special
low-calorie sauce on the side. The **Diet Favors** are:
**Asparagus and Broccoli, Mixed Vegetables,
Chicken and Vegetables, Shrimp with Vegetables, Scallops with Vegetables**, and **Shrimp
and Scallops with Asparagus**. Most other dishes
can be prepared lower in fat - just ask. Sauces are
made of soy sauce, vinegar, and spices - no fat.

Fresh Fruit is available for dessert.

TAM'S

25024 I-45 N
(in Spring)
363-2412

Casual Dining: L,D
Av: $5-7

Meals can be requested without oil, sugar, MSG, or cornstarch - whatever the customer wants. This small family restaurant offers a limited menu. For lunch: **Chicken Chop Suey** or **Moo Goo Gai Pan** ordered with **Steamed Rice** instead of fried and no eggroll.

For dinner: **Chicken Chow Mein, Shrimp Chow Mein, Moo Goo Gai Pan**, and **Chicken with Broccoli**. Meat portions are about 4 oz at lunch and 5 oz at dinner.

YEN JING CHINESE RESTAURANT

7364 Louetta &
1951 W TC Jester
370-8220/861-9647

Informal Dining: L,D
Av: $5-10

Menu identifies four dishes as **"Diet Dishes"**. Each is prepared in the steamer and served with the **Chef's Special Sauce**. These are: **Steamed Mixed Vegetables**, **Chicken with Vegetables**, **Shrimp with Vegetables**, and **Scallops with Vegetables**. But other dishes can be prepared in the steamer with the special sauce.

No MSG is added to the foods; soups can even be special-ordered without MSG.

Both meats and vegetables are boiled in water before the final stage of stir-frying. Some of the vegetable dishes are: **Buddhist Delight** - 10 kinds of vegetables, **Broccoli** with oyster sauce, **Snow Peas with Water Chestnuts**. **Eggplant with Garlic Sauce** can be prepared steamed if requested. The tofu dishes are either pan-fried or deep fried.

There are many dishes with plenty of vegetables such as **Moo Goo Gai Pan**. Also: **Chicken, Beef, or Shrimp with Vegetables**; **Chicken, Beef, or Shrimp with Snow Peas**; **Chicken, Beef, or Shrimp with Broccoli**; or the **Seafood Platter** - lobster, crabmeat, shrimp, and scallops with 6 kinds of vegetables.

THAI

Thai cooking is considered, by some, to be lighter and healthier than Chinese cuisine. Both use stir-frying as a method of cooking and serve rice with the meals. Thai restaurants use fish sauce (nam pla) made from salted, fermented, and pressed anchovies much in the same way that the Chinese use soy sauce. Ginger and garlic are commonly used in both Chinese and Thai cusines.

Thai food also closely resembles Indian food. Similar spices are used such as coriander, cumin, cardamom, and cinnamon. Curries are also common to both. Coconut milk is used in both Thai and Indian cuisines. Coconut milk has as many calories as heavy whipping cream (800 cals/80 gms fat per cup) so order the curries made without coconut milk. This is usually noted on the menu.

Unique to Thai cuisine are the spices lemon grass, kaffir lime leaves, and basil. Salads are often low fat because they are made with lime juice as a dressing. Steamed Spring Rolls are lean appetizers made of vegetables and/or meat stuffed inside rice paper.

Frying and stir-frying is sometimes done with lard or coconut oil. Every restaurant listed in this book uses vegetable oil, but the amount added varies widely. When ordering, ask for as little oil as possible to be used; request those dishes made with more vegetables than meat. Chinese cooking commonly uses flour or cornstarch for thickening; the Thai do not as frequently.

GOLDEN ROOM RESTAURANT

1209 Montrose
(Downtown)
524-9614

Formal Dining: L,D
Av: $5-10

Fresh Spring Rolls - rice paper wrapped around grilled chicken, fresh vegetables, and noodles; served with their special sauce. Hot, medium, or mild preparation are available.

The salads are made with about 6 oz meat. **Yum Gai** - grilled chicken, lettuce, tomatoes, and cucumber with spicy lime sauce (sauce is made without oil). **Yum Goong** - similar to Yum Gai but with shrimp.

All stir-fried dishes are prepared with about 2 T vegetable oil (request less oil or none at all). Steamed rice is served with the dishes. These entrees are prepared with about 4 oz meat and lots of vegetables: **Chicken Poey-Sean** and **Beef Poey Sean**. Both are made with glass noodles and a mixture of vegetables.

Goong-Ten - charbroiled shrimp topped with a special sauce has no added fats. **Steamed Fish** - steamed fish accompanied by spicy Thai sauce.

NIT NOI THAI RESTAURANT

2462 Bolsover
(near Kirby & Rice Blvd)
524-8114

Informal Dining: L,D
Av: $5-10

Soft Spring Rolls are stuffed with tofu, chicken, and vegetables and are steamed. About 1 T of peanut oil is used to prepare many of the dishes; most can be prepared with just 1 t of oil or none at all if requested.

About 8 oz meat or 8 oz tofu are used in the preparation of most menu items; you can request less meat and more vegetables. These dishes have a high vegetable content: **Chicken with Garlic Sauce and Hot Peppers, Beef with Garlic Sauce and Hot Peppers**, and **Shrimp with Garlic Sauce and Hot Peppers**.

The vegetarian dishes have no meat, but some have fried ingredients. Vegetarian Curry, Panaeng, and Musmun have coconut milk (high in fat) added. The lowest fat dishes include: **Putt Thai Korat with Tofu** - tofu, noodle, and vegetables; **Woon-Sen With Tofu** - soybean noodle, tofu, and vegetables; **Tofu Salad** - tofu, soybean noodle, lettuce, tomato, and herbs; and **Vegetarian Delight**.

Other dishes include: **Stir Fried Tofu and Bean Sprouts, Stir Fried Thai Egg Plant, Stir Fried Tofu with Sweet Basil and Hot Pepper**, and **Stir Fried Tofu with Garlic Sauce and Hot Pepper**.

SIAM THAI RESTAURANT

9150 S Main, A-1
(Medical Center area)
660-9955

Casual Dining: L,D
Av: $5-10

The leanest soups are **Hot and Sour Shrimp Soup** and **Vegetable Soup with Tofu or Chicken**.

Many salads are prepared with a spicy lime dressing that has no oil. These are: **Larb Gai** - chopped chicken salad, **Yum Wun Sen** - glass noodle or bean thread salad with shrimp or ground chicken, **Shrimp Salad**, **Squid Salad**, and **Seafood Combination Salad**. Luncheon specials include a Spring Roll (which is fried) and Fried Rice (request **Steamed Rice** and no spring roll instead). Luncheon dishes include about 3 oz of meat; there is about 5 oz in the dinner dishes.

Dinners are served with **Steamed Rice**. **Steamed Fish** is served with a **Chinese Preserve Plum Sauce**. Other dishes are stir-fried with about 1 t of oil plus some chicken stock - that has had the fat skimmed off. **Cashew Chicken** (includes plenty of vegetables so order without cashews). **Pepper Chicken**, **Chicken with Mixed Vegetables**, **Garlic Chicken** (request the chicken to be grilled), and **Broccoli with Chicken**.

Three curries are made without coconut milk. One is **Kaeng Pah Chicken** - a country style red curry cooked with baby corn, green beans and/or broccoli, and bamboo shoots.

Vegetarian Dishes are made with **Tofu** (request fresh tofu, not fried), **Tempeh** - made from soybean, and **Seitan** - wheat gluten. Any dish can be prepared with these items instead of the meat.

THAI ORCHID

8282 Bellaire, Suite 112
(SW Houston)
981-7006

Formal Dining: L,D
Av: $5-10

An appetizer, **Baked Mussel**, is baked in a clay pot without any oil. **Thom Yum** - spicy and sour shrimp soup with a definite taste of lemon grass is prepared without any oil. For a salad, the **Lime Beef Salad** - charcoaled beef and vegetables and served with mint laced lime juice and chili is leanest.

Steamed Fish (**Pla Nung**) is available; be sure to ask them not to add oil to the plate. **Heavenly Chicken** - boneless chicken breast marinated in soy sauce, garlic, and spices has no added oil. The traditional Thai dishes: **Summer Palace**, **Princess Favorite** (can ask for no cashew nuts or eat sparingly), and **Beef A La King** is prepared with about a tablespoon of oil in the wok. You can ask them to use just water to prevent sticking instead.

Curries are prepared with a tablespoon of oil and coconut milk is added - both should be omitted for a lean dish. All meals come with **Steamed Rice**. Entrees include about 6-8 oz of meat.

Fresh Fruit, in season, is available for dessert. The dessert, **Cassava** is a boiled starch with sugar added but no fat is added.

VIETNAMESE

Vietnamese food is similar to the cuisine served in Chinese and Thai restaurants. A great many selections are stir-fried. Rice is a basic component of all Oriental restaurants including Vietnamese cuisines. Rice comes in many forms such as rice paper to wrap around foods, rice noodles, and rice sticks (dried rice-flour noodles).

Food from southern Vietnam is more highly spiced than food from the northern sections. Chilies and chili paste are used for the hot seasoning. The south also depends on more fish, seafood, and the fish sauce (nuoc mam) as in Thai cooking. Northern cooking is similar to the milder Cantonese Chinese cuisine.

Steamed spring rolls, like those offered in Thai restaurants, are frequently on the menu. These are usually very lean. Dipping sauces such as ginger-garlic sauce or fish sauce are offered with the spring rolls as well as with other foods.

Other Vietnamese sauces include shrimp sauce (strong-tasting sauce of mashed, salted, and fermented shrimp) and soybean sauce (made from fermented, crushed and processed soy beans with added sugar and salt). The soybean sauce is a component for making peanut sauce, another dipping sauce.

Request those entrees that offer more vegetables than meat for the leanest choice. Ask for your dish to be prepared with little or no oil.

MRS ME'S CAFE

2100 Waugh
(between W Gray & Fairview)
522-5343

Casual Dining: L,D
Av: $5-10

Offers an extensive selection of **Vegetarian Dishes**. The buffet is even half vegetarian. Appetizers: **Summer Rolls in Rice Paper** can be prepared with only vegetables or with chicken and/or shrimp.

Chefs use teflon pans and only a few drops of oil to cook the dishes. Mixed dishes have only about 2 oz meat and many vegetables. Noodle dishes include: **Bun Ga Nuong** (charbroiled chicken served over rice noodle, bean sprouts and mint leaves); **Hu Tieu Xao** (stir fried rice noodles with bean sprouts, shrimp, and chicken); and **Mi Xao Viet Nam** (stir fried egg noodles with bean sprouts, shrimp, and chicken).

Dinners offers options for accompaniments but select **Summer Roll, Steamed Rice**, and **Won Ton Soup** or Salad (carrot, cabbage, cilantro with vinegar and a few peanuts). Mixed dishes include: **Beef with Vegetables** and **Chicken and Vegetables**. Dishes with mostly meat contains about 4 oz: **Spicy Lemongrass Chicken** and **Stir Fried Beef & Green Onion**.

Vegetarian dishes include: **Fresh Tofu Soup**; **Bun Goi Cuon** (summer rolls, rice noodles, and bean sprouts); and **Bun Mi Cang** (soybean gluten seasoning with ginger, garlic, and lemongrass served over rice noodles, bean sprouts, mint leaves, and cucumber).

NIT NOI

THAI RESTAURANT

Treat yourself to excellent authentic Thai cuisine in
a relaxed, cozy atmosphere. Prepared with only the
finest spices & fresh vegetables. Suited for the
healthy, diet-concious.

Choose from a variety of healthy specials for only
$4.99 - weekdays.

Extensive dinner menu.

No MSG

2462 Bolsover
In the Village
(713) 524-8114

When we think of Italian foods, we most often think of pastas and pizza. Refer to the Table of Contents to find the chapter on "Pizzas".

Olive oil is very popular in Italian cooking. It is considered a "good", healthy fat with no cholesterol, but it still has as many calories as all other oils at 125 calories per tablespoon. To eat lean, avoid fried foods or those foods that have a great deal of oil added.

Here are some general guidelines for Dinin'Lean® in Italian restaurants:

Bread

Hard crusted Italian bread is frequently offered. This bread is very low in fat unless butter or margarine is added. Some restaurants offer olive oil to dip the bread into - this is a caloric disaster. If you can not afford the calories, keep the bread away from your end of the table.

Appetizers

Stay away from the fried appetizers such as fried eggplant and fried cheese. Instead, consider squid, mussels, or clams cooked in an herb wine sauce.

Prosciutto ham is very high in sodium and can be high in fat depending on the quality of the meat. However, an appetizer of Prosciutto generally offers just a couple of thin slices of the ham with fruit such as melon. This appetizer may not be inappropriate if you are ordering a low fat pasta dish as an entree.

Minestrone Soup is a vegetable soup that is generally low in fat. Therefore, this soup would be a recommended selection.

Salads

Caesar salad is made with eggs, Parmesan cheese, and Italian dressing. A much leaner choice would be the dinner salad. Generally, this consists of salad greens such as lettuce, radicchio, arugula, endive, and spinach complimented with other vegetables such as tomato, onions, and mushrooms. Each olive has about 1 gram of fat but, fortunately, most salads do not serve more than a couple. Added pine nuts, in moderation, may not be a problem either if it is just a sprinkle rather than a handful.

Always ask for the dressing on the side or use just lemon or a flavorful vinegar as an alternative.

Pastas

Pasta noodles are very low in fat. They are made of mostly flour and water. Sometimes eggs are used but the amount per serving does not add up to too much - about 50 mg of cholesterol per cup and a few grams of fat. If you watching your cholesterol, ask for those noodles made without egg. Some restaurants reported they provided dried pastas, made without egg, for this reason.

Each half cup portion of pasta has about 80 calories but the serving sizes are often 2 cups. Frequently, appetizer portions can be ordered instead of a large entree portion; or request a doggie bag.

Here's a description of the common pastas:

STRAIGHT PASTAS:
(from very thin to the widest)
Angel hair
Vermicelli
Spaghetti
Linguine
Fettucine
Lasagne

TUBULAR PASTAS:
Mostaccioli - about 1 1/2 " long
Penne
Rigatoni
Cannelloni - stuffed
Manicotti - stuffed
Ziti

STUFFED PASTAS:
Capellitti
Tortellini
Ravioli

OTHER PASTAS:
Gnocchi - little dumplings
Shells - shaped like shells

Most of the calories, in pasta dishes, come from the sauces or stuffings such as in lasagna, tortellini, and ravioli.

Other starches used in Italian cooking include risotto, a short grain rice. This is low in fat by itself but is often mixed with butter and cheese. Polenta, corn meal pudding comprised of mostly cornmeal and water, is often poured into "pancakes". This is low fat but the sauces may not be.

Cheese

The cheeses frequently used are ricotta cheese (100 cals/8 gms fat per 1/4 c), mozzarella cheese (80 cals/6 gms fat per 1 oz), and parmesan cheese (50 cals/3 gms fat per 2 T). Unfortunately, partially skimmed cheeses do not bring the calories and grams of fat down as much as you might think. For example, part skim mozzarella cheese still has 70 cals/5 gms fat per 1 oz.

Sauces

Tomato sauces (such as marinara and pomodori) are typically lower in fat and calories than alfredo sauce and those foods sauteed in lots of butter or oil.

White clam sauce is a little higher in fat than the tomato sauces. Some butter or oil is used but white clam sauce also has wine added.

Pesto sauce begins with basil, but pine nuts, olive oil and parmesan cheese are also added. If you want a dish prepared with pesto - request it to be prepared with "just a little".

Primavera consists of sauteed vegetables and a buttery or alfredo sauce. For a lower fat alternative, order Pasta Primavera to be prepared with steamed vegetables and a red sauce instead.

It is best to avoid alfredo, other cream sauces, and carbonara sauce or request the sauce on the side so you can control the amount.

When ordering a side order of pasta, consider asking for no sauce to be added. Mix the sauce from your meat entree with the pasta instead.

Parmigiana means floured, fried, and topped with a marinara sauce and cheese. Whether the parmigiana is made from veal or eggplant, they are all high in fat. But you can request the meat to be grilled and topped with a marinara sauce but without cheese.

Meat

Meat portions are often 8-10 ounces when ordered as an entree. Portions are more appropriate when you order them with a pasta such as shrimp fettucine.

When ordering a pasta dish with meat, ask what sauces are added. Request either a tomato based sauce or order the sauce on the side so you can decide how much to add.

Chicken and seafood are definitely the leanest "meats" as long as they are not fried. Request the skin to be removed from the poultry dishes.

Veal is fairly low in fat. Most often it is prepared breaded and fried. Sometimes it is offered grilled or sauteed in wine; those choices would be far more appropriate.

Desserts

Fresh fruits are often offered in Italian restaurants. Low fat Italian ices or sorbets may also be available. When you can not resist the temptation, rich creamy desserts such as cannoli, are best split between many friends.

ARRIVEDERCI ITALIAN CAFE

515 Post Oak Blvd &
1900 W Loop South
622-5775/622-3333

Casual Dining: B,L
Av: Under $5

Caesar's Salad or the Grilled Chicken Salad (3 oz chicken on a Caesar's Salad) has eggs & croutons - so always request dressing on the side. **Fresh Fruit Salad**. **Vegetable Soup** is usually available each day. **Tabouli** - cracked wheat, parsley, tomatoes, and very little oil. **Baked Potato** is available dry.

Pasta servings are about 3-1/2 ounces (almost 2 cups). **Spaghetti and Tomato Sauce** is offered. The next two dishes are said to use very little olive oil in their preparation: **Linguine al Pesto** (adds about 1 T sauce made with pinenuts, olive oil & basil). **Pasta alla Carrettera** - a cold dish made with a tomato & olive oil sauce (about 1 T of sauce is added to the dish). Comes with **Fresh Steamed Vegetables** (no fat is added).

Meat dishes are about 4-1/2 oz; nothing is fried. **Fish Special** (such as lemon pepper), **Chicken Special** (such as grilled chicken breast in a marinara sauce), or **Roast Chicken** (remove the skin) are the lowest fat items.

Roast Beef or Breast of Turkey Sandwich on **Wheat or French Bread** are made with about 3-1/2 oz meat (request no mayonnaise).

Smoothies or **Frozen Yogurt** (lite or non-fat is available).

BALLATORI RISTORANTE ITALIANO

4215 Leeland
(at Cullen)
224-9556

Formal Dining: L,D
Av: $10-20

Everything is made to order so your food can be prepared to meet your dietary specifications. For example, the **Special Lasagna** is a vegetarian lasagna with cheese; tell them how much cheese to use. **Ciambotta** is a mixed vegetable dish. **Minestrone alla Sergio** and **Pasta e Fagioli** (bean & noodle soup) are low fat soups. **Insalata Mista** consists of lettuce and tomato (request without olives and with salad dressing on the side).

Any pasta can be requested with marinara sauce such as: **Spaghetti with Marinara** and **Pappardelle Verdi** (green egg noodles in a *marinara* sauce).

Request chicken dishes to be prepared without skin and without oil. **Pollo Arrosto** - 1/4 chicken roasted with garlic & rosemary. **Pollo alla Cacciatora** - 1/4 chicken in wine.

Vitella alla Villa - grilled veal. **Pizzaiola** - grilled veal with fresh tomato sauce.

BERTOLOTTI CUCINA ITALIANA

2300 Richton &
2555 Bay Area
524-3354/480-4494

Formal Dining: L,D
Av: $10-20

Each restaurant uses slightly different terminology for the same or similar items. Therefore, the english translations will be used for some of the items. **Proscuitto e Melone/Proscuitto Di Parma** (2 thin slices of lean ham & sweet melon) or **Peperoni Alla Bagna Cauda/Peperoni Alla Piemontese** - roasted bell pepper, ask for the sauce on side. Request dressing on the side for all the salads. **Asparagus** or **Spinach** can be prepared without any oils. Order the **Mushrooms** to be sauteed in white wine only. Soups: **Bean, Lentil**, or **Tomato & Sweet Pepper Soup**.

Any pasta can be prepared with the **Tomato Sauce** which is lower in fat. **Bucatini Alla Amatricciana** - noodles with a rich tomato sauce with onions (request it without bacon). Have the sauce on the side for: **Panzarotti Con Salza di Noci** - pasta filled with swisschard and veal or **Tagliatelle Verdi Con Porcini** - noodles with wild mushroom sauce.

Meat portions are between 5 and 6 ounces. **Petti Di Pollo Con Carciofi Patate** - grilled breast of chicken with garlic, potatoes, and artichoke hearts. **Grilled Fish** such as Red Snapper, Swordfish, or Rainbow Trout can be grilled dry, poached, or be made with a white wine sauce without butter or oil. **Paillard Di Vitello** (grilled veal) or **Roasted Rabbit**. **Fresh Fruit** is available.

ITALIAN

BIRRAPORETTI'S

6 restaurants in Houston area
For locations, call:
529-9292

Informal Dining: L,D
Av: $5-10

Unbuttered Italian Bread can be requested. A combination of **Minestrone Soup** and **Dinner Salad** (ask for dressing on the side) is available. **Grilled Chicken Almond Salad** - has 7 oz chicken, 1-1/2 oz mozzarella cheese, 3 olives, and 1/2 T. almonds (can request no cheese, olives, or almonds).

Lowest fat choices on the menu include: **Spaghetti with Homemade Tomato Sauce**, **Birraporetti's Grilled Chicken** with fresh vegetables (has about 1/4 t butter or oil), or **Grilled Chicken & Scampi** (specify with *tomato* sauce).

It states on Birraporetti's menu that "We've been concerned with good taste and good health for nearly twenty years...". Be sure to ask the server for any special dietary request, such as the following. **Fettucine Primavera** - request with *tomato* sauce. **Clams & Fresh Mushrooms** - order to be served in a tomato sauce instead of the alfredo sauce topping. **Lasagna Primavera** - fresh spinach, broccoli, pasta and cheese (request to leave off the cream sauce). **Grilled Fish Florentine** is served with fettucine alfredo (request *tomato* sauce instead) or with **Fresh Vegetables**.

Meat portions are about 7 ounces. **Fresh Fruit** is seasonlly available.

BUON APPETITO RESTAURANT

2231 W Holcombe
(Medical Center area)
665-4601

Informal Dining: L,D
Av: $5-10

Order **Unbuttered Bread** instead of the usual.
Minestrone Soup and **Cozzuli Marinara** (mussels
in marinara sauce) are the leanest appetizers.
Request salad dressing on the side for: **Nzala di
Cacocciuli** (sliced tomatoes, artichoke, and olives)
and **Nzalata Verdi** (romaine lettuce, olives, and
cucumbers).

Some pastas are available at a half portion:
Capeddi D'Angelu 'A Marinara (angel hair pasta
with marinara sauce) and **Linguine Trapani** (fresh
garlic, chunk tomatoes, and basil).

Penne Puttanesca - penne pasta topped with
mix of fresh vegetables. **Linguini Pescaturi** - pasta
with seafood assortment & marinara. **Linguini
Vonguli** (request served with *red* clam sauce). Meat
portions vary from between 6 oz within a pasta dish
to 8-10 oz in an entree. For lean veal: **O'Limuni**
(request grilled) or **Custuletti Mariasantissima** -
veal chop (ask for without sauce and vegetables
steamed without butter). There are always a wide
variety of vegetables available.

Any **Fish**, such as snapper, trout, or flounder
can be **Grilled**, **Broiled**, or **Sauteed with Wine**.
Shrimp Marinara and **Jaddina-Nta-Gratiglia** -
grilled breast of chicken marinated with garlic &
lemon are other good choices. **Fresh Fruit** is
seasonally available.

CARMELO'S ITALIAN RESTAURANT

14795 Memorial Drive
(W Houston)
531-0696

Informal Dining: L,D
Av: $10-20

Appetizers: **Grilled Shrimps** (request without sauce) and **Carpaccio** - lean raw beef (3 oz) with a light sauce.

Minestrone and **Oyster and Artichoke Soup** are both lean.

Request salad dressing on the side for **Insalata Italiana**.

Pasta: **Linguine alla Siciliana** - shrimps, calamari, crabmeat, mussels, and tomato sauce. **Linguine with Grilled Chicken** - roasted peppers, basil, tomatoes, and garlic (request very little oil). **Pasta Rustica Hilary** - grilled balsamic marinated vegetables and a touch of marinara sauce. **Capellini with Grilled Scallops** - in a green tomatillo sauce. **Penne Primavera** - pasta with fennel, eggplant, celery, mushrooms, fresh basil, and tomato sauce.

Seafood: **Salmone Fresco** - request *grilled* salmon over spinach but no sauce. **Tara Blackened Tuna & Scallops**. **Grilled Mahi Mahi** (request without butter sauce).

Pollo Griglia - chicken with spinach, garlic, rosemary and oregano, with Italian potatoes. **Grilled Lamb Chops** has visible fat trimmed. **Grilled Veal Chops** - topped with mushrooms and served with Italian potatoes.

All main dishes are served with **Vegetable** (request without margarine) and **Salad** (request dressing on the side).

CARRABBA'S

3115 Kirby &
1399 S Voss at Woodway
522-3131/468-0868

Informal Dining: L,D
Av: $10-20

Management said that about 40% of all orders
are *off* the menu; special requests are encouraged.
For Antipasti: **Cozze in Bianco** (request fresh
mussels to be steamed without any olive oil).
Minestrone is made with chicken stock, refrigerated, and then the fat is skimmed off. Ask for salad
dressing on the side. The house Parmigiana dressing is made of eggs, cheese, and olive oil - you may
want to request another type.

Pizza can be prepared **Te Piace** - you chose the
ingredients that you want. Try the **Primavera** -
mixed grilled vegetables with pomodora sauce
instead of pesto.

Request the **Pomodoro or Spicy Marinara
Sauce** (both are low in fat) for any pasta noodle.
The homemade fettucini and tagliarini noodles are
both made with eggs, the others (including the dry
fettucini) are not.

Tagliarini Picchi Pacchiu - thin noodles in a
sauce of uncooked tomatoes, garlic, olive oil, and
basil. You may want to add grilled chicken or grilled
scallops to your pasta dish (request these meats to
be prepared without oil).

Pollo Parmigiano - can be prepared with a
grilled chicken breast, topped with pomodoro, and
melted mozzarella (less than 1 ounce of cheese is
used).

CAVATORE ITALIAN RESTAURANT

2120 Ella Blvd
(at W 21st)
869-6622

Informal Dining: L,D
Av: $10-20

Request these hot appetizers to be prepared with very little butter/oil: **Escargot Cavatore** - sauteed escargot with vegetables and **Gamberi con Scalops** - sauteed shrimp and sea scallops with herbs and spices. **Minestrone** is a low fat vegetable soup.

Lower fat pasta dishes include: **Spaghetti Bolognese** - spaghetti with meat sauce; **Spaghetti Marinara** - grilled shrimp on a bed of spaghetti with marinara sauce; and **Capelli d'Angelo** - angel hair pasta with mushroom, green onion, and crabmeat in a veal broth.

Full portions come with salad (request the dressing on the side) and garlic bread (request *plain*, **Italian Bread** instead).

The menu also lists four of the **Chef's Low Calorie Specials**: **Pesce con Gamberi alla Griglia** - grilled fish and shrimp; **Petto di Pollo alla Griglia** - grilled breast of chicken; **Fettuccine Casareccie** - sauteed fresh tomato with green onion, basil, and spices on fettuccine; and **Vitello alla Griglia al Limone** - grilled slices of veal. These low calorie specials are served with spaghetti with olive oil (request *marinara* sauce instead) and toasted bread (request it unbuttered).

Fresh fruit is available for dessert.

CENT'ANNI

2128 Portsmouth
(S of Richmond near Shepherd)
529-4199

Informal Dining: L,D
Av: $5-10

Italian Sour Dough Bread is unbuttered. Small and large servings are available for some of the menu items.

Lower fat soups (Zuppe) include: **Pollo Con Riso** - chicken, spinach, and rice and **Zucca E Aglio** - zucchini & garlic.

Request **Lite Italian Dressing** on the side of salads. **Asparago E Gamberi** is an asparagus & grilled shrimp salad.

Pizzas can be prepared with just a sprinkling of cheese - the **Vegetariana** is made with grilled vegetables and roasted peppers.

Lower fat antipasti include: **Granchio Arabiatta** - crab claws in spicy tomato sauce and **Legume Alla Griglia** - grilled vegetables and marinated skewed chicken.

Fresh fish (**Pesce Del Giorno**) can be prepared without any fats. Meat portion size is 7-8 oz. **Linguini Del Mare** - mixed seafood in linguini pasta can be requested to be prepared with *marinara* sauce instead.

Fresh fruit (**Frutta Fresca**) is available for dessert - request the fruit *without* cream.

CHEF RAYKO'S CUCINA ITALIAN

11760 Grant Rd
(Lakewood Forest area)
376-0800

Casual Dining: L,D
Av: $10-20

"For those with special dietary needs, we listen very well. We definitely want people to tell us what they need". **Insalata Mista** - fresh green salad (request dressing on the side or Balsamic Vinegar only). **Plain Bread** comes to the table with butter on the side. **Low Fat Milk** is available.

There are ten specials each night, ask the server for the "Leanest and the Meanest". **Linguine Juliana Adriatico** - sauteed pasta with a touch of olive oil, fresh diced roma tomatoes, white wine, and basil is complimented with scallops and shrimp. **Semi-Fredo Chicken Salad** - 8 oz of hot grilled chicken atop fresh greens (request dressing on the side).

Linguine Vongole - pasta with any fresh clam sauce. **White Sauce** is a touch of olive oil, browned garlic, clam juice, and clams; **Red Sauce** is marinara sauce; **Marachiara Sauce** is white sauce with a little marinara sauce.

Chef Rayko says his **Veal Chop** (about 8 oz meat) is very lean. **Cooked Vegetables** are usually steamed - request without added butter. **Fresh Fruit** for dessert.

CIRO'S CIBI ITALIANI

1000 Campbell, #550
(Spring Branch)
467-9336

Informal Dining: L,D
Av: $10-20

Garlic bread (try to avoid or ask that it be removed) and **Bread Sticks** are brought to the table. Willing to prepare special dietary requests. Meat portions are about 3 oz in the pasta and 5-6 oz in an entree. Luncheon portions can be ordered at dinner for a discounted price.

Offers an "**Off the Menu Menu**" that lists many food items, their fat grams (all are 12 grams or under), and the percentage of fat in each item (all under 30% fat).

Lower fat antipasti include: **Minestrone Soup** and **Dinner Salad** with **Pritikin Raspberry Vinaigrette**. **Spaghetti Pomodoro** and **Spaghetti Marinara** are low fat side orders.

Entree choices are: **Pollo alla Verdura** - steamed chicken and vegetables, **Baked Pollo Mary** - breaded chicken & steamed spinach, and **Mare di Veggie** - steamed sea scallops and vegetables.

Lower fat pasta ideas: **Spaghetti Mama "C"** - grilled eggplant and tomato in an olive oil sauce; **Capellini alla Gamberetto** - angel hair pasta and shrimp in a marinara sauce; **Spaghetti Abdo** - grilled chicken, broccoli, and diced tomato in a wine/margarine sauce; and **Rigatoni Frankie** - grilled chicken, grilled zucchini, diced tomato, and pinenuts in a marsala wine sauce.

Fresh Fruit is available for dessert.

FRED'S ITALIAN CORNER RESTAURANT

2278 W Holcombe
(Medical Center area)
665-7506

Informal Dining: L,D
Av: Under $5

Request that salad dressings be served on the side for **Tossed Green Salad** and **Scungilli Salad** - boiled conch salad. **Unbuttered Bread** is served with margarine. For lean starters: **Minestrone Soup** - vegetable soup or **Shrimp Cocktail**.

Pizza can be prepared with half the usual cheese. No oil is added to the pizzas. For a lean pizza, order the **Vegetable Pizza** without olives.

Marinara Sauce can be ordered on spaghetti, fettucine, or vermicelli. In addition, **Clam Sauce Marinara** and **Shrimp Marinara** are also available. Orders are prepared individually, so you can make special requests. For the **Chicken Cacciatore**, request only 1 t oil to be used in the preparation and for the skin and fat to be removed. A thigh and drumstick is included in each serving.

No smoking is permitted in this restaurant.

GROTTO RESTAURANT

3920 Westheimer
(Highland Village Shopping Center)
622-3663

Casual Dining: L,D
Av: $10-20

Willing to prepare any special dietary requests.
Antipasti: **Shrimp Grotto** has no oil added, **Grilled
Scallops Spiedino** has very little oil added to their
sweet pepper sauce.

Salads: **Vallone** is an Italian home style salad
(request no provolone cheese and dressing on the
side). They can make a vinaigrette without oil if you
ask. **Unbuttered Italian Bread** is served to every
table.

Pizza (9" pizza can be split between 2 persons)
may be requested with *fresh* tomatoes instead of
marinated tomatoes, without oil, and light on the
cheese.

Pasta: **Fedelini Alla "Chicchina". Linguine
Alle Vongole** - made with clams, garlic, and olive
oil can be requested *without* oil. **Linguine
Pescatore** - mixed shellfish (request it to be served
in their *zesty pomodoro* sauce).

Grilled Red Snapper Napoletan and **"A
Scapece"** are brushed with a little oil. **Grilled
Chicken Grotto** - request the cream/vermouth
sauce on the side. **Petto Di Pollo Alla Griglia** is a
grilled chicken breast with grilled Italian vegetables
- request a side of pasta instead of patatine (deep
fried potato chips). **Contorni** - fresh greens of the
day such as broccoli or spinach can be requested to
be steamed in consomme.

J. CHRISTOPHER'S PASTA/PIZZA

17600 Kuykendahl
(in Spring)
353-6899

Casual Dining: L,D
Av: $5-10

Request salad dressing on the side and no croutons when ordering the **Dinner Salad**. Can request **Grilled Marinated Chicken** (8 oz) to be added to the salad if desired.

Pizza is baked in a traditional pizza oven. Pizza pans are brushed with oil when baking the **Whole Wheat Crust** and the **Deep Pan Pizzas** but not with the **Thin Crust**. The leanest toppings are **Fresh Mushrooms**, **Tomatoes**, **Green Peppers**, **Onions**, and **Pineapple**. Normally, a pizza has 6, 9, and 12 oz of cheese on the small, medium, and large pizzas respectively - order with half the cheese and they will weigh out the exact amount.

Mostaccioli and Spaghetti with Marinara Sauce is available as a full portion or as a children's portion (at any age). **Chicken Italiano** is 8 oz of chicken marinated in a solution that has no added fat/oil (request with marinara sauce instead of garlic butter).

The **Diet Platter** includes 8 oz non-marinated chicken with a **Special Salad** (request salad dressing on the side).

LA STRADA

322 Westheimer
(Museum area)
523-1014

Informal Dining: L,D
Av: $9-16

Special requests encouraged. Request salad
dressing on the side for: **Insalata Mista** - tossed
green salad, **Insalata Italia** - arrugula, radicchio,
and greens, or **Tomato and Red Onion Salad** (the
1 oz goat's cheese can be left off).

Pizza can be prepared as you wish. About 4-5
oz of cheese is used for each pizza but less can be
requested. Or one pizza can be split between two
people. Leaner ingredients include: mushrooms,
sundried tomatoes, red onions, roasted peppers,
grilled shrimp, and grilled chicken.

Portions are about 8 oz for entrees such as:
**Grilled Fish, Mixed Seafood Grill, Marinated
Grilled Swordfish**, and **Grilled Chicken** (ask to
have the skin removed). Fish is brushed with olive
oil, then coated with fresh bread crumbs and herbs.
Bread crumbs can be omitted but a small amount of
oil is needed to prevent sticking on grill.

Request pastas with ***Marinara* Sauce** instead of
the usual on pasta dishes such as **Broccoli and
Grilled Chicken, Jalapeno Fettucine**, and
Capellini Pomodoro with Seafood. About 4 oz
meat is used in the pasta dishes.

Fresh Fruit is available for dessert.

LA TRATTORIA

6504 Westheimer
(Galleria area)
782-1324

Formal Dining: L,D
Av: $10-20

Willing to prepare any special diet requests -
please ask. **Bread sticks** and buttered bread are
served (ask for **Unbuttered Bread** instead). At least
3-4 lunch specials are available each day. There's
always one leaner choice, such as **Grilled Amber-
jack** or **Grilled Chicken**.

Gamberetti alla Americana - boiled shrimp
with cocktail sauce. **Minestrone alla Contadina** -
Italian vegetable soup. **Insalata Mista** - tossed
salad (request salad dressing on the side). **Fagiolini
Verdi Alla Toscana** - french green beans marinated with red onions (ask for the dijon vinaigrette
on the side).

Spaghetti al Pomodoro - spaghetti with
tomato and basil sauce. **Penne ai Peperoni** -
angle-sliced pasta in a sauce of pureed red and
green bellpeppers, mint, and basil. Veal portions are
about 4-5 oz; fish is 8-9 oz. **Scaloppine Paillard** -
thin, grilled veal scaloppine served with fresh,
grilled vegetables. **Pesce del Giorno** (catch of the
day) all can be grilled. **Grilled Salmon** is available.
Cozze alla Napoletana is steamed mussels in a
spicy sauce of tomatoes, garlic, and white wine over
linguini.

Grilled Vegetables or **Steamed Vegetables**
can be prepared without any fats or oils. **Low Fat
Milk** is available. **Fresh Fruit** is available for
dessert (request it without cream).

MANGOLA'S

11786 Wilcrest
(SW Houston)
498-7950

Casual dining: L,D
Av: $5-10

Chef Pete Tau said that he would be willing to cook up anything special that the customer would like. Specials are offered each night. He recommended the **Steamed Clams or Mussels** (order it to be prepared without butter) and **Salad** (request no black olives) - dressing is served on the side.

Pizza Primavera (fresh vegetables and tomato) and **Pizza Margherita** (tomato and basil) should be ordered *light on the mozzarella.*

Many dishes can be prepared lower in fat. **Flounder Ala Pietro** - flounder cooked in consomme, lemon, fresh vegetables, and Italian spices. **Pasta e Petti di Pollo alla Marinara** - sauteed chicken breast (request that it be charbroiled instead) on a bed of pasta with marinara sauce (request no black olives). **Scallops**, **Snapper**, and **Mahi Mahi** can be baked with lemon and wine only.

Any of the pasta dishes can be ordered with the sauce on the side so you can control how much to add.

MICHELANGELO'S

307 Westheimer
(5-6 blocks E of Montrose)
524-7836

Casual Dining: L,D
Av: $10-20

Request salad dressing on the side. **Insalata di Granzellola** (4 oz crabmeat) has about 1/2 t oil (can be prepared without oil). **Cozze Marinara** - steamed mussels (6 oz) and marinara sauce.

Pizza is prepared in a pizza oven with about 4 oz cheese (can request *no* cheese or *half* the usual cheese). Tomato and cheese pizzas include: **Pizza Margharita** or **Pizza Michelangelo Classico**.

Half orders can be placed for *any* of the pasta dishes. **Spaghetti or Capelleini with Tomato Sauce**. **Scampi Pomodora** - shrimp in tomato and red wine sauce with spaghetti. **Linguine alle Vongole** in red or white sauce (white sauce consists of only about 1/2 t oil). Pesto dishes include about 1 T oil but you can request less: **Linguini al Pesto** and **Capelleini al Pesto di Mare** - angel hair pasta with scallops and shrimp in tomato and pesto.

Meat portions are about 8 oz; most are served with fettucine alfredo (request pasta with *tomato sauce* instead). **Piccato di Pollo** (chicken) and the **Vitello al Piccata** (veal) includes about 1 t oil and no butter. Both the **Pollo alla Griglia** (chicken) and the **Paillard di Vitello** (veal) are dipped in pesto and grilled.

Pesce del Giorno - fresh fish of the day can often be prepared low in fat such as **Snapper sauteed in Pomodoro sauce**. **Steamed Vegetables** have no added fat. **Fresh Fruit** for dessert.

NASH D'AMICO'S PASTA & CLAM

2421 Times Blvd
(Rice Village area)
521-3010

Casual dining: L,D
Av: $5-10

Many "heart-healthy" choices are listed on the menu. Fresh **Homemade Bread** comes to the table with butter on the side. For an appetizer: **Clams on the Half Shell** or **Steamed Mussels with Marinara Sauce**.

Request dressing on the side for the: **Dinner Salad**, and **Honey Mustard Chicken Salad**. **Marinated Seafood Salad** (request lite on the oil). **Minestrone (vegetable) Soup** is low in fat.

Tomato, Cheese, and Basil Pizza can be ordered with half the usual cheese.

For a lower fat pasta try the next three menu items listed. **Taglierini** - fine ribbons of fresh pasta tossed with slow roasted roma tomatoes, sliced garlic in extra virgin olive oil & fresh basil. **Pasta Pomodori** - a fresh tomato, garlic & basil sauce with grilled shrimp on pasta. **Pasta Letizia** - pasta tossed with very little oil, fresh tomatoes, sliced garlic & fresh basil. **Half orders** (2 ounces pasta) are available with salad (hold the garlic bread).

A **Fresh Fish of the Day** is always offered. **Linguini with Red Clam Sauce** or with a **White Clam Sauce** is available - both are said to be prepared with very little oil. **Mixed Steamed Vegetables** are available. Offers **Fresh Fruit** for dessert.

ITALIAN

OLIVE GARDEN

For locations in the
Houston area, call:
1-800-O-GARDEN

Casual Dining: L,D
Av: $5-10

Request their **Garden Salad** with the dressing
on the side and **Unbuttered Breadsticks** instead
of the usual. **Minestrone** or **Pasta e Fagioli Soup**
(beans/ground beef). **Pizza Americana** with
tomato and *half* the usual cheese can be ordered as
an appetizer.

Dinner entrees include about 6 oz meat; lunch
portions are 3 oz. Entrees are served with **Steamed
Vegetables** (request no added butter) or **Pasta**
(order with *marinara* sauce).

Venetian Grilled Chicken is served with
marinara sauce. **Grilled Swordfish** - grilled with a
marinade which includes olive oil. **Spaghetti with
Tomato Sauce**. **Grilled Chicken Sandwich** is
made with a 3 oz skinless chicken breast; order no
butter on bun. **Linguini with *Red* Clam Sauce.
Veal Piccata** and **Veal Marsala**. Garden Chef Salad
is large - 6 oz meat plus 2 oz cheese.

Order the sauce on side for those dishes that
use a cream or cheese sauce, if you just must have
them. That way you can add just a little to dishes
such as: Fettucini Alfredo, Pasta Primavera, and
Chicken Florentine - strips of chicken breasts
sauteed with fresh spinach and served over
fettuccine.

Fresh Fruit will soon be offered for dessert.

PAPPAMIA CUCINA ITALIANA

10211 I-10 W
(at Gessner)
464-8975

Informal Dining: L,D
Av: $10-20

Willing to prepare most special requests and weigh portions. Half portions can be ordered for most entrees. Order the **House or Dinner Salad** with salad dressing on the side and no olives, feta cheese, or parmesan cheese (cheese totals 1-2 oz).

Minestrone Soup has about 2 t olive oil. **Pizza** (request no oil, *fresh* onions, and half the usual 4 oz of cheese). Order any of the pastas in a red sauce such as **Spaghetti alla Marinara**. When placing an order, request *no oil* for *all* menu items. Meats will then be prepared steamed or grilled (the grill will still be brushed with oil); vegetables will be steamed.

Spaghetti con Funghi - with mushrooms, **Capelli d'Angelo di Gamberi** (request without pesto), **Fettuccine Primavera** - with vegetables, **Fettuccine di Mare** - with seafood, and **Tagliatelle di Pollo** - chicken and vegetables (request without cheese).

The following chicken/veal dishes are 6 oz meat portions. Ask that the skin be removed for the chicken dishes. **Vitello (Veal) Piccata** (request without butter and with boiled crabmeat, not sauteed). **Veal or Chicken Parmesan** - topped with marinara sauce; request less or no cheese (cheese portion is 1-1/2 - 2 oz).

Fish portions are 8-10 oz. Request **Mesquite Grilled Fish** with no oil and no sauce. **Fresh Strawberries** or **Raspberry Ice**.

PASTA LOMONTE'S

14510 Grisby
(HW 6 & I-10)
496-0030

Informal Dining: L,D
Av: $10-20

Willing to cook to your special dietary requests. Average meat portion is 3 oz at lunch and 6 oz at dinner. Luncheon portions can be ordered at dinner for a discounted price.

Small House Salad consists of romaine lettuce, onions, artichokes, and pepper (request dressing on the side and

no cheese). **Low Fat Milk** is available.

The next three dishes are prepared without any added fat. **Chicken Barbie** - chicken breast poached in chicken stock with mushrooms, broccoli, and garlic. **Linguini Conpesce** - clam juice with minced garlic, shrimp, fresh tomatoes, mushrooms, and tossed with linguini. **Pasta Pomodora** - dry roasted red peppers, onions, and tomatoes with chicken stock and marinara sauce over linguini. Rainbow Trout is typically dredged in bread crumbs and browned in 1 T olive oil, squeezed with fresh lemon and served with **Steamed Broccoli**. But **Rainbow Trout** can also be prepared in chicken stock and lemon instead of oil. **Stuffed Shrimp Artichoke** is boiled shrimp in cajun seasoning mixed with bread crumbs and stuffed into artichoke. **Veal Parmigiano** can be prepared as a *Grilled* **Veal in a Marinara Sauce**.

Any pasta can be prepared with a *marinara* sauce instead.

PREGO

2520 Amherst
(Medical Center)
529-2420

Informal Dining: L,D
Av: $10-20

Customers are encouraged to customize their own meals. Simply request what you would like on your salad, pizza, or pasta and they will combine it for you. **Sauteed Crab Fingers** is served over a smoked tomato sauce with grilled polenta. **Pizzas** can be ordered without cheese or easy on the cheese. Meat portions within pastas are 3 oz; about 6 oz in an entree.

Lean Duck Salad is 4 oz skinless duck (fat trimmed) with warm beans (beans are prepared in chicken stock), roasted red peppers, and arrugula (order the sundried tomato vinaigrette on the side). **Ragu of Duck with Spinach Pappardelle Eggless Noodles** - 4 oz of lean duck tossed with scallops, tomatoes, chianti wine, white beans, arrugula, and sprinkled with goat cheese (less than 1 oz). Other salads include: **Grilled Salmon Salad** (request without pesto, mozzarella, or pistachios) and **Prego Greens** (request no olives). **Steamed Spinach and Asparagus** are both available.

South of the Border Fettucine is topped with grilled chicken, fresh tomato, black beans, cilantro, and jalapeno. **Gamberi con Capellini y Porcini** - shrimp sauteed in olive oil with fresh tomatoes, mushrooms, peas, and marsala wine.

Or order pastas with whatever components you desire. Whole wheat linguini may be substituted for any pasta. **Fresh Fruit**.

PRIMA PASTA

6811 Kirby
(at Holcombe)
666-4047

Informal Dining: L,D
Av: $5-10

Special orders are encouraged. **Unbuttered
Bread** can be requested instead of the usual.
Request salad dressings on the side of the **Tossed
House Salad** (small or large).

Average portion of meat is 6-8 oz, even on
salads such as the **Grilled Chicken Salad. Grilled
Chicken Breast** (request without mayonnaise or
butter on the bread).

Steamed Vegetables are available instead of
sauteed. Order any pasta dish with **Marinara** (red
sauce) such as with: **Spaghetti, Angel Hair Pasta,
Fettucini,** or **Linguini** noodles.

You can also order these same noodles as a
Primavera (with vegetables) and/or with **Grilled
Chicken, Grilled Shrimp,** or **Salmon Steak.**

Fettucine or Linguini Veracruz is pasta with
marinara sauce & sauteed mushrooms, onion, red &
green bell pepper, and yellow squash (request to be
prepared with only a teaspoon of oil). **Fettucine or
Linguini Veracruz** can also be served with **Grilled
Chicken, Shrimp, or Salmon.** Mix or match as
you like.

Low Fat Milk is available.

RENATA'S RESTAURANT

2006 Lexington
(Summit area)
523-2428

Formal Dining: L,D
Av: $10-20

Willing to prepare special requests. Bread can be served **Unbuttered** if requested. **Skim and Low Fat Milk** are available. An appetizer of **Grilled Vegetables** is served with a non-fat **Orange/Lime Sauce**. **Yogurt** (low fat plain)**, Basil, & Garlic Dressing** is appropriate with salad or with **Shrimp Cocktail**. Request other salad dressings to be served on the side. **One on One on One** - hearts of palm, fresh asparagus, tomato, and artichoke heart. Luncheon salads include: **Orient Express Chicken Salad** - snow peas, lettuce, tomato, and grilled chicken breast. **Spicy Sicilian Shrimp Salad** - skewered shrimp marinated in blackening spices and grilled, served over vegetables.

Linguine with Mushroom & Marinara, Capelinni with Pesto Scented Vegetables (includes about 1 T oil), **Zitti with Green Onion & Plum Tomato, Linguine with Red Clam Sauce, Linguine Pescatore** (Shrimp, Calamari & Marinara), **Vegetable Ravioli,** and **Mediterranean Vegetable Lasagna** - grilled vegetables with 1 layer of pasta and cheese on top only. **Steamed Fresh Vegetable Bouquet** available.

Grilled items (6 oz at lunch & 8 oz at dinner): **Marinated Breast of Chicken, Chicken Pomodoro** (mushroom, bell pepper & marinara), **Shrimp Scampi Giganti with Red Sauce, Snapper Au Natural** (charbroiled), and **Veal Marsala. Fresh Fruit** and **Sorbet**.

TRATTORIA PASQUALE

2325 University Blvd
(at Greenbriar)
665-6116

Casual Dining: L,D
Av: $10-20

Lunch comes with a salad (ask for dressing on the side) but is ala carte for dinner. **Minestrone Soup** - all vegetables with very little oil used in its preparation.

Everything is sauteed in a small amount of butter, often with white wine and lemon. They are willing to saute with *only* white wine and lemon if requested.

Some lower fat menu items that are not listed on the menu: **Grilled Chicken Breast Salad** - ask for dressing on the side; **Veal Paillard** - grilled veal scallopine with garlic and Italian herbs; **Fettucine Primavera with Marinara** - fettucine noodles, vegetables, and red sauce; and **Grilled Fish** without butter or oil. Entrees come with spinach, spaghetti, or Angel hair pasta (request a *marinara* sauce instead).

Vegetables can be steamed if requested. **Fresh Fruit Plate** is available for dessert.

TUTTO BENE! ITALIAN FAMILY RESTAURANT

4618 Feagan
(near Memorial & Shepherd)
864-0209

Informal Dining: L,D
Av: $5-10

Order the salad dressing on the side with the **Dinner Salad**. Garlic bread is served with dinner, but it can be requested **Plain**.

The **Pastas** (**Cappellini, Farfalone, Fettucine, Linguine, Rotelle, Spaghetti, Spirali, Penne Ziti,** and **Spinach Fettucine**) are made without egg. These can be topped with **Tomato Sauce, Tomato with Chicken** (boneless, skinless chicken breast), or **Clam Sauce** (tomato with clams). **Tomato with Beef Sauce** is made with 85% fat-free beef but is "pressed" after being cooked.

About 1 T. oil is used in the preparation of the **Veal Picatta** (sauteed with lemon and mushrooms) and the **Veal Marsala** (sauteed with marsala wine and mushrooms). **Fresh Vegetables** (no oil is added) and Fettucine Alfredo (request a tomato sauce instead) is served with these dishes. No oil is added when making the **Chicken Cacciatore**. About a 4 ounce portion of meat is used in the dishes. The Fettucine Alfredo "Tutto Bene" is made with (instead of cream) whole milk, margarine, and parmesan cheese - although not low in fat or calories, it may be a healthier alternative than the traditional recipe.

For dessert, order the **Ricotta Cheesecake**. It is made with Ricotta cheese instead of cream cheese (159 cals/7 gms fat).

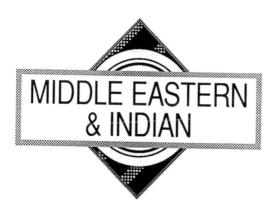

MIDDLE EASTERN & INDIAN

MIDDLE EASTERN

Middle Eastern cuisine includes food which is native to areas such as Greece, Syria, Lebanon, Iran, Iraq, Turkey, and Armenia.

Some of the foods common to this area include: eggplant, olives, wheat, rice, legumes, yogurt, dates, figs, and lamb. Frequently seen spices are parsley, mint, cilantro, and oregano. The common Indian spices such as cinnamon, coriander, cumin, and ginger are also used.

Olive oil is commonly used in Middle Eastern cooking. The oil is used in the preparation of many dishes and a small spoonful is dropped on top of some of the vegetable dishes such as ground chick peas and whipped eggplant. You may not always be able to order a salad such as tabouli to be prepared without oil. But always request that they not add the oil on top of their food. Yogurt is a frequent ingredient, most commonly homemade with whole milk. Rice is served with most meats.

Middle Eastern food is rather healthy food with a few exceptions. You still want to avoid the fried foods such as falafel or the buttered deserts such as baklava. Eggs are added to dishes such as the Avgolemono Soup.

Here's a description of some of the Middle Eastern Menu Items, spelling and pronounciation can vary greatly:

Avgolemono Soup - Greek soup made with rice, vegetables and lemon. Eggs are whirled in.

Babaghnoush or Melitzanosalata - a mild dish prepared with whipped eggplant and spices.

Baklava - a sweet and rich dessert made of layers of phyllo dough, honey, butter and nuts.

Cous Cous - cooked cracked wheat.

Falafel - a fried patty consisting of fava beans and chick peas.

Feta cheese - a white crumbly cheese, high in fat, often added to salads.

Gyros - combination of beef and lamb

Grape Leaves - green leaves of a grape vine stuffed with a rice, meat, and spice mixture then boiled. Usually served with a sauce or yogurt.

Hommos or Hummus - ground chick peas (also known as garbanzo beans).

Kabob or Souvlaki - meat cooked on a skewer.

Pita Bread - a flat, round bread with a hollow center that is low in fat. It is eaten as an accompaniment to a meat or stuffed as a sandwich. Pita bread is often buttered and grilled.

Phyllo - paper thin dough made from flour, egg, water, and some added fat. Not high in fat until the layers are seperated and buttered as in the dish baklava.

Rice Pilaf - a rice dish made with sauteed vegetables and cooked rice.

Tabouli - salad consisting of cracked wheat, parsley, onion, tomato, olive oil, lemon, and mint.

Tahini - sesame seed paste (which is mostly fat)
with lemon juice and spices is added to many
dishes and used as an accompaniment to others.
Tzateki - a spicy yogurt-based sauce.

ABDALLAH'S

3939 Hilcroft, Ste 100
(at North Park)
952-4747

Informal Dining: B,L,D
Av: $5-10

Sandwiches are served with tomato, lettuce, and
garlic sauce (smashed garlic) in a white or whole
wheat pita (wheat pita is an additional charge).
Shish Taouk is chicken on skew - marinated and
grilled. **Kafta Kabob** is said to be *lean* beef.
Turkey Breast is also available.

Grill Platters include: **Roasted Chicken, Shish
Taouk** - grilled chicken, and **Shish Kabob** - beef or
lamb. Platters come with **White Rice** and
Vermicelli Noodles and a **Tossed Salad**.

Grape Leaves are served with homemade
yogurt (made with half skim and half whole milk).
Tabbouli has less than a teaspoon of oil. **Cucumber and Yogurt** is spiced with garlic & mint.

AL BASHA

6374 Richmond
(Galleria area)
784-2727

Formal Dining: L,D
Av: $10-20

Hommos and **Salad** (lettuce, tomato, mashed garlic, cucumbers, radishes, green onion, parsley, spices, lemon juice, and oil) are served with meals. Toasted **Pita** bread is also served. Average meat portion is 8 oz but a smaller portion can be ordered for a discount.

Request no olive oil to be added on top of foods such as **Hommos** and **Babaghnoush. Stuffed Grape Leaves** and **Tabbouleh** have a small amount of oil added during the preparation. **Cucumber and Yogurt** has none added.

Shish-Taouk - charbroiled chicken pieces on skewers comes on 3 skewers (7-8 oz) or 2 skewers (5-6 oz). **Spicy Fish** is marinated in lemon, garlic, coriander, cumin, red pepper, and oil - then baked.

CAFE NASA

1305 Nasa Rd
(in Clear Lake)
486-8854

Informal Dining: B,L,D
Av: $5-10

For lunch, **Lentil Soup**, has a little oil used to
brown the onions. **Chicken Gyros Salad** is made with
4 oz of chicken breast; ask for the dressing on the side.
Fruit Salad is all fruit.

Chicken Breast Sandwich - request the pasta to
be served with the sauce on the side. The lowest fat
hot plates for lunch are: **Chicken Kabob** and **Up Side
Down (Maaloubi)** - a rice and chicken casserole.

The dinner appetizers: **Yogurt and Cucumber**
and **Baba Gannouje** (baked eggplant, smashed with
garlic) have no oil or fats added. **Hommos** and **Lab-
neh** (dried yogurt) are served with a topping of olive
oil (request these menu items to be served without oil).
Minestrone Soup, made with beef broth, has no fat
added.

Tuna Salad and **Chicken Salad** are typically
made with mayonnaise, but they can be prepared dry
if requested. Order the dressing on the side of the
House Salad. Oil is added to the: **Seafood Salad**, **Pasta Salad**, **Tabbouli Salad**, and the **Fattoush Salad**
(tomato and parsley salad) but can be left off if you
ask.

The entrees can be prepared without any oil if requested; the average portion of meat is 7 oz. The leanest are: **Chicken Kabob**, **Seafood Kabob** - shrimp
and scallops, and **Chicken Breast** (ask for the chicken
to be grilled without oil and for the garlic sauce to be
served on the side).

GREAT GREEK

80 Woodlake Sq
(corner of Westheimer at Gessner)
783-5100

Casual Dining: L,D
Av: $10-15

Request salad dressing on the side of salads.
Many of the Greek-style appetizers have vegetable
oil added on top of the item such as **Hummus** and
Melitzanosalata - whipped eggplant. Request them
not to add the oil on top. **Tahama** has oil in the
dish itself; but you can request that it be made
without. **Yogurt and Cucumber** has no added fat.
Yogurt is homemade with whole milk. **Vegetarian
Platter** consists of an assortment of many of these
appetizers.

Pasta dishes are made with seafood and a
tomato sauce similar to an Italian marinara sauce so
they are low in fat. Feta cheese can be left off if
desired.

Beef, Lamb, and Chicken entrees are 16 oz, but a
smaller portion (called an appetizer plate) can be
ordered for a discount.

Leanest entrees include: **Chicken Souvlaki**,
Oven Roasted Lamb, and **Roasted Chicken
Plaka**. These dishes are served with **Vegetable** and
Rice Pilaf which do have some margarine added.
Steamed Vegetables are occasionally available
(request with no margarine added).

Fresh Seafood such as **Mahi Mahi** and
Orange Roughy can be grilled with only oregano
and lemon if requested. **Blackened Fish** is prepared on the grill with a small amount of oil. **Fresh
Fruit** is available for dessert.

GYROS GYROS SANDWICH SHOPPE

1536 Westheimer
(Museum area)
528-4655

Casual Dining: L,D
Av: Under $5

Sandwiches are served with french fries but
Salad can be substituted. **Small Greek Salad**
consists of lettuce, tomato, and about 1 oz feta
cheese (request salad dressing on the side). Buttered and grilled pita bread is served with the salad.

Grilled Chicken Sandwich is 3 oz chicken
breast served on a bun with lettuce and tomato
(request no mayonnaise or cheese). **Vegetarian
Sandwich** - stir-fried broccoli, cauliflower, carrots,
bell pepper, and onion on regular or whole wheat
bread (request tzatziki sauce on the side which has
about 3 gms fat/T).

Grilled Chicken Plate is 6-7 oz grilled chicken
served with **Rice** and **Salad**.

MAMA'S PO-BOY

3235 Hillcroft
(at Richmond)
783-4145

Casual Dining: L
Av: Under $5

Each serving of **Tabouli Salad** has about 2 t oil. **Hommos** has no oil, it is sprinkled with paprika. **Kosher Dill Pickles** are also offered.

No oil is added when grilling the steaks or the onions. **Gyro Sandwich** is made of 4 oz of beef/lamb, topped with **Tahini Sauce. Shawarma or Middle Eastern Steak** - 4 oz shaved steak grilled in spices and onions, served with Tahini Sauce. The other dressing used on the sandwiches is oil and vinegar with Italian spices. Request these dressings on the side.

INDIAN

Indian restaurants use some of the same ingredients as the Middle Eastern countries such as rice, yogurt, onions, tomatoes, eggplant, legumes, and lamb. But Indian food more closely resembles the cuisine from Thailand because of the commonality of spices and curries. Spices used in Indian cooking includes: cardamon, cinnamon, clove, coriander, cumin, fennel, mint, saffron, and tumeric.

The many religions practiced in this country play a large role in what is served in the particular regions of India. Vegetarianism is practiced by many Buddhists. Moslems avoid pork and pork products while Hindus do not eat beef.

South Indian cuisine is hotter than foods from the northern part of India. Chilies, peppers, and hot pickles are more common. Rice, seafood, and chutney are served frequently. The Northern region is milder and uses more wheat products. Restaurants in the United States serve food from all over India.

Sesame oil and coconut oil are the fats commonly used in Indian cuisine. While sesame oil is a unsaturated fat, coconut oil is a highly saturated fat. Ask which fat is being used before you make your selection.

Curries are often made with very high fat coconut milk but can also be prepared without. Yogurt is used in most recipes; typically whole milk or low-fat yogurt is the norm.

Appetizers

Most appetizers such as samosas, fried turnover filled with vegetables and/or meat, are fried. These dishes are best avoided. Papadum (thin, crisp, lentil wafer) is also fried and served with dipping sauces. Limit your intake of the papadum as well.

Salads often have no dressing other than lemon juice and, therefore, would be low in fat.

Entrees

The leanest entrees are meats baked in the tandoor, a clay oven, without any added fats. Tandori meats are often marinated in a yogurt, vinegar, lemon juice, and spice mixture first. Look for tandori chicken or chicken tikka. Kabobs or skewered meats are often prepared low fat in the tandori as well.

Other meats are often sauteed in oil or ghee (clarified butter) as a first step. Vandaloo is meat cooked with potatoes and spices.

Curry is a sauce flavored with garam masala, a combination of spices, not a single spice. In order to make curries or a sauce, the onions (the major component of the curry) are browned in a little oil. The onions are then blenderized. At that point, yogurt, paprika and other spices are added. Coconut milk or cream may also be added; these are usually noted on the menu.

Paneer is a homemade cream or cottage cheese that is used in a vegetarian dish. Not very high in fat by itself, it is often covered with a high fat sauce.

Accompaniments

Low fat breads served include chapati or tandori roti (unleavened bread similar to pita) or nan (leavened bread). Avoid the high fat, fried breads paratha and poori.

Basmati rice, an aromatic long grain rice, is commonly served with the meal. It has a nutty taste. Served plain, as plain pullao, it is very low in fat. When mixed with vegetables and fat, it has a slightly higher fat content.

Yogurt is frequently used in side dishes and sauces. Dahi refers to plain, unflavored yogurt. Raita is yogurt mixed with selected vegetables. Dahl is a lentil-based sauce that is spicy.

THE BOMBAY OVEN

10703 Gulf Frwy
(S of Edgebrook)
944-0193

Formal Dining: L,D
Av: $5-10

The owner's wife is very knowledgeable about
fats and low fat cooking - be sure to request what you
need and she will prepare it whenever possible. Yogurt is used throughout the Indian cooking and is
homemade from whole milk. **Allu Chat** - appetizer
with diced potatoes, chopped tomatoes, cucumber,
lemon and spice; no oil is added. The soups: **Lentil
and Mulligatawny** are also made without any fats.

To make the **Tandoori Specials**, about 8 oz of
meat is used. The meat is marinated in a yogurt, vinegar, lemon juice, and spice mixture. Then the chunks
are skewered and baked in a clay oven. Select from:
Tandoori Chicken (half or full chicken), **Chicken
Tikka** (boneless, skinless chicken), **Lamb Boti Kabob**, and **Fish Tikka Kabob**.

All visible fats are removed and in most recipes
the meat is cooked (boiled or microwaved without
any oil) first before making the **Curries**. Whenever
cream is mentioned in the menu description, the
cream is made from low fat sour cream for a lower fat
product. Try the: **Chicken Vindaloo** (boneless chick-
en cooked with hot spices), **Shrimp Curry,** or **Fish
Curry**.

Entrees are ala carte and can be served with Basmati Rice Pullao (**Plain Rice** can be requested) or
Nan (plain Indian bread).

MAHARAJAH RESTAURANT

9593 Country Creek Dr
(SW Houston)
270-6644

Informal Dining: L,D
Av: $5-10

Green Salads are served with Tandori dishes; salad dressings are brought to you at the side. **Dahi Raita** is a yogurt dressing with diced cucumber. All yogurt is made with whole milk.

Any of the **Tandoori Specials** would be appropriate. They are cooked in a charcoal fired clay oven; 10 oz of meat are served. The Tandoori Specials include: **Boti Kabob** (lamb), **Fish Tikka, Tandoori Shrimp**, and **Chicken Tikka**.

Tandoori Roti and **Nan** are both low fat breads but the Nan does has egg yolks added. The lowest fat chicken curries are: **Chicken Vindalloo, Chicken Ceylon, Chicken Dahiwala,** and **Chicken Curry**. For lamb, order: **Lamb Madras, Lamb Ceylon,** or **Lamb Vindalloo**. The shrimp dishes: **Shrimp Curry, Shrimp Madras, Shrimp Ceylon,** or **Shrimp & Mushrooms** would also be low in fat.

Vegetarian meals are also available. The leanest ones are probably: **Mushrooms Bhaji, Dal Tarka** (ask to be prepared without cream), **Allo Gobi Masala** - medium to hot cauliflower and potatoes, and **Bengan Bhartha** - baked eggplant mashed with onions and tomatoes, garnished with tangy spices.

MEXICAN

If you like hot, spicy foods, Mexican restaurants may top your list of favorite ethnic cuisines. Common foods served in Mexican restaurants include beans, rice, and tortillas as well as tomatoes, onions, salsa, and jalapeno peppers.

Most people think that Mexican restaurants are definitely off the list when watching their fat intake. However, there are some lean choices available.

Appetizers

Typically, fried chips and salsa are served to the table. Fried chips have about 15 cals/1 gm fat for each individual chip. Some restaurants now offer baked chips without any added fats. Salsa is made with little or no fat added and can be used freely.

Ceviche is fish "cooked" without heat with lemons or limes and onions and jalapeno; this would be a very lean entree.

Soups

Gazpacho soup is a low fat, cold soup made with tomatoes and other vegetables. Black bean soup is another lower fat soup.

Chili (beans) or chili con carne (beans with

meat) can be prepared in a low fat manner; the chili with added meat would not be as lean. Watch for added toppings such as cheese.

Breads

Corn tortillas (70 cals/1 gm fat) are a lean choice. The fried shells would add more fat. Flour tortillas (110 cals/3 gms fat) are usually made with lard. Vegetable oil or shortening is being used more often than in the past. One or two soft flour tortillas would not be a nutritional disaster for most people. On the other hand, fried flour tortillas would not be recommended.

Salads

Lettuce and tomato salad is low in fat. Use the picante sauce for a low calorie dressing. Taco salads and fajita salads, are often served in a fried flour tortilla shell; request that the salad be served on a plate for a savings of hundreds of calories. Cheese, avocado, and sour cream are common additions to these salads; note their calories and grams of fat under the section *"Toppings"* in this chapter. Any or all of these can be omitted if requested.

Entrees

The leanest way to order in a Mexican restaurant is ala carte. Chicken fajitas or chicken tacos al carbon can be ordered singly in most restaurants. Lettuce, tomatoes, and onions, can be requested to accompany this order. When ordered as a dinner, the fajita dinner is usually served with sauteed green peppers and onions as well as side orders of lettuce, tomato, guacamole, sour cream, and cheese. It is these extras that really add up the calories and fat.

Other soft tacos made with corn or flour tortillas would be acceptable option. A burrito is a soft flour tortilla filled with chicken, beef, or cheese and served rolled up.

Fried corn tortillas are definitely higher in fat than soft corn tortillas but one or two may still fit into your fat budget. Chalupas are flat, fried corn tortilla topped with beans, meat, and/or cheese. Tacos are fried corn tortilla filled with chicken, beef, beans, and/or cheese.

Enchiladas, corn tortillas dipped in hot oil and then rolled with chicken, cheese, or beef, are generally served with a tomato-based enchilada sauce. Again, an ala carte order of one or two enchiladas would be a better choice than the typical order of three plus the extras.

Higher fat items to be avoided include the chimichanga, a flour tortilla filled with beef, chicken, cheese and/or beans and then deep fried. This is often covered with a picante or cheese sauce.

Accompaniments

Mexican rice is first fried to brown the rice and cook the vegetables such as onions, garlic, and tomatoes. Consequently, Mexican rice can be high in fat depending on how much fat is added.

Beans ala charra or cooked pinto beans are prepared with bacon or other fat. It is best to eat the beans and leave the broth and added fat in the bowl. Beans ala charro is usually a better choice over the refried beans. There are many recipes for refried beans but normally quite a bit of fat is added - some restauranteurs told the author that it was half beans and half lard! Beans ala charra can often be substituted for dinners than include the refried beans.

Toppings

Many dishes are served with guacamole (mashed avocado), sour cream, and cheese which are all very high in fat. Avocados are nearly pure fat;

just 1/4 of an avocado has 80 cals/7 gms fat. Sour cream has 50 cals/5 gms fat for a dollop which contains 2 level tablespoons. Shredded cheese has 120 cals/10 gms fat per 1/4 c.

Salsa and pico de gallo generally have very little fat added.

Salsa verde is a green sauce made from a green tomato, tomatillo. It usually is made with little or no fat.

Dessert

Fruit is rarely offered. Flan, a baked custard, is made with egg and whole milk and does have some fat. But because of the usual small portion served it would be a better choice than sopapillas. Sopapillas are fried flour dough sprinkled with sugar and cinnamon.

ADRIAN'S RESTAURANT Y CANTINA

1919 Louisiana
(Downtown)
951-9651

Informal Dining: L,D
Av: $5-10

Fried Chips are brought to the table. Smaller portions of some food items can be ordered for a discount. Many items are available **Ala Carte.**

Adrian's Ensaladas - garden salad with chicken fajitas, shrimp, or cabrito (request no sour cream and dressing on the side). Refrain from eating the fried flour tortilla shell that the salad comes in.

These entrees include 2 tacos (less than 2 oz meat in each taco): **Tacos Al Carbon** - chicken fajita meat, **Tacos Al Pastor** - fajita cooked in a blend of chiles, or **Tacos de Cabrito** - goat meat sauteed in ranchero sauce (request no guacamole). Leanest accompaniments are **Salsa** or **Pico de Gallo** *and* **Borracho Beans** or **Black Beans**.

Grilled menu items should be requested without guacamole. **Half order of Fajitas de Gallo** (chicken) is still 6-8 oz and could be shared. **Cabrito Pancho Villa** - goat meat cooked like a stew with onions and bell peppers (request no guacamole). **Grilled Shrimp** are available. **Pollo a la Parrilla** - half chicken marinated with a blend of chiles, cilantro, and onions.

Chargrilled Zucchini and **Steamed Broccoli** are available.

MEXICAN

CUELLAR'S CAFE

2101 W Loop South
(between Westheimer & San Felipe)
960-1669

Casual Dining: L,D
Av: $5-10

    Baked Chips are available. One section of the menu lists the "Lite" menu items. Most meat portions are 6-8 oz.
    Corn Tortillas can be ordered with fajitas. **Beef, Chicken, and Shrimp Fajitas** can be requested without any oil. **Steak Tampico**, **Tacos Al Carbon**, or **Red Snapper** should also be ordered to be prepared without any oil.
    Instead of the usual accompaniments of rice, beans, and guacamole - a dinner salad is served for these lower calorie entrees. Always ask for dressing on the side. A dinner salad can be substituted for *any* of the regular menu items that typically serve rice, beans, and guacamole.
    If you want **Chicken Enchiladas**, ask them to leave off the cheese.

EL PALENQUE

1416 Spring-Cypress &
21161 Tomball Parkway
353-4055/376-6960

Casual Dining: L,D
Av: $7-12

Many menu items are available "A La Carta" such
as **Rice**, **Borracho Beans**, and **Taco al Carvon** so
you can make up your own meals. **Borracho
Beans** have bacon - less than 1/2 oz per serving.
Can substitute **Borracho Beans** instead of "Beans"
(which is refried beans) or **Lettuce & Tomato**
instead of Guacamole for any of the plates.

Chicken Fajita *for one* is a 12 oz serving; but you
can order as a **Chicken Taco al Carvon** with just 3
oz meat in a flour tortilla. Or order an extra flour
tortilla to split the 3 oz of meat into 2 tacos.

Pechugas Jeovani - a 7-8 oz chicken breast
topped with a Mexican sauce (request no cheese or
cheese puff). **Vera Cruz** - a 7-8 oz chicken breast
covered with a sauce made from bell peppers,
onions, mushrooms, and wine.

Camaron Acapulco - 6 jumbo shrimp cooked
in fresh tomatoes, jalapenos, and onions. **Steak
Mexicana** - a 6-7 oz chicken cooked in fresh
tomatoes, jalapenos, and onions.

Ensalada Palenque has 8-10 oz chicken meat
and 4 oz of cheese.

IGNACIOS

6013 FM 1960
(Champions area)
893-8760

Casual Dining: L,D
Av: $5-10

The **Hot sauce**, **Spanish sauce**, and **Salsa Verde** (green sauce) all have no oil - but at present, only fried chips are available. **Enchilada Verdas** - 2 chicken enchiladas topped with salsa verde sauce and about 1 to 1-1/2 ounces of cheese (you can request little or no cheese).

Pollo or Fajita Asado - request that it be prepared dry; request a dinner salad instead of the guacamole. **Lite Italian Dressing** is available; dressings are always brought on the side.

Vegetarian Burrito - prepared with vegetables sauteed in water with spices, rolled in flour tortilla and salsa verde. Can also be prepared as 2 enchiladas in corn tortillas.

When ordering the **Tampico Plate**, request a chicken enchilada topped with Spanish sauce, tostada with a thin layer of refried beans, and a chicken taco (request no cheese).

JALAPENOS MEXICAN RESTAURANT

2702 Kirby Dr
(between Westheimer & Richmond)
524-1668

Informal Dining: L,D
Av: $5-10

Baked Chips are available if you ask. The **Pico De Gallo** has no oil but their Picante Sauce does. **Black Bean Soup** can be requested without the usual toppings of cheese, sour cream, and bacon.

Grilled Chicken Salad can be requested without olives. **Taco Salad Deluxe** can also be requested without cheese or avocado. Ask for salad dressing on the side. Order the **Club Cancun** without the bacon, avocado, or cheese and with the mayonnaise on the side.

The **Grilled Snapper**, **Grilled Quail**, **Grilled Chicken**, **Grilled Frog Legs**, and **Grilled Shrimp** (or combinations of each) can be cooked dry with butter on the side. Portions are about 6-7 ounces cooked. Request the grilled items to be served with **Rice and Salad** (instead of the beans and guacamole).

Side orders of **Onions and Chilies** can be ordered *grilled* for less fat but will take longer. The Molcajete Salsa is about half avocado so it is high in fat.

LAREDO'S TOO

2110 Bay Area Blvd
(in Clearlake)
488-0286

Casual Dining: L,D
Av: $5-10

Features a "Diet Center Approved Menu" with
no added fat or salt. All eight menu items listed
below include a 4-1/2 oz meat portion.
Ensalada Saltillo - grilled chicken breast served
on a bed of Romaine salad with onions, tomatoes,
and mixed vegetables; topped with oil-free dressing. **Ensalada Del Mar** - grilled shrimp and
scallops, served on a bed of Romaine salad with
onions, tomatoes, and mixed vegetables topped
with oil-free house dressing.

The following six entrees are served with
steamed vegetables and green salad. **Flautas De
Pollo** - grilled chicken stuffed in 2 lite rye wasa
crisps rolled and broiled in oven. **Pollo Relleno** -
chicken breast stuffed with cumin, cottage cheese,
breaded with 2 wasa crisp, broiled and topped with
a red pepper sauce.

Pollo Ala Parilla - grilled chicken breast served
on a bed of onions, peppers and topped with a
lemon sauce. **Catch of the Day** - grilled, broiled, or
poached fish topped with Hauchinango sauce.
Camarones Ala Parilla - grilled shrimp served on
a bed of grilled onions and peppers. **Scallops Ala
Parilla** - grilled scallops served on a bed of grilled
onions and peppers.

LOLITA'S ON THE PARK

6002 Washington
(near Memorial Park)
861-5246

Casual Dining: B,L,D
Av: $5-10

Salad dressings come on the side of all salads. The Taco Salad and the Fajita Taco Salad are prepared in a fried flour tortilla shell - but may be requested on a plate instead. This is how the other salads are prepared.

Tampico Special - chicken fajita, tomatoes, and boiled popcorn shrimp, served on a bed of lettuce (request without avocado or bacon). **Chicken Fajita Taco Salad** (request without cheese, guacamole, or sour cream).

Pollo Blanco - lettuce, tomato, and shredded white chicken, served with Spanish sauce (request no cheese or avocado). **Shrimp Salad** - lettuce and tomato salad topped with miniature shrimp and served with red sauce (request no cheese, avocado, or sour cream).

Caldo de Res is a beef soup with fresh vegetables. But the meat is cooked separately and added just before serving so you can order the soup without meat. It is served with rice and tortillas.

Tacos al Carbon or **Chicken Fajitas** may be ordered ala carte. Meat portions are about 4 oz at lunch and 6 oz at dinner.

NINFA'S MEXICAN & SEAFOOD RESTAURANTS

10 restaurants in Houston area
for locations, call:
228-6906

Casual Dining: L,D
Av: $5-10

Baked Chips are available if you order in advance or if you don't mind waiting a few extra minutes.

Frijoles ala Charra-pinto bean soup, can be substituted for beans (which are refried beans).

All menu items can be ordered **A La Carte** so you can order just what you want without all the extras.

Tortilla Soup-mushrooms, onions, and tomatoes and **Oaxaquena**-black bean & tortilla soup, should be requested without the crispy tortillas.

Ceviche-shrimp and scallops, can be ordered as an appetizer or as a meal; this is served with cocktail sauce.

Request salad dressing on the side of the **Dinner Salad** -lettuce and tomato, or the **Chicken Fajita Taco Salad** (about 3 oz chicken).

Fajitas can be ordered in as little as a 1/4 lb (4 oz) serving. **Charbroiled Chicken, Broiled Shrimp**, and **Broiled Scallops** are also offered and are available in combinations with other meats.

PAPPASITO'S CANTINA

8 restaurants around Houston
for locations, call:
784-5253

Informal Dining: L,D
Av: $10-20

Don't hesitate to ask for special dietary requests. Fried chips are served to the tables.

An order of **Ceviche** includes 9 oz of fresh fish, shrimp, & scallops. **Sopa de Tortilla** is Mexican vegetable soup.

Pappasito's Salad includes 6 oz chicken fajitas and vegetables (request no cheese). Request the chicken fajitas to be prepared without the usual splash of butter.

Tiajuana Platter consists of 6 oz chicken fajita and 4 jumbo shrimp.

Chargrilled Quail - each contains about 3 oz edible meat portion. **Pechuga de Pollo** is a 10 oz chicken breast (request no skin).

Camarones Diablo - 6 jumbo shrimp, can be requested to be prepared without butter. There is usually a **Mesquite Fish of the Day** offered, request toppings on the side.

For a taste of your favorites but in smaller portions, request menu items ala carte. A **Single Taco al Carbon** includes 5 oz meat.

RICARDO'S MEXICAN RESTAURANT

I-45 at Gulf Bank &
120 E FM 1314, Porter
445-2550

Casual Dining: L,D
Av: $5-10

Fajitas can be prepared without oil, if requested. Menu suggests 8 oz of fajitas per person but can be split amongst more people for a smaller portion. Leanest order is probably the **Chicken Fajitas** without guacamole. **Corn Tortillas** can be requested instead of flour tortillas. Frijoles a la Charra is prepared with bacon.

The same beef meat used in the fajitas is used for **Al Carbon Taco** - one or two can be ordered ala carte. Or order **Single Chicken Taco** - chicken in a soft corn tortilla. When ordering a full order of the Chicken Taco, guacamole and sour cream come on the side and may be left off.

Request salad dressing on the side or **Salsa** for all salads. Chicken Salad would be a leaner choice than the Taco Salad. **Chicken Salad** - lettuce, tomato, sliced chicken (4-5 oz) and cheese (1 oz). Can request without the cheese. Taco Salad has 1 cup of beef (probably about 4-5 oz), 1 oz of cheese, and crisp chips (1 oz) on the side.

Low Fat Milk is available.

SOUTHWESTERN

Southwestern cuisine is actually a menagerie of many types of cooking. The menu will usually include a wide variety of dishes such as Mexican foods, beef and wild game, seafood, and a wide variety of salads.

Follow these general suggestions for Dinin'Lean® in Southwestern restaurants:

Appetizers

Tortilla soup is usually prepared from a simple low fat vegetable soup. The added bacon, cheese, avocado, and strips of fried tortilla is what contributes most of the calories and fat; some or all of these components can often be omitted.

As discussed in the chapter on Mexican restaurants, fried tortilla chips are loaded in fat and calories. When you pile on the cheese, beans, and/or meat, an order of Nachos can exceed your maximum daily allotment of fat.

Salads

Vegetable salads are low in fat, but Southwestern cuisine also features a variety of other salads that are not served in a low fat manner. Always order the dressing on the side. On a large salad, restaurants can add as much as 1/3 c or nearly 500 calories of nearly pure fat. The Spinach salad consisting of spinach, onion, sliced mushrooms is low in fat until the hot bacon dressing is added.

The calories and grams of fat for the components commonly added to salads are discussed in the chapters on "Salad Bars" and "Mexican". To cut fat and calories, the Cobb salad (diced avocado, chicken, bacon, tomato and blue cheese crumbles over crisp greens) can be ordered without the bacon or avocado. When ordering the taco or fajita salad, ask for it to be served on a plate instead of a fried tortilla shell. Request some of the higher fat components to be omitted as well. Greek Salads prepared with romaine lettuce leaves and feta cheese will usually have an ounce or two of cheese; some of this cheese can be omitted.

Entrees

Refer to the previous chapter titled "Mexican" for suggestions on how to minimize fat intake when ordering Mexican foods in a Southwestern restaurant. Fish and shellfish are covered under the chapter "Seafood Restaurants". There you will discover that grilled shrimp, catfish, and snapper are low fat entrees; frying, however, doubles the calories and fat.

Beef is another food that is commonly served in the Southwestern United States. Grilled chicken sandwiches are leaner choices than burgers, but burgers are still acceptable on occasion - if chosen wisely.

Consider these suggestions:

	CALS	FAT (gms)
Order the Smaller Burger:		
1/2 lb ground beef, cooked	580	42
1/4 lb ground beef, cooked	290	21
SAVINGS:	290	21
Request the Buns to be Grilled without Butter:		
Bun with butter	260	12
Bun without butter	160	1
SAVINGS:	100	11
Use Mustard instead of Mayonnaise:		
1 T mayonnaise	100	11
1 T mustard	15	1
SAVINGS:	85	10
Forget the Extras:		
1 crisp slice bacon	35	3
1/4 Avocado	80	8
1 oz slice cheese	100	8
1/4 c mushrooms sauteed in 1 T butter	110	11
SAVINGS:	325	30
Compare these Burgers:		
1/2 lb burger, buttered bun, 2 oz cheese, 2 sl bacon.	1110	76
1/4 lb burger, buttered bun, 1 oz cheese, 1 T mayo.	750	52
1/4 lb burger, no butter on bun, mustard, tomato.	465	23

The other frequently ordered beef and pork menu items such as steaks, chili, and beef ribs are discussed within the "Barbeque and Steakhouse" chapter. Grilled quail, roast rabbit, and smoked pheasant are all very lean choices, but inquire about the sauces - they can add significantly to the calories and grams of fat.

Oriental dishes frequently appear on the menu in Southwestern cuisine restaurants. Stir-fried menu items such as Oriental stir-fry chicken can be ordered steamed or prepared with very little oil. Other suggestions are mentioned in the "Oriental" chapter.

Italian dishes, especially pasta, are also common in many Southwestern restaurants. Pesto is made from basil, pine nuts, and oil. A menu item such as "Angel Hair Pasta with Basil and Pine Nuts" should be ordered with very little oil. Pasta with tomato sauce is typically low fat; the calories and fat grams escalate rapidly when meat is added. A tomato sauce can often be substituted when a particular selection is made with alfredo sauce or other creamy sauce. If not, ask for the sauce to be served on the side.

Accompaniments

Baked potatoes are low in fat and calories; a medium sized potato will have only 200 calories and negligible fat. A huge potato weighing in at 1 pound (16 oz) will have 400 cals/< 1 gram fat. It's the butter, sour cream, and cheese that contribute most of the calories and fat. Baked and stuffed potatoes are discussed in the Barbeque chapter.

Char-grilled vegetables and steamed vegetables (without butter added) are both lean accompaniments.

Desserts

Fresh fruit for dessert is always a lean choice.

BRASSERIE

5150 Westheimer
(in JW Marriot Hotel)
961-1500

Informal Dining: B,L,D
Av: $10-20

Angel Hair Pasta - request to be prepared with chicken stock and without pinenuts. Meat portions at lunch and dinner are about 6 oz. **House Salad**, **Fresh Fruit**, or **Lettuce & Tomato** can be substituted for fries.

Request **Diet Vinaigrette Dressing** on the side for: **House Salad**, **Spinach Salad**, **Grilled Marinated Chicken Breast Salad**, or **J.W Salmon Salad** - 6 oz poached salmon with greens.

Lunch: **Chicken Burger** - ground skinless chicken breast. **Turkey Sandwich** on *sliced bread* instead of a croissant (request without bacon or mayonnaise). **Oriental Stir-fried Chicken** (ask for it to be prepared with chicken stock instead of oil). **Napa Valley Chicken**. **Fresh Swordfish Picatta**. **Fresh Red Fish Ponchartrain** - request plain crawfish and crab meat, not sauteed. **Grilled Salmon** with a black bean sauce that has no oil. **Brasseried Shrimp** (request them broiled). **Grilled Texas Tapas** (request no sauce).

Dinner: **Fruit Salad Platter** with low fat plain yogurt. **Snapper Sandwich** - request fish grilled without fat and bun toasted without butter. **Chicken Diablo** - 6 oz marinated grilled chicken. Request sauce on the side for: **Salmon Cilantro** with blackbean & corn salsa and **Snapper Sunrise**. All entrees are served with **Fresh Vegetable** (request to be prepared without any fats) and **Steamed Rice** or **Baked Potato**. **Fresh Fruit Plate** for dessert.

CHILI'S GRILL & BAR

13 restaurants in Houston area
for locations, call:
780-3611

Informal Dining: L,D
Av: $5-10

Will accomodate any special dietary request that a guest has. These requests can significantly decrease the number of calories and grams of fat that a menu item contains.

For example, Chili's Research & Development has provided the following information on three of their products:

Chicken Fajitas consisting of charbroiled chicken breasts, grilled onions, 3 flour tortillas, and pico de gallo (order without cheese, guacomole, and sour cream) contains 557 cals/9 gms fat.

Carribbean Chicken Salad with a substitute of **No-fat Vinaigrette Dressing** has only 374 cals/7 gms fat.

Grilled Chicken Platter includes a marinated chicken breast, pineapple slice, rice, steamed fresh vegetables, and cinnamon apples. As ordered, this platter has 742 cals/21 gms fat; without apples it has only 498 cals/11 gms fat.

DEVILLE RESTAURANT

1300 Lamar
(Downtown in Four Seasons Hotel)
650-1300

Formal Dining: B,L,D
Av: $15 and over

Diet Salad Dressings will be made to order. Breads brought to the table include: Cornbread, **Grain Bread**, and **Baguette**. Both **Skim Milk** and **Low Fat Milk** are available.

The menu has stars next to a variety of items that are reduced in calories (appetizer and entree does not exceed 555 calories for lunch or 650 calories for dinner). Some of these choices are listed below:

Appetizers: **Charred Anaheim Chili and Snapper Cake** in a tomato broth with cilantro and **Barbecued Pharaoh Quail on Baby Frissee** with a watermelon and onion salad.

Lunch entrees: **Charbroiled Breast of Chicken** glazed with a New Mexico chili syrup on a salad of spinach and sweet corn; **Grilled Filet of Salmon** on a honey lavender sauce with celery ribbons and charred corn; or **Black Olive Pasta with Fresh Organic Vegetables** sauteed in an olive oil infused with lemon and basil.

Dinner entrees: **Filet of Salmon** cooked campfire style nested on a pear, cucumber, and pickled beet salad and **Roasted Red Snapper in a Cornmeal Herb Crust** on tiny green beans and a carrot saffron sauce.

Steamed Vegetables can be ordered without any added fats. A **Fresh Fruit Plate** is available for dessert.

JACK'S ON WOODWAY

5055 Woodway
(Galleria area)
623-0788

Formal Dining: L,D
Av: $10-20

Unbuttered Bread can be requested instead of the usual. Some items on the menu are noted with a heart to be lower in cholesterol. **Black Bean Soup** has no oil added. **Radicchio, Arugula, and Fennel Salad** (request without walnuts or Parmesan cheese and dressing on the side).

Linguine "Tutti Fruitti Di Mare" - seafood is cooked with 1 T olive oil but can be cooked in white wine instead; marinara sauce is added. **Capellini with Marinated Roma Tomatoes** - request to be prepared without oil. **Capellini Primavera Marinara With Spring Vegetables** uses 1 T oil but can be prepared without any oil if you ask. **Steamed Asparagus** has no fats added.

Grilled fish is a 7 oz portion. Can request **Grilled Salmon or Red Snapper** without sauce. **Mahi Mahi** with papaya salsa can be prepared without any oil. **Farm Raised Catfish** - request no hushpuppies.

Smallest filet offered is the **Beef Tenderloin** at 8 oz. **Free Range Chicken Breast** has no oil in it's tomatillo sauce.

Fresh Berries are offered for dessert.

NICOLE'S CAFE

6540 San Felipe
(San Felipe & Voss)
780-1120

Casual Dining: L,D
Av: $7-15

Thick **White Bread** is served along with butter
(margarine is available upon request). **Grilled
Chicken Caesar** - 5 oz char-broiled breast strips
over a bed of romaine lettuce (request dressing on
the side). **Seafood Cobb Salad** - crabmeat, crawfish, shrimp, and tomato (request no avocado, egg,
or cheese); dressing is on the side.

Request no butter on the buns when grilling and
no mayonnaise for *all* sandwiches. **Grilled
Chicken Club** (ask for without cheese or bacon).
Sandwiches are served with potato chips and **Fresh
Fruit** - if you don't want potato chips, they will give
you more fruit.

Fresh Tomato Sauce and sauteed mushrooms
over whole egg fettucine. Any dish can be prepared
grilled without butter, such as **Grilled Jumbo
Shrimp.**

Fresh Fish of the Day, **Orange Roughy** and
Red Snapper (each about 8 oz) can be ordered to
be *grilled without butter* and served with grilled
tomatoes, onions, & poblano peppers along with
some **Steamed Vegetables** (request no butter
added). Or select a 5 oz **Grilled Chicken** entree.

Fresh Fruit or **Margarita Mousse** (egg whites,
lime rine and touch of triple sec and tequila at less
than 50 calories) for dessert.

OLD BAYOU INN

216 Heights Blvd
(Inside loop)
861-6300

Informal Dining: L,D
Av: $5-10

Request salad dressing on the side for all salads.
Dinner Salad consists of just vegetables. **Chicken Fajita Salad** contains 6 oz chicken (order without guacamole, cheese, or tostada chips). Homemade **Salsa** is available as a very low fat salad dressing.

All sandwiches come with french fries; **Vegetables** are available Mondays through Friday and can be substituted instead. A substitution of a **Salad** will cost a little extra. Request that the sandwich buns be grilled without butter. **Chargrilled Chicken Breast** is 6 oz (request no grilled onions, bacon, cheese, or mayo).

Request "Texan Dinners" with **Salad** and **Vegetables**. The **Bayou Delux Chicken** is 6 oz (request without cheese and for the onions to be cooked without butter).

PAPPY'S GRILL

9041 Katy Frwy &
2651 Richmond
827-1811/524-4410

Casual Dining: L,D
Av: $4-11

Salad dressings are served on the side of all salads. **House Salad** and **Grilled Chicken Salad** can be prepared without bacon bits, eggs, croutons, or cheese. Chicken salad has 6 oz of meat. **"Original" Chicken Sandwich** should be ordered without honey mustard dressing. **Chicken Chicken Fajita Taco** can ordered a la carte (without all the extras).

Hawaiian Chicken is served with rice, new potatoes, and cinnamon apples. **Southwestern Grill** is served with rice, char-grilled vegetables, and baked beans (request without sour cream).

New Potatoes can be prepared dry with seasonings. **Char-Grilled Vegetables** - only the grill is sprayed with a non-stick spray.

Fresh Strawberries are available in season.

RIVER CAFE

3615 Montrose
(Museum district)
529-0088

Casual Dining: L,D
Av: $8-18

Will gladly accomodate any special diet requests. **Ceviche** - seafood marinated in lime juice & spices. **Grilled Eggplant** - eggplant is cooked on active charcoal grill; served with cilantro marinara (made without oil). **Gazpacho Soup** is seasonal. Order salad dressing on the side for **Green River Salad** or **Hearts of Palm Salad**.

Vegetables are cooked in water that has oil added or can be requested *steamed.* **Smoked Brook Trout** is about 4 oz. **Smoked Chicken Salad** has about 3 oz chicken (request salad dressing on the side). **Steamed Vegetable Plate**. **Seafood Salad** has about 8 oz poached fish, ceviche, and *marinated* calamari on a lettuce bed. **River Cafe Pizza** is made with traditional dough, fresh vegetables, sundried tomatoes, and about 2 oz crumbled feta cheese.

Request marinara sauce for pastas such as: **Capellini with Grilled Fish**, **Pasta Primavera** (with fresh vegetables), or **Fettucine with Shrimp**. About 8 oz of meat is served with the "Specialties": **Grilled Seafood**, **Grilled Chicken Breast** - marinated in cilantro, garlic & topped with green tomatillo sauce; **Chicken River Cafe** (request *grilled* chicken instead and vegetables cooked without oil); or **Sauteed Sea Scallops** - grilled with less than 1 T oil (request no sauce). **Fresh Fruit** for dessert.

SAM'S CAFE OF HOUSTON

1800 Post Oak Blvd
(Galleria area)
622-9292

Casual Dining: L,D
Av: $10-20

Request salad dressings on the side for the **Sam's Salad** - mixed greens and fresh julienne vegetables. Average portion of meat entrees are 8 oz at both lunch and dinner; 6 oz in salads.

Steamed and/or Grilled Vegetables are available on the **Vegetarian Plate** or as a side order. **Vegetarian Plate** also has black beans and corn sauteed in chicken stock with wild rice.

Shrimp Pillow - homemade phyllo pillows stuffed with grilled shrimp & spinach, served with ancho chili sauce & sweet corn relish.

Pizzas are prepared in a traditional pizza oven using only about 1-1/2 oz of cheese for a 10" pizza. Request no brushing of garlic oil on the **Margherita Pizza**. **Pizza Primavera** with fresh vegetables has just a sprinkling of parmesean cheese.

Angel Hair Pasta and **Rigatini al Fresco** may add as much as 1-2 T of oil per serving (request that less be used).

Grilled Shrimp - marinated grilled shrimp on a bed of mushroom fettucine with a southwestern vegetable sauce. **Chinatown Chicken Salad** - mixed greens, grilled chicken, baby corn, snow peas, water chestnuts, and crispy rice noodles in a ginger sesame vinaigrette.

Chocolate & Vanilla Frogurt (all nonfat) or **Fresh Fruit**.

Brasserie

"WHATEVER IT TAKES"

When it comes to your health, the Brasserie Restaurant at the JW Marriott Hotel will do "Whatever It Takes" to accommodate your dietary needs. While many of our menu items are already geared toward today's health and fitness minded individuals, if it's not on our menu . . . just ask! We'll be happy to customize one of our meals to your liking.

Newly remodeled, and with recent International selections added to our menus, the Brasserie is more than just a hotel dining room. Our plant-filled atrium, decorative fountain, and gracious wait staff help to make your dining experience one of the best the Galleria area has to offer. Come visit us soon — reservations are optional, or call **961-1500** for more information.

JW MARRIOTT HOTEL
ON WESTHEIMER BY THE GALLERIA

5150 WESTHEIMER • HOUSTON, TEXAS 77056
(713) 961-1500

BARBEQUE & STEAKHOUSES

Beef in a book on how to dine low fat? That's right! Remember, everything in moderation. Lean beef, is in the same caloric range as skinless poultry, but it is still higher in saturated fat. However, lean beef is still part of a healthy diet if it is consumed just a few times a week.

The recommended portion size for all meats is 3 oz at lunch and 3 oz at dinner. An average portion size at restaurants is 6-8 oz so ask for a doggie bag with your meal.

Chicken and fish are often available at these traditional beef restaurants. Remove the skin from chicken before eating it. Fried fish isn't any leaner than prime rib, so order your fish grilled. Lettuce salads, coleslaw, and potato salad are frequently offered at both barbeque restaurants and steakhouses. For more details on ordering any of these non-beef foods, review the appropriate chapters within this book.

BARBEQUE

A barbeque plate has about 8 oz of meat; a sandwich usually includes 3-4 oz of meat. A sandwich is a better idea when trying to cut calories and fat because the portion size is smaller and it is not often served with all those fattening extras.

Always trim the visible fat when your order is delivered. An ounce of lean brisket has only 70 cals per ounce, while fatty brisket and sausage have close to 100 cals. Compare these examples before ordering:

	CALS	FAT (gms)
8 oz sausage	720	64
4 oz sausage	360	32
8 oz fatty brisket	800	72
4 oz fatty brisket	400	36
8 oz lean brisket	550	30
4 oz lean brisket	275	15

When comparing the "extras" offered with a plate, the best choices are lettuce and tomato salad with the dressing on the side and unbuttered corn on the cob. Bread can be requested unbuttered as well.

Beans are usually prepared with added fat such as bacon or sausage and each restaurant has their own secret recipe. Using data found in the USDA food composition tables, consider these selections:

	CALS	FAT (gms)
1 c beans with fat	300	15
1 c chili with beans	350	20
1 c chili without beans	400	30

Bottled barbeque sauces have about 25 cals/<1 gms fat per tablespoon. Restaurants may add more fat than that. It is always best to order the sauce on the side so you can control the portion served.

The usual barbeque stuffed baked potato is not a diet meal. Consider this:

	CALS	FAT (gms)
Huge baked potato	400	<1
2 T butter	200	22
2 T sour cream	50	5
4 T shredded cheese (1 oz)	110	9
2 oz barbeque meat and sauce	200	16
TOTAL:	**960**	**52**

BROWN SUGAR'S BAR-B-Q

10100 Kleckley
(will have new location soon)
944-6544

Casual Dining: L,D
Av: $5-10

Loaf Bread and **Fresh Baked Rolls** are low in fat. But chips and crackers are also served to the table.

For the BBQ lover who wants to have "just a little", menu items are offered in the menu section under "**For the Light Appetite**". Each meat entree is about 3 oz. To substitute **Baked Potatoes** for the other side orders, there is an additional upcharge.

This restaurant uses a RAIR (Rotating Air Cooking System) to cook some of their foods. This is a sealed cooking chamber that rotates hot air - it allows food to cook faster without additional grease. The **Chicken Breasts** and **Fish Filets** are cooked in a low fat way in this machine.

They also cook the Cajun Coated French Fries and the Battered and Fried Zucchini and Okra in the Rair instead of the fryer to produce a crisp product. These products are purchased *with fat added* to the potato, zucchini, and okra already. The Rair cooks them *without additional fat* and then actually draws some of the fat out of the product as well.

According to one research study, 10 pieces of french fries (1-1/2 oz) would have 110 cals/4.3 gms fat cooked in the Rair and 158 cals/8.3 gms fat when fried. While still not low calorie, it has significantly less calories and fat than their fried in grease counterpart.

EMBER'S BBQ

14741 Memorial Dr
(at Dairy Ashford)
497-0022

Casual Dining: L,D
Av: $5-10

Smoked BBQ Turkey Sandwich has no dressing. **Smoked BBQ Turkey and Chicken** are available for take-out by the pound. Plates include all high fat food items, but Texas toast is unbuttered. **Baked Potato** can be ordered with what you want on it - such as only sour cream and chives.

HICKORY BARN

11534 Wilcrest
(at Belfort)
530-9382

Casual Dining: L,D
Av: Under $5

Request salad dressing on the side for **Tossed Salad** and **Chef's Salad**. **Chef's Salad** is available with lean beef, ham, or smoked chicken. About 4 oz is on the small salad; approximately 6 oz meat is served on the large chef's salad. Request Chef's Salad without cheese and bacon.

Smoked Chicken Half can be ordered separately (remove skin). **Corn on the Cob** can be requested without butter. **Baked Potato** can be ordered dry.

HICKORY HOLLOW RESTAURANT

101 Heights Blvd &
10219 Fairbanks N Hou
869-6300/469-5323

Casual Dining: L,D
Av: $5-10

For both lunch and dinner, order **Broiled or Grilled Chicken** (6 oz) with **Baked Potato** - tell them what you want on it: bacon, chives, butter, sour cream, and cheese are available and **Salad** - you make your own. **Broiled or Grilled Chicken Sandwich** (4 oz) comes with lettuce & tomato or **Chef Salad with Grilled Chicken Strips**. **Grilled Catfish** can be ordered with baked potato and salad.

JOE'S BARBEQUE COMPANY OF PEARLAND

2911 E Broadway
(in Pearland)
485-4999

Casual Dining: L,D
Av: $5-10

Dinner Salad from the Cold Bar consists of a variety of raw vegetables, 4 kinds of fruit, and cottage cheese. **Diet Dressing** is also available.

BBQ Chicken (remove the skin) can be ordered ala carte to avoid the high fat additions on the Plate Dinner. **Diet Plates** are served with soup and salad; these include 8 oz **Grilled Chicken** or 7 oz **Grilled Catfish** with cajun seasoning.

Served with the **Salad Bar** and **Baked Potato** are: **Marinated Chicken** and **Blackened Catfish**. **Baked Potatoes** weigh about 16 oz each, but can be ordered dry.

STRACK FARMS RESTAURANT

5707 Louetta Rd
(near Kuykendahl)
376-0901

Casual Dining: L,D
Av: $5-10

Buttered bread is brought to the table but **Unbuttered Bread** can be requested. Request salad dressing on the side for the **Dinner Salad**. **Turkey Noodle Soup** is available most days.

Meat portions are about 6-7 oz. **Bar-B-Que**

Chicken Plate - be sure to remove the chicken skin. Can substitute a **Small Salad** and **Vegetables** for the potato salad and slaw. **Marinated Breast of Chicken** has no skin and is served with a small salad and vegetables. Vegetables are steamed but typically have some fat added. **Baked Potato** can be ordered dry.

Turkey Sandwich is made with 4 oz cold smoked turkey (request without cheese) on Texas Toast (ask that it be grilled without butter) with lettuce, pickle, tomato, and onion.

Dinner includes much of the same as well as **Broiled Snapper** and **Broiled Salmon**. Ask that these be prepared without margarine. Request *Unbuttered* Texas Toast, **Small Vegetable Salad**, and **Baked Potato**.

SWEET MEATS BAR-B-Q

12343 Murphy Rd, Stafford
(at W Airport Rd)
530-9190

Self-Service: L,D
Av: Under $5

Request **Unbuttered Bread**. Plates include 8 oz meat and include 2 vegetables. For leanest choice: **Smoked Chicken** (remove skin) with **Unbuttered Corn on the Cob** and **Baked Potato** (small substitution charge). Sandwiches consist of about 4 oz meat portions; leanest is **Turkey Sandwich**. Buy by the pound: **Smoked Turkey** or **Smoked Chicken**.

STEAKHOUSES

When ordering beef in a restaurant, there are three guidelines to keep your order lean. First, order a small portion. Secondly, order the leaner cuts of beef. And lastly, request your steak to be grilled without added fats.

Many restaurants are offering 4 and 6 ounce cuts of beef. Some restauranteurs reported that they cut their own beef and would be willing to serve *any* size requested. A petite steak of 3 or 4 oz would definitely be a leaner choice than the 16 ounce steak. If the smallest portion size offered is more than 4 ounces, bring home tomorrow's lunch in a doggy bag.

The cuts of beef that are lowest in fat are: top round, top loin, round tip, eye of round, sirloin, and tenderloin. On the menu, look for the smallest "filet". If the filet is wrapped with bacon, remove it before eating.

Most steaks are prepared on an open grill so some fat will cook out of the meat. When cooked on a flat top grill, additional fat may be added; request for no fats to be used.

Over a decade ago, high protein diets were so popular that restaurants started serving a "diet dish" consisting of a hamburger patty, cottage cheese, and a salad. The high protein diets have been discredited due to the high fat content. A more sensible selection would be a small filet with a salad and just 1 T of dressing.

BONNIE'S BEEF & SEAFOOD CO.

6867 Gulf Frwy
(Woodridge & I-45)
641-2397

Casual Dining: L,D
Av: $12 - 15

    Salad Bar has fruits and vegetables. **Low Calorie Italian Dressing** is available.
    Vegetable Platter consists of steamed broccoli, cauliflower, zucchini, squash, mushrooms, and tomatoes. **Grilled Chicken and Fish** are offered. The smallest steak is an 8 oz **Filet**. **Baked Potatoes** are available upon request.

BRENNER'S STEAKHOUSE

10911 Katy Frwy
(at the Westbelt)
465-2901

Formal Dining: L,D
Av: $25-30

    Leanest dishes are the **8 oz Grilled Filet**, **Broiled Fish Filet of the Day** (10-16 oz), and **Half a Chicken, Broiled** (remove the skin before eating).
    All dishes come with **Salad** (dressing is served on the side) and **Baked Potato** (request dry). **Steamed Broccoli** and **Asparagus** are also offered instead of potatoes. **Cold Asparagus Salad** is another option (request the dressing on the side).
    Fruit Salad can be ordered without the poppy-seed dressing.

CATTLE GUARD RESTAURANT & BAR

2800 Milam &
1010 N Hwy 6
520-6696/493-5094

Informal Dining: L,D
Av: $5-10

Sandwiches comes with french fries but **Salad** can be substituted (request **Diet Italian Dressing**). Buns are buttered before grilling (request no butter on buns). Lower fat sandwiches include: **Baked Ham** or **Sliced Turkey** (no cheese or mayonnaise) or **Filet of Chicken Sandwich** - grilled with lettuce and tomato. Chicken, fish, and the sandwiches listed above are 7-8 ounces meat portion.

Smoked Chicken is served with Mexicana rice. **Grilled Catfish** (request no lemon butter). **Hawaiian Chicken** is served over rice pilaf.

Fish can be grilled without any fats if requested. **Grilled White Fish** - halibut. Breads served include: cornbread, biscuits, and Texas Toast (can request toast without butter). **Drunken beans** is made with beer and no oil. **Baked Potatoes** are ala carte - they will ask you what you want on it.

When ordering a **Mexican Chicken Salad**, order without cheese and bacon, dressing on the side, and refrain from eating the fried shell.

Fresh Fruit is available for dessert.

FREY'S BEEF & BREW

1050 Uvalde Rd
(Northshore area)
453-2196

Casual Dining: L,D
Av: $5-10

Willing to accommodate any special requests.
Salad Bar offers a variety of **Fresh Fruits and
Vegetables**. **Lite Italian Dressing** is available.
Chicken De-Lite is a 6 oz boneless, skinless,
marinated chicken breast sandwich (request no
butter on buns and without cheese). **Grilled
Onions** can be prepared in wine only, no butter.
Baked Potato is 12-18 oz but can be ordered dry.
Marinated Chicken Breast is also available as
an entree; served with **Baked Potato**, **Dinner Roll**,
and **Salad**.
Fresh Fruit off the salad bar is available for
dessert.

GOLDEN CORRAL FAMILY STEAK HOUSE

4 restaurants in Houston area
for locations, call:
445-8700

Casual Dining: L,D
Av: $5-10

All you can eat Salad Bar with Raw Veg-
etables, Fresh Fruits, Cooked Vegetables, Soups, etc.
Many **Low Calorie Salad Dressings** are available:
Italian, French, Thousand Island, and Catelina.

Grilled Chicken (5 oz), **Chicken Teriyaki**, or **Chicken Italian** are available. Each is served with a **Baked Potato** (request plain) and **Texas Toast** (request dry).

Smallest beef portion is a 5-1/2 oz **Sirloin Steak**.

Minestrone and **Chicken Noodle Soup** are offered each day. Soup ladle is 3 oz.

Frozen dessert is ice cream, not yogurt.

HOFBRAU STEAKS

1803 Shepherd Dr
(1 block S of I-10)
869-7074

Casual Dining: L,D
Av: $10-15

House Salad (request without olives) should be ordered with dressing on the side.

Grilled Chicken is served with **White Rice**; chicken breasts are 6-8 oz skinless (request it to be grilled dry). Steaks should be ordered to be grilled without the butter sauce; the smallest and leanest cut of beef is a 5 oz **Filet**.

No baked potatoes are offered, only **Rice Pilaf** and fried potatoes.

LYNN'S STEAKHOUSE

955 1/2 Dairy Ashford
(between I-10 & Memorial)
870-0807

Formal: L,D
Av: over $20

Salad (lettuce, tomato, cucumber, and mushroom) comes with every entree; dressing is served on the side. **Unbuttered French Bread** is served with dinner.

Salmon, **Tuna**, and **Red Snapper** (10-14 oz) can be grilled dry with sauces on the side. **Lobster** can be ordered without drawn butter.

Asparagus and **Broccoli** are available without Hollandaise sauce, if requested. **Baked Potato** can be ordered dry. Other vegetables can be made available for a **Vegetarian Platter** if ordered in advance.

NEW TEXAS TUMBLEWEED

20814 Gulf Freeway
(in Webster)
332-7872

Casual Dining: L,D
Av: $8-18

Salad Bar offers **Fresh Fruits** and **Vegetables**. **Light Dressings** are offered: Ranch, Blue Cheese, and Italian.

Grilled Snapper and **Catfish** are served with sauteed vegetables, **Baked Potato**. **Grilled**

Chicken is served with **White Rice** (baked potato is extra). Smallest beef portion is 8 oz.

OLD SAN FRANCISCO STEAK HOUSE

8611 Westheimer
(between Hillcroft & Fondren)
783-5990

Formal Dining: L,D
Av: $13-25

Request salad dressing on the side for either the **Caesar** or the **House Salad**. **Low Calorie Ranch and French Dressings** are available. **Hot Sourdough Bread** and aged Swiss cheese are served at every table. **Shrimp Cocktail** and **Fresh Fruit Cup** are offered as appetizers.

Grilled Seafood is 8-1/2 - 9 oz: **Grilled Snapper**, **Grilled Swordfish**, and **Grilled Salmon** - request sauces on the side. Orders come with **Baked Potato** prepared as you desire. **Steamed Vegetables**. Smallest steak is the 6-1/2 oz **Filet** (ask them to remove the bacon).

OUTBACK STEAKHOUSE

5710 FM 1960 W
(near Champions Forest Dr)
580-4329

Casual Dining: D
Av: $10-20

Order the **House Salad** or **Caesar's Salad** without croutons and with salad dressing on the side.

Chicken on the Barbie is an 8 oz grilled chicken breast. **Grilled Fish** (10 oz) varies, but may be **Grilled Tuna** or **Grilled Swordfish**. The grilled chicken and fish are both brushed with vegetable oil prior to being flame grilled. Both entrees are served with **Fresh Vegetables** (request without seasoned butter).

Smallest steak is a 9 oz filet - seasoned and seared in clarified butter. **Baked Potato** (Jacket Potato) can be served dry upon request.

RUTH CHRIS STEAK HOUSE

6213 Richmond
(between Hillcroft & Fountainview)
789-2333

Casual Dining: L,D
Av: $17-29

Order salad dressing on the side and without croutons for **Garden Salad**. **Vegetables Platter**: broccoli, cauliflower, mushroom, and new potato (order without Hollandaise sauce). **Baked Potato** can be ordered as you wish.

Chicken Salad consists of broiled chicken (4 oz) with vegetables. **Broiled Chicken** is served with a medley of carrots, broccoli, and cauliflower (request no butter). **Swordfish** is 8 oz at lunch and 15-16 oz at dinner. Steaks should be ordered without oil or butter; an 8 oz filet is offered.

U R COOKS STEAKHOUSE

6100 Westheimer
(between Hillcroft & Chimney Rock)
266-9750

Casual Dining: L,D
Av: $13.95

Limited salad bar with lettuce, cherry tomatoes, and croutons. **Baked Potato Bar** allows you to dress your own. **Grilled Rainbow Trout**. **Grilled Chicken** (includes three 5 oz pieces). Smallest beef portion is 14 oz.

SEAFOOD

Fish and shellfish comprise the leanest "meat" category. However, the calories and grams of fat range widely within this group.

Specific fish and shellfish are often referred to as either lean fish and fatty fish. Even the fattier fish such as trout, salmon, and mackerel are not very high in calories, they simply have more fat than the white fishes like cod, flounder, and snapper. The fat found in fish, fish oil, is very unsaturated. Therefore, it is one of the "good" fats. One class of fats, omega-3 fatty acids, appear to be able to lower serum cholesterol and triglycerides.

The recent refinement of measuring procedures have demonstrated that shellfish does not have as much cholesterol as was once thought. Chicken and beef have about 70-80 mg per 3.5 oz portion; clams, mussels, oysters, scallops, and Alaska King Crab have even less. Comparing the same portions, Rock Lobster has 70 mg while Maine Lobster has 90 mg.

Shrimp and squid, however, are significantly higher in cholesterol. Shrimp has 150 mg and squid contains 230 mg cholesterol per 3.5 oz portion. Because shrimp and squid are so low in fat, they can still be included in a low fat/low cholesterol diet. Depending on what else is eaten, small portions once or twice a week would not be inappropriate. For comparison purposes, one egg yolk has about 250 mg cholesterol.

The addition of butter or other fats during food preparation raises the fat content of fish and shellfish significantly. In restaurants, fish is often brushed with butter before grilling, pan-fried in 1-2 tablespoons of fat, dipped (as with lobster) in a dish of melted butter, or deep fat fried in oil or fat.

Just one level tablespoon of butter or margarine (100 cals/11 gms of fat) can nearly double the calories found in a low fat fish dinner. While vegetable oils and margarine have no cholesterol, 1 T butter contributes another 33 mg cholesterol.

Request your fish order to be prepared with little or no butter or oil. Instead ask that it be seasoned with lemon, wine, and spices. If you want a large portion of fish, order the fish or shellfish from the Very Low Fat or Low Fat list. Compare the calories and fat grams of beef and chicken below with the list of fish and shellfish on the following page:

	CALS	FAT (gms)
4 oz White Chicken (no skin)	190	5
4 oz Dark Chicken (no skin)	210	9
4 oz Lean Round Beef	210	9
4 oz Prime Rib Beef	400	35

Nutritional Information for 4 oz Edible Portion
of Fish and Shellfish:

		<u>CALS</u>	<u>FAT (gms)</u>
Very Low Fat:		90-120	1-3

Clams	Red Rockfish
Cod	Red Snapper
Crab Legs	Redfish
Flounder	Scallops
Grouper	Shark
Haddock	Shrimp
Halibut	Sole
Langostino	Squid
Lobster	Surimi
Mahi Mahi	Tilefish
Monkfish	Tuna
Perch	Turbot
Pollock	

Low Fat: 100-160   4-6

Ocean Perch	Rainbow Trout
Bass	Sockeye Salmon
Bluefish	Swordfish
Mussels	Yellowfin Tuna
Oysters	

Medium Fat: 120-200   7-12

Catfish	Norwegian Salmon
Lake Trout	Pompano
Mackerel	

High Fat: 200-400   15-40

Fried Calamari	Fried Oysters
Fried Clams	Fried Shrimp
Fried Fish	

ANCHORAGE

2504 North Loop West
(5 minutes N of Galleria)
688-4411

Formal Dining: B,L,D
Av: $10-20

Unbuttered Bread is brought to the table with butter; margarine may be requested instead. Ask for salad dressing on the side. **Skim Milk** is available.

Grill Selections (such as **Mahi Mahi**, **Yellowfin Tuna**, **Grilled Gulf Shrimp**, **Boneless Chicken Breast**, **Halibut Steak**, and many other specials) can be requested to be grilled without any butter. The restaurant will still flavor the fish with herbs and spices. You may still want to ask for the sauces on the side. They are willing to make a **Seasoned Skim Milk "Cream" Sauce** - skim milk thickened with cornstarch and seasoned. Add the sauce to your grilled red snapper, sole, or scrod for an alternative topping.

Luncheon portions are 7-8 oz and dinner portions are 10 oz. You may order **Half Portions** at a discounted price. These entrees come with a **Steamed Vegetables** (no fat is added), **Potato du Jour** (usually red-skinned **Potatoes** with butter but can request without), or rice of the day (seasoned with vegetables and butter). At dinner, ask that the **Chicken Celestine** or the **Shrimp Diane** be prepared without oil, only white wine.

BOCA DEL RIO SEAFOOD

6508 Washington
(I-10 at 610)
862-8622

Informal Dining: L,D
Av: $10-20

French Bread can be requested unbuttered.
Fat-Free Crackers are also offered. **Oysters on
the Half Shell, Boiled Shrimp**, and **Shrimp
Cocktail** are available for appetizers.

Request salad dressing on the side of the **Salad**,
and without cheese, croutons, or bacon. Request
the dressing on the side when ordering **Lump
Crabmeat Salad** and **Tuna Salad** - and ask for
without the egg.

Willing to do special requests. Meat portions are
about 8-10 oz. **Mesquite Grilled** choices include:
Shrimp and Lobster (ask that the linguini be
prepared without oil), **Shrimp** (request no bacon),
and **Grilled Chicken Breast**.

Request no lemon butter when ordering **Mesquite Grilled Red Snapper, Catfish**, or other
Catch of the Day. Blackened Fish and **Blackened Chicken** can be prepared without any oil.

A **4 oz Filet Mignon** can be requested. **Vegetables of the Day** and **Baked Potato** is available
without any fats, if you ask.

LAVACA BAY

474 S HW 6
(West Houston)
558-0600

Informal Dining: L,D
Av: $8-20

For appetizers: **Shrimp Cocktail, Boiled Shrimp, Oysters on the Half Shell**. Sandwiches are served with **Salad** and french fries. Request **Steamed Vegetables of the Day** to be substituted instead of the fries.

Sandwiches include: **Lavaca's Blackened Fish Sandwich** (6 oz piece) or **Grilled Chicken Breast** - 7 oz served with a honey mustard sauce made with no oil.

Broiled or blackened meats are brushed with oil but can be prepared without oil if you ask. These fish can be prepared broiled or blackened: **Shrimp, Fresh Fish of the Day, Flounder, Green Lake Catfish**, or **Snapper**. Request the sauces on the side. If you order a **Baked Potato**, tell the server what you want added.

The smallest cut of beef (6 oz) is the **Small Filet Mignon** (request that it be cooked without the bacon). **Fresh Fruit** is available seasonally.

PAPPAS SEAFOOD HOUSE

5 in Houston & 2 Little Pappas
Call for locations:
784-4729

Informal Dining: L,D
Av: $10-20

Appetizers: **Cold Boiled Shrimp**, **Fresh Gulf Oysters**, **Shrimp Cocktail**, and **Crabmeat Cocktail** - all are served with red sauce.

Request salad dressing on the side for: **Dinner Salad**, **Shrimp Salad**, **Crabmeat Salad**, or **Combination Salad** (with shrimp and crabmeat). The above fish salads are simply boiled fish over a green salad.

Request no olives or feta cheese and dressing on the side when ordering the **Greek Salad**.

Live Lobster or **Lobster Tail** without drawn butter are available. **Baked Potato** is 16-22 oz but can be dressed as you wish.

Oven Broiled Fish is the leanest; a perforated baking dish is used to cook the fish and a scampi butter blend is poured over the top of the fish. Instead of the usual toppings of seafood in a butter sauce request the respective seafood to be boiled, and used as a simple topping instead.

The two heart healthy entrees listed are: **Oven Broiled Fillet** - a 10 oz fish fillet seasoned with olive oil, lemon, oregano, and spices. **Jardin Fillet** - fresh garden vegetables in olive oil and spices.

Fresh Fruit is available upon request.

PLATTERS SEAFOOD BAR & GRILL

8125 Katy Frwy
(W of 610 Loop at Wirt Rd)
683-7226

Informal Dining: L,D
Av: $10-20

For appetizer: **Boiled Gulf Shrimp** or **Gulf Shrimp Cocktail**. Salad dressings are brought on the side. **Chicken Salad** - 6 oz boneless, skinless chicken; **Tossed Salad** (request no cheese toast); **Platters' Salad** - includes 4 shrimp and 2 oz lump crab (ask for without egg), or **Jumbo Lump Crabmeat Salad** - 4 oz crabmeat.

Mesquite Grilled Seafood is an 8 oz portion. There are 8-10 fish specials each day. **Fresh Swordfish Filet, Grilled Catfish, Fresh Gulf Red Snapper, Rainbow Trout, Frog Legs, Gulf Shrimp, Mesquite Grilled Seafood Platter** (6 oz fish filet, 4 shrimp, and 3 frog legs), or **Live Maine Lobster** (ask for no drawn butter). Grilled fish is brushed with oil (request to be prepared without oil, but still seasoned).

Blackened Fish of the Day - filet is dipped in olive oil and then spices before blackening. Can not be prepared with less fat, but be sure to ask for no drawn butter. Dishes come with dirty rice or rice pilaf but you may request **White Rice**. Request no butter on **Steamed Vegetables**.

Fresh Fruit - ask for without whipped cream.

RED LOBSTER

19 restaurants
in the Houston area,
Call for locations

Casual Dining: L, D
Av: $5-10

Request salad dressing on the side of your salad. **Low Calorie Blue Cheese and Ranch Dressings** are available. Request dry **Baked Potato** and **Steamed Vegetables** without butter or sauce.

A wide variety of fresh fish are available daily. Lunch portion is about 4-5 oz; dinner portion is 8-10 oz cooked. Fish are available **Grilled**, **Broiled**, or **Blackened** such as **Broiled Flounder**, **Broiled Sea Scallops**, and **Grilled Halibut Steak**. Fish are brushed with butter in each case.

Venetian Flounder - baked with Italian herbs, Parmesan cheese, and fresh mushrooms. **Shrimp Seville** - shrimp with fresh tomatoes, black olives, green peppers, and red onions in a zesty tomato sauce over linguini. **Flounder Veracruz** - broiled fillets topped with a seasoned blend of tomatoes, olives, peppers, and onions.

Live Maine Lobster - order steamed. **Alaskian Snow Crab Legs** or **King Crab Legs**. Request each of these without the drawn butter.

Grilled Chicken Breasts - 8 oz. **Grilled Chicken and Shrimp** - 4 oz chicken with shrimp.

WILLIE G'S SEAFOOD RESTAURANT

1605 Post Oak
(Galleria area)
840-7190

Informal Dining: L,D
Av: $10-20

Shrimp Cocktail, Lump Crab Cocktail, Crawfish Cocktail, and **Oysters on the Half Shell** should be requested with red sauce. Lower fat salads are the **Lettuce and Tomato Salad** and the **Sliced Tomato Salad** (dressing comes on the side). **Lump Crab Salad, Shrimp Salad,** or the **Shrimp and Lump Crab Salad** are just the seafood and lettuce. Salads are available at an appetizer (small) size or as a meal (large).

All Broiled Seafood (**Whole Gulf Flounder, Swordfish Steak, Speckled Trout Filet, Gulf Red Snapper, Broiled Shrimp, Broiled Scallops**) and **Charbroiled Chicken Breast** can be broiled dry without butter. Or you may want to ask them to use lemon juice.

Fish filets are about 8 ounces; chicken about 8 ounces. Available with a choice of six different sauces (request sauces on the side since all are high in fat).

Steamed Live Maine Lobster would also be a good lowfat choice without the drawn butter. **Baked Potato** is served with all condiments on the side. **Vegetable of the Day** (green beans and new potatoes) - you can request no butter or bacon.

Fresh Berries are available for dessert.

SALAD BARS

It is often a misconception of people watching their weight that salads are low calorie meals. It *can* be, but more often the dieter chooses the wrong items and end up with far more calories than even a hamburger and fries.

Salad

The lettuce, other raw vegetables, and fresh fruit are very low in calories and fat. But, additions like mayonnaise-type salads (potato salad, macaroni salad); marinated vegetables (cucumbers, mushrooms); and salad dressings (even the Light ones) can really add up the total calories and grams of fat.

Salad Dressing

Typically, the Low Calorie or Light dressings available at salad bars are not the Fat-Free or the Very Low Calorie dressings that are available at the grocery store. Instead, they may have almost as many calories and fat grams as the regular variety. Ask the manager about the specific brand used in their salad bar area. Very low calorie and no-fat options for a salad include Picante Sauce, Lemon, and Flavored Vinegars (such as red wine, balsamic, and tarragon vinegars).

Soups

Most salad bars also offer soups; the broth-type soups are typically lower in fat and calories than the creamy variety. The cream soups in this chapter have been analyzed with *milk* added, if *cream* has been used, the cals/fat grams will be much higher, some can be as high as 400-500 calories per cup.

Breads and Muffins

Muffins and breads are often much higher in calories and grams of fat than most people think. Yeast rolls are very similar to bread and can be expected to have about 80 calories/0 gms fat *per ounce* (the equivalent of a slice of bread).

Muffins, cornbread, and sweet breads have eggs and fat added. They are also denser than yeast rolls. For these two reasons, they have a much higher calorie content per piece. Expect them to have about 100-125 cals/3-5 gms fat *per ounce*. A *small* muffin that is in a cupcake cup and extends no higher than the cup itself is 1 or 1-1/2 oz; if it "mushrooms over" expect it to be 2 or 2-1/2 oz. A softball size muffin is 3-4 oz. A 2 inch cube of cornbread is about 1 oz.

On the next few pages you will find nutritional information for most of the food items available at a salad bar. Information was obtained from USDA food composition tables and not from the restaurants directly.

First, let's look at how a plate of salad increases in calories and grams of fat as it gets built. A salad can start off low calorie (but not necessarily low fat):

	CALS	FAT (gms)
Basic Salad:		
2 c Raw Vegetables	100	0
1/4 c Cottage Cheese	60	5
2 T Chickpeas	20	0
2 T Shredded Cheese	60	5
2 T Salad Dressing	160	16
1 Spoon Croutons	45	3
1/2 c Fresh Fruit	50	0
SUBTOTAL:	**495**	**29**
Unless you add extras such as:		
1/4 c Potato Salad	100	7
1/4 c Broccoli/Caul/Ranch	100	9
2 extra T Salad Dressing	160	16
SUBTOTAL:	**855**	**61**
And then have just one:		
Blueberry muffin (small)	120	4
GRAND TOTAL:	**975**	**65**

Not too low calorie is it? Keep these numbers in mind when you build your salad.

SALAD BARS

NUTRITIONAL INFORMATION FOR
SALAD BAR ITEMS:

(Keep in mind that all portions are for level
measures - not heaping!)

	CALS	FAT (gms)
1/2 c Fresh Fruit	50	0
1/2 c Raw Vegetables	25	0
5 Olives	25	3
1 T Croutons	15	1
1 T Bacon Bits	30	2
1 spoon Chow Mein	15	1
1 spoon Sunflower Seeds	40	3
2 T Chopped Egg	30	2
2 T Chickpeas (Garbanzo)	20	0
1/4 c Cole Slaw	80	5
1/4 c Macaroni Salad	110	7
1/4 c Potato Salad	100	7
1/4 c Tuna Salad	190	10
1/4 c Fluff	15	0
1/4 c Jello	40	0
1/4 c Pudding	80	2
1/4 c Mixed Fruit Salad	80	2
1/4 c Three Bean Salad	100	5
1/4 c Pea Salad	70	6
1/4 c Broccoli/Caul/Ranch	100	9
1/4 c Rotelli Pasta Salad	110	5
1/4 c Cottage Cheese	60	5
2 T Ham	20	1
2 T Shredded Cheese	60	5
2 T Parmesan Cheese	45	3

Salad Dressings (1 T):
(most ladles = 2-4 T)

Blue Cheese	80	8
French	80	9
Honey Mustard	85	9
No Oil Dressings	6-12	0

	CALS	**FAT (gms)**
Low Calorie Dressings	30-50	3-5
Italian	80	9
Olive Oil	120	14
Oil and Vinegar	70	8
Ranch	60	5
Thousand	60	5
Vinegar	2	0

SOUPS (1 c):

Bean w/Bacon Soup	175	6
Cheese Soup	230	15
Chicken Noodle Soup	80	2
Clam Soup	125	7
Cream of Chicken	200	12
Tomato Soup	160	6
Tomato Bisque	200	7
Vegetable Soup	70	2

BREADS

Blueberry muffin (small)	120	4
Bran muffin (softball size - 3 oz)	360	12
Cornbread (2" X 2")	130	3
Gingerbread (2" X 2")	100	2
Yeast Roll (small - 1 oz)	80	1
Yeast Roll (large - 2 oz)	160	2

FATS

1 t margarine/butter	35	4
1 T margarine/butter	100	11

LETTUCE EAT

1020 FM 1960 W
(W of I-45)
537-8969

Casual Dining: L,D
Av: $5-10

All you can eat Buffet. **Salad Bar** offers a variety of **Fresh Vegetables** and **Fresh Fruits**. Four **Kraft Fat-Free Dressings** are available each day: **Italian, French, Thousand Island**, and **Ranch**.

Soups: Four soups are offered each day; two are **Broth-Based Soups**. Serving size ladle is 8 oz.

Bread: **Unbuttered Rolls**, Garlic Rolls, **Corn & Blueberry Muffins**, and Chocolate Chip Cookies.

Other: **Pasta Bar** offers **Spaghetti with a Tomato Sauce** or **Spaghetti with a Meat Sauce**. **Baked Potatoes** (10 oz) are dry; you add the toppings as desired.

Yogurt: **Low Fat Frogurt**, self-serve.

LETTUCE SOUPRISE YOU

10001 Westheimer
(between Briarpark & Beltway 8)
974-6552

Casual Dining: L,D
Av: $5-10

All-you-can-eat self-service **Salad Bar** with three kinds of lettuce, a variety of fresh cut veggies, and freshly prepared meat, vegetable and pasta salads.

Four Weight Watchers light dressings are rotated:
Poppyseed, **Italian**, **Ranch**, and **French**. Ladles
are 1 oz (2 T) each.

Soups: Rotating menu of homemade **Soups** are
available each day, including **Vegetable Soup.** Soup
Ladle is 4 oz.

Other: **Baked Potatoes**

Bread: Homemade muffins, **Pita Bread** and
Wheat Rolls.

Dessert: **Fruit Bar** with seasonal fruits.

SOUPER SALAD RESTAURANT

10 locations in Houston area
for more information, call:
453-3912

Casual Dining: L,D
Av: $5-10

Self-service **Salad Bar**. Three **Fat-Free Salad
Dressings** are available - **French**, **Italian**, and
Ranch. Dressing ladle is 1 oz. **Fresh Fruit** is also
available.

Soups: Four are offered each day; 2 are **Broth-
based Soups**. Ladle size is 8 oz.

Bread: **Blueberry Muffins**, **Corn bread**, and
Ginger Bread.

Other: Self-serve **Baked Potatoes**. You can
"dress" yours with **Picante Sauce** and **Vegetables**.

SUPREME SOUP & SALAD

4 locations in Houston area:
for more information, call:
785-1155

Casual Dining: L,D
Av: $5-10

Crystal Light is available in addition to **Diet Coke**. Self-service **Soup and Salad Bar** offers **Fat-Free Italian and French Dressings** as well as **Low Calorie Ranch and House Dressing**. **Fresh Fruit** is on the Salad Bar.

Soup: Six soups are available each day - 3 are broth-based. Portion size is 12 oz.

Breads: **Cornbread, Gingerbread, Unbuttered French Bread**, and **Blueberry Muffin**.

Other: **Turkey** or **Ham Sandwiches** (request no cheese) are served; light mayonnaise is available. **Baked Potato** - you dress your own.

Dessert: **Fresh Fruit** or **Non Fat Frozen Yogurt**.

INTERNATIONAL

The theme, atmosphere, and food selections in most restaurants can be traced to a specific country or region. The wide variety of restaurants in this chapter have the flavor of so many countries that it can be best be termed "eclectic".

Below are some suggestions for Dinin'Lean® in international restaurants. More specific guidelines will be found in the chapter related to the particular cuisine.

Always order the salad dressing on the side of your salad. Request additional information about the components of the salad; some of the higher fat items may be omitted.

Sandwiches should be ordered dry, with the dressings on the side, so you can control the amount to be added.

Avoid the fried foods. Entree servings are often 6 - 10 oz meat portions so choose the leaner offerings such as chicken fajitas, grilled chicken, or baked fish. Steamed vegetables, plain rice, or dry potato are frequently available. Ask that little or no oil/fats be used in the preparation of your dishes; request all sauces on the side.

BARRONS/UNIVERSITY CLUB

4600 Calhoun
(U of H Hilton College)
749-1690

Formal Dining: L,D
Av: $10-20

Lunch offers a variety of lower fat salads (ask for dressing on the side). Salads include: **Tossed Green Garden Salad**, **Crab Louise** - fresh crab and lettuce only, **Smoked Turkey and Artichoke Salad**, **Fruit Platter** - fresh fruit with **Sorbet** or **Cottage Cheese**, and **Grilled Chicken Salad** with 4 oz chicken (request no pistachio nuts or egg).

Sandwiches include: **Smoked Turkey** (request on bread instead of a croissant and without mayonnaise) and **Cajun Chicken Grill** (request sauce on side).

Hot entrees include **Steamed Vegetables** (no fats are added). **Grilled Tuna** is about 4 oz; sauce is made of thickened, concentrated orange juice with ginger but no fat.

Dinner features several food choices from the country chosen for that particular evening; it may be difficult to accommodate special dietary requests. **Grilled Chicken** is always available with **Steamed Rice**.

BOMBAY BICYCLE CLUB CAFE & BAR

9110 Southwest Frwy
(SW Houston)
776-3512

Casual Dining: L,D
Av: $5-10

Has a "Yes I Can" program - whatever the consumer wants, they'll get. Ask them to weigh/measure foods (most meats are 8 oz); half portions are available for a discounted price.

Appetizer: **Punjabi Chicken or Beef Kabobs** - 5 oz meat charbroiled on a grill with rice noodles and peanut sauce on the side (peanut sauce is high in fat). Request **Diet Ranch Dressing** on the side for all salads. **House Dinner Salad** (ask for no croutons). **Grilled Chicken Salad** includes 5 oz meat and 2 oz cheese (can request no cheese).

No oil is used for either chargrilling or blackening **Chicken** or **Fresh Fish**. **Chicken Fajitas** includes 5 oz meat, tortillas, ranch-style beans, and rice pilaf (request **Plain Rice**); request without guacamole or sour cream. **Teriyaki Chicken** - chargrilled chicken with a Teriyaki glaze, served with vegetables and Indian rice (can request **Plain Rice** instead).

Mayonnaise comes on the side for all sandwiches. **Cajun Blackened Chicken Sandwich**. **Grilled Chicken Sandwich** (request no Swiss cheese and that the mushrooms to be cooked without oil). A special of 6 oz **Top Sirloin** is offered most days.

Fresh Steamed Vegetables, **Parsleyed New Potatoes**, and **Baked Potatoes** are available without fat if you ask.

INTERNATIONAL

DEERFIELD'S

6580 Fannin
(in Marriot/Medical Center)
796-0080

Casual Dining: B,L,D
Av: $5-10

Soups: **Beef or Chicken Broth**; Chicken
Noodle Soup is roux based, therefore, is high in fat.
Appetizers: **Shrimp Cocktail, Grilled Vegetable
Fajita** - vegetables marinated in a minimal amount
of oil and charbroiled, served with 2 flour tortillas.

Fresh Fruit Plate is served with **Honey
Yogurt Dressing** made with nonfat plain yogurt.
Stuffed Tomato - with shrimp or chicken salad
(mixed with light mayonnaise) garnished with fresh
vegetables. **Grilled Swordfish** (4 oz) **and Spinach Salad** (request the dressing on the side).
Shrimp Pasta Salad - boiled shrimp pieces and
corkscrew pasta tossed in an Italian marinade.

Sandwiches are served with chips or fries. You
can substitute **Steamed Vegetables** upon request.
Swordfish Sandwich - ask for without the tartar
sauce. **Chicken Breast Sandwich** - 6 oz grilled
chicken served on wheat bread with lettuce and
tomato. **Open Face Turkey Sandwich** - toasted
English muffin, 3 oz turkey, spinach, and shredded
carrot.

Entrees include **Grilled Shrimp** - on rice pilaf,
Fresh Salmon - broiled or poached, **Herbed
Chicken Breast** - grilled chicken and served on
rice pilaf, and **Stir Fry Chicken** - stir fried chicken
and vegetables served with rice.

For dessert: **Orange Sherbet** or **Fresh Berries**.

RAGS BAR & GRILL

14933 Bellaire Blvd
(SW Houston)
561-5074

Casual Dining: L,D
Av: $5-10

Request salad dressing on the side for **House Salad**. **Chicken Salad** (4 oz charbroiled chicken) comes with **Pico de Gallo** as a dressing (request no guacamole or sour cream to be served). Can also request the Chicken Salad to be served on a plate rather than on the usual fried flour tortilla shell.

Fajita Platter - can split a half pound serving with another person. Request no guacamole or sour cream and *fresh* onions, tomatoes, and green peppers instead of *sauteed*. Or order **Tacos al Carbon** (fajita meat rolled in flour tortilla) ala carte.

Spaghetti with Meatballs in Red Sauce includes 5 oz of meatballs but you can request less. Request unbuttered bread instead of garlic bread.

Chicken Burger - 6 oz charbroiled chicken served with lettuce, tomato, pickles, and onions. **Baked Potato** can be dressed as you request.

HEALTH FOOD & VEGETARIAN

There is no one definition of "health food" but rather a whole gamut of descriptions. The common perception is that health food refers to getting back to nature.

That approach may consist of cutting out all red meats, while still eating chicken and fish. A lacto-ovo vegetarian diet includes eggs, milk, and cheese but no meat (beef, chicken, or fish) at all. Vegan diets are defined as no meat (beef, chicken, or fish) or meat products (cheese, eggs, and milk).

Health food usually refers to whole grains rather than the refined grains. Wheat, corn, rice, and other grains are presented whole; this includes the germ and bran. More legumes and vegetables are also offered.

Fruits and fresh fruit juices are often increased in quantity when eating healthy. Fruit juices are high in vitamins and minerals but if you are watching your weight, keep in mind that juices, ounce for ounce, have just as many calories as soda pop. Both have about 100 calories per 8 oz; the fat content is negligible.

Not everyone is willing to give up meat and the

meat products, but going without eating meat can be a desirable alternative. Even if it means giving up meat for just one meal every week or so.

Leaving off the meat and substituting more whole grains, legumes, and vegetables can definitely be a healthier alternative. Vegetarian and health foods can still be high in calories and fat, especially when cheeses, nuts, or excess oil is used in the preparation.

Cheeses have about 100 cals/8 gms fat per ounce. This is twice as many calories and fat as lean chicken and beef. Some lower fat cheeses are available in the grocery store but are not used in most restaurants. Part skim cheeses are equivalent to lean chicken and beef at about 50-75 cals/5 gms fat per ounce.

Seeds and nuts are healthy because they are high in fiber as well as vitamins and minerals. They are also a good source of protein for vegetarians but they are not low calorie.

Seeds and nuts have between 200 to 250 calories per handful or 1/4 c portion. Pumpkin seeds and pine nuts are on the lower end of the scale (200 cals/16 gms fat). Peanuts, almonds, cashews, and sunflower seeds comprise the midrange (225 cals/ 20 gms fat). Pecans and macadamia nuts are the highest in fat and calories (250 cals/27 gms fat).

A MOVEABLE FEAST

2202 West Alabama
(at Greenbriar)
528-3585

Casual Dining: L,D
Av: Under $5-10

    Menu consists of vegetarian foods, chicken, salad, and tuna salad - no red meats. Those foods prepared without any added fats include: **Steamed Vegetables**, **Pinto Beans**, **Black Beans**, **Organic Brown Rice**, **Beans & Rice**, **Greens**, **Soups of the Day**, **Vegetarian Chili**, and **Gazpacho** (chilled soup).

    Sandwiches and burgers include about 1 T eggless mayonnaise (50 cals/5 gms fat) on **Whole Wheat Bread** or **Whole Wheat Pita**. The mayonnaise can be left off if desired. Sandwiches and burgers are served with corn chips but you can request rice crackers (which are made without fat) instead.

    The sandwich choices include: **Tuna with Celery & Onion** or **Hummus** - mashed chickpea with a small amount of oil. **Happy Burger** (413 cals/11 gms fat) or **Tempeh Burger** (481 cals/11 gms fat) are both vegetarian.

    Salads include the **Tossed Salad** and the **House Green Salad**. You select your own dressing; a no-oil **Lemon Tahini Dressing** is available. Although blackboard specials change daily, the **Macrobiotic Plate** is generally low in fat.

    Frozen Yogurt is really the brand "Skinny Dip".

HEALTH FOUNTAIN RESTAURANT

1331 August Drive
(in Post Oak YMCA)
266-7600

Casual Dining: B,L
Av: Under $5

Fruit, **Fresh Juices**, **Smoothies**, and **Home-made Muffins** are available - they are described in the Breakfast chapter. **Salads** are plenty; all dressings are fat-free. Soups are all water-based (no fats added) and include: **Vegetable Medley** and **Vegetarian Chili**.

Lite mayonnaise or mustard is served on the sandwiches upon request. Sandwiches include: **The Augusta** - chicken salad, alfalfa sprouts, shredded cabbage, and carrots plus seasoning on honey wheat bread. **The Neptune** - tuna salad, bean sprouts, and seasonings on honey wheat bread (request without sunflower seeds or swiss cheese).

The Garden - lettuce, tomatoes, fresh mushrooms, carrots, cabbage, alfalfa sprouts, cucumbers, and seasonings on honey wheat bread. **Tuna Salad** and **Chicken Salads** are described as "almost dry" with just enough *light* mayonnaise to keep it together.

Vegetarian meals include: **Red Beans & Rice**, **Steamed Veggie Plate with Organic Rice** & Whole Wheat Cornbread. All of these are prepared without fats except for the cornbread which is very high in fat.

WONDERFUL VEGETARIAN RESTAURANT

7549 Westheimer
(at Hillcroft, Galleria area)
977-3137

Casual Dining: L,D
Av: $5-10

This is a Chinese vegetarian restaurant; any reference to a meat is actually an imitation item. Calorie and protein estimates (but not fat) are listed for over half the menu items. Every dish on the menu can be requested to be steamed or sauteed without any oil. Best to avoid (or ask for different preparation) for fried items. **Pickled Cabbage** is brought to the table. Orders come with **Steamed White or Brown Rice**.

Appetizers include: **Seaweed Sushi** (100 cals) and **Steamed Dumplings** (178 cals). Dishes are made up of lots of vegetables, bean curd (tofu), imitation shrimp & squid (potato flour & carrots) and imitation fish (soybean sheets & seaweed).

Dishes include: **Sauteed Marinated Mushrooms & Vegetables** or also called Vegetarian Steak (365 cals); **Hot & Spicy Fish Rolls** (398 cals); **Wheat Gluten & Broccoli in Szechuan Style** (380 cals); **Stewed Wheat Gluten in Curry Sauce** (374 cals); **Sesame Chicken**; **Sauteed Mushrooms, Bamboo Shoots & Tree Mushrooms in Spicy Sauce** (376 cals); **Moo Goo Soybean Gluten** (375 cals); **Vegetable Lo Mein** and **Sauteed Eggplants in Spicy Ginger Sauce**.

HOME DELIVERY & CARRY OUT

Many restaurants listed in this book offer catering to large groups and will accommodate pick up orders. These services were not addressed due to the scope of this book.

How many times have you just not felt like cooking, but the only other option you could think of was to call for a pizza. Well here's five other options!

These companies are part of a new and emerging category of food establishments that offers you an alternative to dining out. One of these restaurants offers a pick-up service for their homemade pasta and pasta dishes; there is no server or tables that we have become accustomed to in traditional restaurants. You can buy a whole pan of low-fat lasagna in quantities adequate for more than one meal.

Four other companies listed in this classification deliver food to your front door. Most focus on delivering only healthy food. What could be easier than Dinin'Lean® in Houston without leaving your home?

BUSHEL & PECK

222-1915

Offers "delivered dining"; presently limited to areas within the loop. Although not all foods on the menu are low fat, several entrees can still be appropriate.

Entrees include: **Breast of Chicken** (skinless) and **Orange Roughy Filet**; each is a 4-1/2 - 5 oz portion. **Skinless Roast Chicken** is also available.

Choose from the sauces that have little (less than 1 t) or no fat: **Bigarade** (zest of lemon & orange in a brown base), **Robert** (flavored with dijon mustard and capers), **Madeira** (dark brown sauce with madeira wine), and **Au Poivre** (black pepper and mushrooms). **Broccoli Florets, Parsleyed New Potatoes**, and **Carrots** are steamed in approximately 1 T of butter but this can be drained off if requested. **Sweet Corn with Peppers** and **Green Beans** also have added butter.

Garden Salad consists of lettuce, red bell pepper, carrots, black olive, and a sprinkle of sesame seed. **French Country Roll** is available.

DIET GOURMET

3435 Westheimer
(at Buffalo Speedway)
850-0900

This company concentrates on keeping all of their food low fat (23% of total cals), low sodium (1221 mg per 1000 cals), and low cholesterol (112 per 1000 cals). All food is made from scratch.

Meals are individually packaged in microwave safe containers and is calorie regulated on a computer. You can order 1 to 21 meals a week. Food can be picked up at different sites or can be delivered throughout Houston for a nominal fee.

Breakfasts include: **Zucchini Muffin, Bagel with D.G. Cream Cheese, Fruity Oatmeal, Rice Ambrosia, Blintzes with Fruit Sauce,** or **Blueberry Bran Muffin,** with **Fresh Fruit** or **Juice**.

Lunches include: **Greek Salad and Wheat Bread; Pasta Primavera and Orange Wedges; Pita Veggie Sandwich, Almond Dressing, and Grapes; Potato Bean Salad, Raspberry Chiffon, and Wheat Bread;** or **Turkey Salad Sandwich and Fruit**.

Dinners include: **Lasagna, Yellow Squash, and Brussel Sprouts; Texas Turkey Chili, Cornbread, and Rice; Pineapple Sesame Chicken, Poppyseed Garlic Noodles, and Ginger Carrots;** or **Fish with Cheese Sauce, Green Beans, and Kale**.

FERRARI FRESH PASTA

1345 S Voss
(at Woodway)
785-6337

Pasta and pasta dishes to go. Each is sold by weight so you can select your own portions. To ensure the freshness of their product, limited quantities are made daily; they may run out of popular items. They encourage you to call ahead of time and reserve your favorites.

Most of the **Pasta Noodles** are made with eggs. But 2-3 varieties are available each day that are made with only the whites of the egg (referred to as **No-Yolk Pasta**). One half cup of **Boscaola Sauce** over 1 cup of **No-Yolk Pasta** has 198 cals/1 gm fat; One half cup of **Marinara Sauce** over 1 cup of **No-Yolk Pasta** has 203 cals/2 gms fat.

Pasta dishes include: **Diet Lasagna** - no-cholesterol pasta layered with low fat ricotta cheese, vegetables, and a spicy no-fat added chunky tomato sauce covered with a layer of skim milk mozzarella. Other pasta dishes can be requested (with a 24 hour notice) to be prepared with low fat cheese.

HEALTH FOOD EXPRESS & CAFE

4400 Memorial Dr
(Bayou Park Club)
868-2412

Healthy and balanced vegan meals are packaged in bulk for pick-up or delivery once or twice a week. Cafe serves lunch Monday through Friday. No animal or dairy products are used, therefore, foods do not contain cholesterol.

Eight different foods are delivered and include a pasta dish, a whole grain such as brown rice, two vegetable dishes, beans, salad with fixins and green leafy vegetables, soup, and a dessert sweetened with fruit juice or grain. A snack of seeds or nuts (which should be omitted on a low fat diet) are also included in the package.

Little oils are said to be used in the preparation of most of the meals except in the desserts. For a lower fat intake, you can request another item instead of the dessert. The leanest day is probably Wednesday; minimal amounts of oil and spices are used in food preparation on this day.

A sample menu includes: **Yellow Squash Soup with onions, Szechuan Noodle Salad** with peanuts, **Blue Corn Bread with red peppers, Mexican Kidney Beans with sauteed onions, Steamed Cauliflower Salad with red onions and parsley, Fresh Kale Greens with Chinese cabbage**, Almond Peach Cobbler with Granola, and Toasted Sunflower Seeds as a snack.

NATURAL FOODS DELIVERY & CATERING SERVICE

523-0171

Delivered gourmet vegetarian food. No meat or dairy products are used. Foods are delivered twice a week in amounts to cover about 2-3 days of dining. They can be delivered anywhere around town (an add-on price may be required).

Meals are packed prior to delivery into eight containers so you can mix and match and only heat up what you want. The "mini" is 8 oz, "regular" is 16 oz, and "family" is 32 oz. There's typically two bean dishes, two grain dishes, two different vegetables, a soup, and one dessert. Sauces are on the side.

Very little oil is said to be used in the production of the meals; probably under a half teaspoon per serving.

An example of sample menus: **Wild Rice Pilaf and Black Bean Cavier**; **BBQ Beans**; Bulghar Cashew Pie; **Garlic & Poppyseed Noodles**; **Chinese Veggies: snow peas, bok choy, sprouts**; **Yams with lime sauce**; **Leek Soup**; and Tofu Cheesecake.

Another menu: **Chick Pea Salad**, **Red Beans and Squash**, **Vegetarian Lasagna**, **Cornbread Stuffing with mushroom gravy**, **Cauliflower and Red Onion Salad**, **Cole Slaw**, Cream of Mushroom Soup, and Great Cake.

A Health-Oriented
Diet Plan That Works!

3 COMPLETE MEALS DAILY
21 MEALS WEEKLY

Not frozen or dried   No additives or preservatives

Three calorie levels

Ideal for anyone who wants to maintain good health and /or lose weight, lower cholesterol, fat, sodium and feel better. Meals are made from scratch and analyzed by a dietitian. All for what you would normally spend on food.

NO MORE

COOKING   ◆   CALORIE COUNTING
SHOPPING   ◆   PLANNING

CALL NOW 850-0900

YOGURT & FROZEN DESSERTS

Many restaurants are serving frozen yogurt as an option to high fat desserts. In addition, free-standing frozen yogurt and ice cream shops sell a variety of frozen yogurt, ice milks, and other frozen desserts.

Frozen Yogurt is Low in Calories and Fat

Frozen Yogurt is considerably lower in calories and fat grams than ice cream. While 1/2 c of frozen yogurt has about 100 cals/0-2 gms fat, 1/2 c of Haagen-Dazs Butter Pecan ice cream has 310 cals/24 gms fat.

A Warning about Sizes

Be careful when deciding which size to order. Ordering a large size of frozen yogurt may not be any lower in calories than a moderate portion of ice cream.

Most people should order the kiddie cup, child's cup, or the small size. These usually range between 4-6 fluid ounces of dessert. The regular size is about 8 fluid ounces; many frozen yogurt shops offer sizes as large as a quart.

The small-sized cones, cake or sugar, have

negligible fat and only about 25-40 calories respectively. The large waffle cones are considerably higher in fats and calories; chocolate and nut dips add even more.

Fluid Ounces Versus Weight Ounces

A glass of water has both 8 **fluid** (volume) ounces **and** 8 **weight** ounces. This is probably why most people think of fluid ounces and weight ounces as the same. They are not always.

When your cup of frozen yogurt is **weighed** (for quality control or for pricing) keep in mind that you can not calculate the calories directly from this number. The **weight ounces** of the product within the cup **are not** the same as the **fluid ounces** from which calories are most often calculated.

Frozen Yogurt has air incorporated into the product. Companies refer to this in terms of "percent overrun". If the company has a 50% overrun (as most do), multiply the weight ounces by 1.5.

Therefore, a cup of frozen yogurt weighing 4 oz (4 weight ounces) will equate to 6 fluid ounces. Six weight ounces is about 9 fluid ounces.

An Example

A company states that their product contains 20 calories per **fluid** ounce and you buy a cup of frozen yogurt that **weighs** 4 ounces. How many calories does this product have?

First, convert the **weight ounces** into **fluid ounces**:

4 **weight ounces** X 1.5 = 6 **fluid ounces**.

Now multiply the **fluid ounces** by the number of calories per fluid ounce:

6 **fluid ounces** X 20 calories per fluid ounce = 120 calories.

YOGURT & FROZEN DESSERTS

A Note About Sweetners

Frozen yogurt is most often sweetened with sugar. Sugar-free frozen yogurts often use aspartame, sorbitol, or fructose.

Sweeteners, if not sugar, are listed within parentheses when applicable. Nutrasweet is the brand name for aspartame. Sorbitol is a sweetener that has the same number of calories as sugar but is absorbed slower than sucrose. Fructose also has the same number of calories as sugar but is sweeter so less is needed.

NUTRITION INFORMATION

Per Fluid Ounce:

	CALS	**FAT (gms)**
Ambrosia	18	0
American Glace - Sugar free ice milk (aspartame & sorbitol)	9	0
Baskin Robbins, Sugar Free (Nutrasweet)	20	<1
Columbo Frozen Yogurt		
Lowfat	28	0.5
Nonfat	25	0
Sugar Free Diet (Sorbitol & aspartame)	15	0
Frogurt (Coca Cola)		
Lowfat	28	<1
Nonfat	25	<1
Gise (fructose)	9	0
Heidi's Frogen Yozurt (fructose)	15	0

	CALS	FAT (gms)
Honey Hill Farms (fructose)		
Low Fat	26-35	0
Nonfat Frozen Yogurt	20	0
Sugar Free (Nutrasweet)	10	0
Jersey Maid Yogurt (fructose)	8	0
Just 10 (aspartame)	10	0
Ms. Karen's		
Original	20	0
Premium	26	1
Chocolate	26	1
Non-Fat	22	0
Non-fat Chocolate	24	0
Diet (Nutrasweet)	13	0
Skinny Dip Frozen Dessert (fructose)	9	0
TCBY Yogurt		
Regular	30	0.8
Nonfat	28	0
Sugar Free (Aspartame)	20	0
Wispy Premium Soft Serve (fructose)	**12**	**0**
Yogurt Culture		
Nonfat	22	0
Ultra Light	8	0

Nutritional information for this chapter was obtained from the companies or from their product information flyers.

SUGGESTIONS AND COMMENTS
FOR NEXT EDITION:

Restaurants, menu items, and their personnel change rapidly. Therefore this restaurant guide will be revised every year or two. I need your assistance for the next edition. Let me know:

- If you visited a restaurant that is noteworthy of inclusion in this book.
- If a specific menu item should be mentioned.
- If you were disappointed in a restaurant or menu item listed in this edition and feel it should be re-evaluated before the next edition.

_____

_____

_____

_____

_____

_____

_____

_____

Please send your comments and suggestions in
writing to: Nutrifit Consulting, Inc.
P.O. Box 690452
Houston, TX 77269-0452